THE
EARLY
YEARS

AVIATION CENTURY

THE EARLY YEARS

RON DICK AND DAN PATTERSON

The BOSTON
MILLS PRESS

A BOSTON MILLS PRESS BOOK

National Library of Canada Cataloguing in Publication

Dick, Ron, 1931–
Aviation century: the early years / Ron Dick and Dan Patterson.

Includes bibliographical references and index.

ISBN 1-55046-407-8

1. Aeronautics — History.
I. Patterson, Dan, 1953–
II. Title.

TL515.D52 2003   629.13'009   C2003-902724-4

Publisher Cataloging-in-Publication Data (U.S.)

Dick, Ron, 1931–
Aviation century the early years / Ron Dick and Dan Patterson. — 1st ed.

[240] p.: ill., photos. (chiefly col.) ; cm.

Includes bibliographical references and index.

Summary: From the achievements of the Wright brothers, to the researches and
adventures of early flying pioneers, and the military aviation of World War I to
the rise of commercial aviation. Biographical information is included.

ISBN 1-55046-407-8

1. Airplanes — History. 2. Aircraft industry – History.
3. Aeronautics—Biography. I. Patterson, Dan, 1953– II. Title.

629.13'09 21   TL670.3.D52 2003

Published by BOSTON MILLS PRESS
132 Main Street,
Erin, Ontario N0B 1T0
Tel 519-833-2407
Fax 519-833-2195
books@bostonmillspress.com
www.bostonmillspress.com

IN CANADA:
Distributed by Firefly Books Ltd.
3680 Victoria Park Avenue
Willowdale, Ontario M2H 3K1

IN THE UNITED STATES:
Distributed by Firefly Books (U.S.) Inc.
P.O. Box 1338, Ellicott Station
Buffalo, New York 14205

Aviation Century series editor: Kathleen Fraser
Design: PageWave Graphics Inc.

Printed in Canada by Friesen Printers

07 06 05 04 03   1 2 3 4 5

The publisher acknowledges the financial support of the Government of Canada through
the Book Publishing Industry Development Program (BPIDP) for its publishing efforts.

HALF-TITLE PAGE *This photograph of the Wright brothers' first flight was recorded on a 5-by-7-inch glass plate. It was developed by Orville in 1903 and stored with their other plates. In the spring of 1913, Dayton, Ohio, suffered a catastrophic flood. Though they survived the deluge, many of the Wrights' early flight photographs, as well as the 1903 machine, were damaged. This full print of the image clearly shows a broken corner at lower left. Orville considered this a flaw and after 1913 cropped the image.*

PAGE 2 *This image from the Caproni Museum in Trento, Italy — an interesting collection of tails featuring the early years of Italian aviation. The small round rudder at right is from the Caproni Ca.9, the white rudder at top left from the Ca.6, and the rudder in the center, the Ansaldo S.V.A.5, a combat veteran from WWI.*

TITLE PAGE *The Deperdussin Monocoque of 1912, now at the Musée de l'Air, Le Bourget.*

PAGE 6 *A collection of Henry Botterell's WWI artifacts, from his experiences flying over the Western Front. See page 114.*

FRONT JACKET

MAIN IMAGE *The 1903 Wright Flyer seen from above. This history-making machine is in the collection of the National Air & Space Museum in Washington, D.C.*

BOTTOM ROW

FAR LEFT *The Nieuport 28 in the collection of the USAF Museum, Dayton, Ohio, is powered by a Gnôme rotary engine.*

CENTER LEFT *The rotary engine warms up on this still flyable Blériot monoplane at Le Bourget in France.*

CENTER RIGHT *The wingtip of the 1905 Wright Flyer, at Carillon Historical Park in Dayton, Ohio. The Wright brothers considered this their first practical "aeroplane."*

FAR RIGHT *This Vultee airliner from the early years of air travel is at the Virginia Museum of Flight in Richmond, Virginia.*

BACK JACKET

The Boeing 247 at Seattle's Museum of Flight is finished in United Airlines colors and maintained in flying condition. The trail-blazing design of the 247 led the way in revolutionizing air travel in the 1930s.

Dedicated to aviators,
past, present
and of the future.

APRIL, 1918.

19 FRIDAY
Down to Chatham &
got teeth. Up to town
for lunch and out to
Manston in evg.

20 SATURDAY
First flips on Camel. Did
formation. Flew low
& gunned over cliffs
at Ramsgate. Also
low over towns.

21 SUNDAY 3rd after Easter.

16 TUESDAY
do
Edith.

WEDNESDAY
do

18 THURSDAY
do
Up to town on my
bike at Waldot
13th Chant.

AL NAVAL AIR SERVICE.

PILOT'S FLYING

LOG

H.J.L. Botterell
PROBATIONARY FL.
OFFICER

Remarks.

MACHINE FROM RELY.   RAINING.

                FIRED 400 ROUNDS
                INTO BALLOON OVER
BOMBING.   BRAYELLE. SAW OBSER-
                VER IN PARACHUTE. DROP-
                PED FOUR BOMBS IN
                VITRY. OBSERVED HITS
                BALLOON GRADUALLY
                CRUMPLED UP AND WENT
                DOWN.

                DROPPED 4 BOMBS NEAR
                HENIN L'ETARD & FIRED 100
                ROUNDS ON GROUND TARGETS.

                DROPPED 4 BOMBS AND
LOW BOMBING.   FIRED 150 ROUNDS
                INTO VITRY.

                TEST.

LOCAL.   FROM A.D. AT RELY.

NG NEW MACHINE FROM UNEVE

16TH SEPT AM 10.30
17TH SEPT 1.15
           AM 9.00
           PM
           2.30
18TH SEPT PM 100
           AM 7.55
19TH SEPT
21ST SEPT

Contents

ACKNOWLEDGMENTS

THE AUTHORS ARE most sincerely grateful to all those who have contributed their time and resources to the *Aviation Century* project since its inception in 1997. An undertaking as large as this could not have been accomplished without considerable help and advice from a host of people in many countries on three continents. We hope that we will have thanked them all by the time the fifth and final volume of the series is published, but we are well aware that perfection in this endeavor may be beyond our reach. Even with the best intentions, it is possible that a person or organization will be missed, or that a mistake will be made and credit perhaps given where it does not belong. If such proves to be the case, the authors would be glad to have errors brought to their attention so that apologies can be offered and the necessary corrections included in future printings.

> *"Flight without feathers is not easy."*
> PLAUTUS, 254–184 BC

The home base for the project has been Dayton, Ohio, home of the Wright brothers and the "Birthplace of Aviation." Members of the Wright family encouraged our efforts throughout, and Mary Mathews, Director of Dayton's Carillon Park Museum, gave us unfettered access to the 1905 Wright Flyer. At Wright State University, Dawne Dewey and John Sanford dug deep into the archives to find Wright brothers memorabilia and unpublished aviation photographs. In downtown Dayton, the Engineer's Club and the Packard Museum helped us with artifacts, and at nearby Wright-Patterson AFB, the Director and Teresa Lacy opened the doors to us on the huge USAF Museum collection.

Starting in 1998, our travels took us to museums and archives in Canada, the United Kingdom, France, Italy, Sweden, Poland and all over the United States. Earlier trips and correspondence added material from Russia, Sweden, Finland, Germany, Australia and New Zealand. For their help in providing the material for *Aviation Century,* the authors would like to offer particular thanks to the following individuals and institutions: The National Air & Space Museum, Smithsonian Institution (Don Lopez, Ted Maxwell, Trish Graboske, Dom Pisano, Bob van der Linden, Peter Jakab, Ron Davies, Tom Allison, Scott Wiley); USAF History Office (Dr. Richard Hallion); Museum of Naval Aviation, Pensacola (Bob Rasmussen, Hill Goodspeed); Museum of Flight, Seattle (Dennis Parks, Katherine Williams, Eden Hopkins); Virginia Aviation Museum (Kim Leigh, David Hahn); U.S. Marine Corps Museum, Quantico; National Aviation Hall of Fame (Director Mike Jackson, Director of Marketing Ron Kaplan, Tara Engle); International Association of Eagles (David McFarland); National Aviation Museum, Ottawa; Canadian Warplane Heritage Museum; Royal Aeronautical Society (Brian Riddle); Imperial War Museum, Duxford (Ted Inman, Colette Byatt); General Lester L. Lyles, USAF, Commander Air Force Materiel Command, Wright-Patterson AFB; Royal Air Force Museum, Hendon and Cosford (Michael Fopp, Henry Hall, P.J.V. Elliott, Ewan Cameron); Fleet Air Arm Museum, Yeovilton (Graham Mottram); Museum of Army Flying, Middle Wallop (Brigadier Edward Tait); Science Museum, London (Andrew Nahum); The Shuttleworth Trust (Tony Podmore); Musée de l'Air et de l'Espace, Le Bourget (General Sifre); Jean Salis Collection, La Ferté Alais; Lafayette Escadrille Memorial, Paris; Museo Storico Aeronautica Militare, Vigna di Valle (Colonel Marco Scarlatti and Lieutenant Egidi); Museo Caproni, Trento (Contessa Maria Fede Armani Caproni); and the Royal Australian Air Force Museum, Point Cook. Individual help and encouragement came from Bob Ready of LSI Industries, Cincinnati; Floyd McGowin, Chapman, Alabama; Jerry Ellis, Delta Airlines; Clive and Linda Denny; Paddy Worth; Jean-Louis and Shirley Marro of Chateau Fosseuse; Larry Pisoni of Gourmet Italia: Piera Graffa, author, in Trento; Lieutenant General Antonino Lenzo in Rome; and Air Marshal Alan Reed in Melbourne.

All the original color photography was completed by Dan Patterson. Generous support and advice in the provision of photographic equipment was given by David Brown of KJP, London (now Calumet Photo).

Archive photographs in *The Early Years* came from the collections of Wright State University; Smithsonian National Air & Space Museum; Museum of Flight, Seattle; USAF Museum, Dayton; National Museum of Naval Aviation, Pensacola; Packard Museum, Dayton; Imperial War Museum, London; Royal Air Force Museum, Hendon; Royal Aeronautical Society; Museum of Army Flying, Middle Wallop; Musée de l'Air et de l'Espace, Le Bourget; Museo Caproni, Trento; and from the private collections of the Caproni family and the authors.

Many distinguished artists generously agreed to contribute their work to *Aviation Century*. *The Early Years* includes paintings or drawings by Jim Dietz, Bill Marsalko, Robert Taylor, Nicolas Trudgian, and Michael Turner. HMS *Hibernia* at the end of Chapter 1, Early Powered Flight, is reproduced by permission of Air Commodore Mark Tomkins, RAF Benevolent Fund. The painting by Henri Farré in Chapter 2, Aerial Warfare, is from the USAF collection, and is presently on display at the Virginia Aviation Museum, Richmond. The portraits in Chapter 4, Great Names, are by Milton Caniff and are owned by the National Aviation Hall of Fame, Dayton. The authors are particularly grateful to Pat Barnard of the Military Gallery, Bath, U.K., for all his encouragement and for permission to reproduce works by many of the artists.

We would like to thank Boston Mills Press of Erin, Ontario, for their continuing belief in and support of this project, which has had its share of challenges and bumps in the road: publisher John Denison, managing editor Noel Hudson and particularly Kathy Fraser, who seems to have become our personal editor. Thanks also to PageWave Graphics of Toronto, for establishing a friendly and professional atmosphere which has brought this project to a very happy conclusion.

Before bringing these acknowledgments to a close, the authors would like to add an assurance of their gratitude to their wives, Paul and Cheryl, for the forbearance they have shown and the unfailing support they have offered over five challenging years. They have fed and watered us, lifted us when we were down, followed us on our peregrinations, borne our idiosyncrasies, consoled us in failure, applauded us in success, and on occasion even carried our bags. We are greatly in their debt. Our love and thanks are humbly offered to them both.

Ron Dick and Dan Patterson

FOREWORD
Amanda Wright Lane

"VIEWED FROM ABOVE, the flat monotonous landscapes take on a new beauty not seen from the ground; the plowed fields, the patches of grass and grain, and the wooded spots appear as a quilt of beautiful colors; the hills and valleys are scarcely distinguishable; the earth appears to be a flat plain, marked and colored with a beauty not appreciated except when seen this way."

These words that describe our Earth as seen from aloft were not spoken by a modern-day aviator, but by the world's first successful pilot of a heavier-than-air, controlled flying machine. My great-granduncle, Orville Wright, shared this observation in February 1917, fourteen years after he and his brother Will made aviation history on the dunes of the Outer Banks in North Carolina. Little did they know how many others would glimpse this heavenly view over the next 100 years, as mankind soared ever higher, faster and further.

In this volume, my family today is pictured fittingly on a quiet grassy pasture known as Huffman Prairie. It hasn't changed a bit in 100 years. While most of the world remembers Orville and Wilbur's 1903 flight at Kitty Hawk, the future of aviation truly began in this cow pasture in Dayton, Ohio, one year later. It is here that my great-granduncles tackled the problems of consistent takeoff and landings, air safety, machine maneuverability, and endurance in the air. But, perhaps more important, it was on this spot that Uncle Orv and Uncle Will taught themselves how to fly. Reflecting on their earliest flights, Uncle Orv once said, "The termination of these first flights was brought about entirely by our inexperience as operators and not through any failure of the machine itself to perform."

As the technology of early airplanes and pilot proficiency rapidly improved, Uncle Orv and Uncle Will pondered the future of aviation.

"The sporting side of the aeroplane development will, I believe, speedily follow, and be continuous with, the experimental stage, in which all flying machines are at present. The exhilaration of flying is too keen, the pleasure too great, for it to be neglected as a sport." — Wilbur Wright, January 1909.

"After the war we are told we shall have a new world and a new type of civilization; in my opinion one of the factors that will contribute to this changed order will be the part which will be played in it by the aeroplane. We shall have an entirely new form of transportation; which will serve many ends and contribute in many ways to the welfare and happiness of mankind." — Orville Wright, April 1917.

Uncle Will did not get to see most of the swift, incredible changes that aviation brought to mankind. He died in 1912. But Uncle Orv saw the airplane go from a flimsy bird of bicycle parts and "Pride of the West" muslin, to a streamlined, multi-passenger carrying aircraft, capable of speeds beyond all early imagination.

The people, "flying machines," and memorabilia photographed in this book tell aviation stories as varied as the patchwork picture of Earth that Uncle Orv described. Each contributed to the first 100 years of flight, some simply, some quietly, some more dramatically than others. All of these snapshots of history, however, share one thing in common — a "view from above" that is the legacy of my great-granduncles, Orville and Wilbur Wright.

Amanda Wright Lane,
November 5, 2002

FOREWORD
Contessa Maria Fede Caproni di Taliedo

DURING THE FIRST DECADE of the 20th century, a few remarkable men thought they could free humankind from earthly constraints and make real the ancient dreams of flight. They were visionaries who believed that people could take to the air and exploit the third dimension, and they set out to construct machines that would defy gravity. The Wright brothers led the way, but they were quickly followed by others — among them such far-sighted men as Santos-Dumont, Farman, Bleriot, Curtiss, and A.V. Roe. My father, Gianni Caproni, Conte di Taliedo, was one of those inspired and determined pioneers. In common with his contemporaries, he relished the challenge of tackling apparently insurmountable difficulties, persevering in his researches and experiments until the aeronautical problems were solved and success was achieved. By their efforts, aviation's pioneers expanded human horizons and forever changed the way we live. They were imaginative, courageous and persistent, exploring realms until then unknown and pointing the way to a future in which even the remotest regions of the world became accessible by air.

The machines with which the pioneers launched these revolutionary developments were often delicate and unreliable. They were constructed of basic materials and they operated at the edge, or even beyond, the frontiers of human knowledge. My father's first aircraft was built in a dilapidated workshop with the help of small-town carpenters using simple tools — saws, hammers and chisels. Early designers everywhere faced similar conditions, buying success dearly with endless hours of mental and physical labor, and all too frequently as a result of destructive accidents, the inevitable price of progress made by trial and error.

This volume covers the early days of aviation, starting with the Wright brothers and tracing the evolution of manned flight through the conflagration of the First World War to the interwar development of civil airlines. There are stories of great fighter aces and of courageous aerial trailblazers alongside accounts of changes in military thinking and of expanding commercial enterprise. Aircraft are shown as they evolve from small, fragile, fabric-covered creatures, often seriously underpowered, into mighty machines capable of crossing the world's oceans while carrying loads of passengers and freight. The all-up weight of my father's early aircraft seldom rose much above 700 pounds, but by 1929 his Ca.90 was flying at ten times that weight. The Caproni Ca.8 of 1911 was capable of reaching a speed of 45 mph and a height of perhaps 2,000 feet. By the 1930s, there were several Caproni designs achieving speeds of well over 300 mph, and in 1938 the Ca.161 bis climbed to 56,046 feet, a world record for piston-engined aircraft that still stands today. Other designers managed similar improvements, branching out into a bewildering variety of aircraft types with incredibly diverse capabilities.

Such remarkable advances were made possible by men who were prepared to attempt the impossible, and who countered public skepticism with that most irrefutable response — success. This book tells the story of their achievements and, at a time when all of us have a tendency to take aviation for granted, reminds us that we owe our three-dimensional freedom to the flair and imagination of a few great men.

Maria Fede Caproni di Taliedo,
September 21, 2002

INTRODUCTION
Air Vice-Marshal Ron Dick

THE 20TH CENTURY was preeminently the era of aviation. Beginning with the first successful powered flight of the Wright brothers in 1903, aviation progressed, in little more than one human lifetime, until aircraft reached into every region of the globe. The effects of their operations were felt in one way or another by all people no matter where on Earth they lived. Human accomplishments in the air irrevocably changed the world's societies in countless ways — both for better and for worse.

In historical terms, human aviation is a relatively recent phenomenon. At the dawn of the 21st century, people still lived who were alive when the Wright brothers first flew. Despite its relative youth, however, most of us tend to take the consequences of flying for granted and give little thought to how very different our world would be if human flight had remained in the realm of dreams, where it had been for thousands of years. Aviation's social, political and economic effects, and the consequent changes brought about in the way people think and behave, are countless and all-encompassing. It would be difficult to do justice to the subject of aviation in a complete library of books, let alone a series of five.

In this first volume of *Aviation Century* the story begins with a look back at man's eternal fascination with flying, before reviewing the achievements, thoughts and aims of early aviators and the reactions to their efforts of those still anchored to the ground. The ideals framed during the early days of flying did not always coincide with later developments; events often led airmen in directions other than those intended. In 1917, for example, Orville Wright remarked ruefully, "When my brother and I built the first man-carrying flying machine we thought that we were introducing into the world an invention which would make further wars practically impossible." The Schneider Trophy is another example. It was originally conceived before World

> *"If there be a domineering, tyrant thought, it is the conception that the problem of flight may be solved by man. When once this idea has invaded the brain it possesses it exclusively. It is then a haunting thought, a kind of nightmare, impossible to cast off."*
>
> LOUIS-PIERRE MOUILLARD,
> "L'EMPIRE DE L'AIR," 1881

War I as a competition to encourage the development of aircraft capable of operating quickly and safely across oceans. Those qualities of range and seaworthiness were progressively set aside as it grew into an outright trial of speed, which in turn had an effect on the course of World War II.

The first steps in the evolution of aircraft as weapons, both before and during WWI, often drew criticism from officers in the established services. As air combat began and tactical doctrines for aircraft were devised, opinions changed, and the operational concepts of both armies and navies inevitably were affected. The idea that air power had a strategic dimension grew to influence not only the size, shape and role of air forces in general, but also political thoughts and decisions, the results of which were felt by the populations of every continent. British Prime Minister Stanley Baldwin's remark in 1932, that "The bomber will always get through," reflected a widely held belief and, even though it was unsupported conjecture, it drove policy.

The interwar years were also notable for the rise of commercial aviation, starting with early adventures in mail delivery. The growth in the demand for passenger services and the subsequent struggle for commercial viability by budding airlines gave the first hints of the very real changes these developments would bring about in the way people travel and conduct their business. In this golden age of flight, great names emerged. Air power strategists followed the ideas of Trenchard, Douhet and Mitchell. Aircraft industries were founded by Donald Douglas, Geoffrey de Havilland, Igor Sikorsky, Gianni Caproni, Willi Messerschmitt and many others. Trailblazers such as Charles Lindbergh, Wiley Post and Charles Kingsford-Smith, and record breakers, among them Sadi Leconte, Francesco Agello and John Macready, all brought their imagination, flair and courage to the business of continually expanding aviation's possibilities, reaching for goals that grew greater with each passing year, set by the faster, higher and further demands of those who flew.

This first volume of the *Aviation Century* series closes with a look at some of the great men who pioneered the world's aviation industries. Further volumes take the story of human flight through the era of exploration and adventure to the dramatic rise of air power in World War II and beyond. The revolutionary impact of turbo-jet engines and the explosion of commercial air transport after WWII are covered, as are private flying and gliding, air shows and museums, rotary wings, lighter-than-air, flight safety, and aeronautical research and development.

Looking back on the Aviation Century, there can be no doubt that human flight and its multifarious effects changed the way people live their lives in every part of the globe. Politics, trade, travel, warfare — all these things and many more were transformed in only a hundred years. The world became a smaller, more convenient and more dangerous place than it was before the Wrights had flown. Aircraft, with all their blessings and their curses, shaped the 20th century and left an indelible mark on the history of our planet.

Ron Dick,
May 2003

PHOTOGRAPHER'S PREFACE
Dan Patterson

ON THE TITLE PAGE of this first volume of *Aviation Century* is the famous photograph of the first powered flight of the Wright brothers' airplane. There were three other flights made that day in 1903, and all of them were also photographed, but none of them was so dramatic. As Ron and I have worked on this project for the past five years, I have had a lot of time to consider this photograph. After all, the Wrights were also the first aviation photographers, so their work in photography was also the beginning of my profession.

A photograph by its nature captures a moment in time, freezing for that instant all of the elements in front of the lens. This remarkable image has captured more. Look at the photograph and divide it in half, top and bottom, first just beneath the Flyer and then reverse that, the Flyer and the sky.

Consider the scene on the sands of Kitty Hawk that morning. It was cold, really cold, and windy. Orville and Wilbur decided that this was it, the morning they would fly. They put up the signal flag on top of their shed to summon the men of the Life Saving station to come to the two wooden buildings, to help them get their machine out and ready to fly. There the small group assisted the Wrights in hauling the flying machine from the hangar to the 60-foot launching rail. They placed the Flyer on top of the cradle, which ran on bicycle hubs, at the south end of the track.

Look carefully at the bottom half of the photo. You can see the outline of the lower right wing in the sand, surrounded by hundreds of footprints, the footprints of the

Caught inside the original Wright brothers' camera, aviation's most famous image comes to life once more.

Wrights and of the others as they readied the machine to fly. From that mass of overlapped prints some significant footsteps emerge.

In all of the prints along the trailing edge of the wing, Orville's are there, as he climbed onto the wing, around the wires and the propeller chains, and as he settled onto the lower wing, next to the engine. Orville's footprints also appear in the lower right corner, along with another set, those of Lifesaving Crewman John T. Daniels. Orville set up his camera and focused it where he and Wilbur had figured the Flyer would take off. He asked Mr. Daniels to stand behind the camera and trip the shutter when the Flyer left the track. Those footprints leading to and from the bottom right of the photo are Orville Wright's.

The final set of footprints are those of Wilbur Wright, who stood at the wingtip of the Flyer and steadied it as it gathered speed, moving down the track. They emerge from the mass of overlapping prints, a lone track of steps that stop at the point the Flyer took off. These footsteps significantly cross over the two halves of the photograph.

The footprints in the sand, the outline of the wing, the tools, the bench, the launch rail — all represent time *before* flight. Wilbur's footsteps emerge from that time and cross over into the time *of* flight. Mr. Daniels tripped the shutter and captured the Flyer just a foot or two above the sand. In the background you can make out some shore birds who, before that moment, had the skies to themselves.

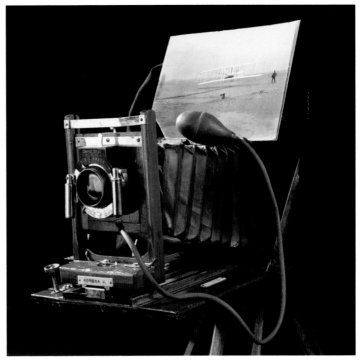

The Wright brothers' camera seen with its most celebrated image. The Korona V 5-by-7-inch camera is in the collection of Carillon Historical Park, Dayton, Ohio.

This volume and the ones to follow are about the top half of the photo, and how that moment changed our world forever.

Dan Patterson,
May 2003

CHAPTER 1

Early Powered Flight: 1900 to 1914

"Forward, forward let us range,
Let the great world spin for ever
Down the ringing grooves of change."

ALFRED, LORD TENNYSON

As THE VICTORIAN ERA ended and gave way to the 20th century, there was plenty of evidence that the world was indeed spinning down Tennyson's "ringing grooves of change." The British Empire might still encompass almost a quarter of the world's landmass, but it was apparent that the United States was eclipsing its European rivals and growing rapidly into the most powerful country on Earth. In 1900, even though the average age of the population at death was a meager forty-seven years, there were 76 million Americans, and their burgeoning society was brimming with new ideas. In little more than a century since its birth as an independent nation, the U.S.A. had become the world's most productive industrial society, and Americans were proud of the technological advances that promised them a future in which they might enjoy unprecedented convenience and prosperity.

Typical of these popular developments was the Eastman Kodak company's introduction, in 1900, of the Brownie box camera. For only $1, the wonders of photography were brought within reach of almost everyone. Horseless travel was more expensive, but that was on the rise, too. Thirty-one exhibitors were attracted to the first National Automobile Show held at Madison Square Garden, New York, in November 1900. A chain-driven Packard, powered by a one-cylinder 12-horsepower engine and with the luxury of three forward gears, was among the vehicles prominently displayed. Enthusiasm for the new-fangled automobiles was high, and there were 13,284 motorcars on American roads by the year's end, even though, from sea to shining sea, there were just 144 miles of hard-surfaced pavement for them to drive on. Nevertheless, even at this early stage, drivers strove to reach higher and higher speeds, and Albert C. Bostwick put himself among the leaders by covering 10 miles in the astonishing time of 15 minutes, 9 seconds. Some concern was expressed as to whether the human body could long withstand the stresses of travel at so great a pace.

As they had for thousands of years, some imaginations soared beyond the constrictions of earthly achievements and looked to the skies of the 20th century for their inspiration. At the Paris International Exhibition of 1900, the aeronautical exhibits encouraged Europeans to think that powered manned flight might soon be possible. A prize of 100,000 francs was offered for the first aviator to fly the 7 miles between the Paris headquarters of the Aero Club de France and the Eiffel Tower. While heavier-than-air flight was the Holy Grail, it was always more likely that the prize would be won by an airman who relied on hydrogen gas to defeat gravity. In 1900, the Brazilian Alberto Santos-Dumont delighted Parisians by appearing over their city in his cigar-shaped dirigible and, in October 1901, winning the prize.

> *"Sacrifices must be made."*
>
> WORDS USED BY GLIDING PIONEER OTTO LILIENTHAL AND ENGRAVED ON HIS TOMBSTONE IN 1896.

The possibilities of manned flight were discussed at the inaugural meeting of the International Congress of Aeronautics, held in Paris during September 1900. In his speech, Henri Deutsch de la Meurthe, the French oil magnate and patron of aeronautics, went so far as to say: "Let us hope that automobiles of the air will one day exceed the speeds of all automobiles on land." Meanwhile, reaching far beyond this cautious aspiration, the British writer H.G. Wells started work on the manuscript of *The First Men in the Moon*. On the other side of the Atlantic, two bicycle mechanics in Dayton, largely unknown and unnoticed in the wider world, went quietly and methodically about the business of designing an experimental glider.

CONTROL IS THE KEY

It is probable that Wilbur and Orville Wright first became intrigued by the idea of human flight in 1894 after reading an article on the exploits of Otto Lilienthal, the German gliding pioneer, but it was not until 1899 that they gave serious consideration to the problem of how man might fly. After some studious bird-watching, Wilbur came to an important conclusion. "My observations of the flight of buzzards," he said, "led me to believe that they regain their lateral balance ... by a torsion of the tips of the wings." Later, in a letter to the aviation historian Octave Chanute, he showed a healthy skepticism for Lilienthal's method of control in the air, saying "birds use more positive and energetic methods of regaining equilibrium than that of shifting the center of gravity." Wilbur had hit the nail on the head. His concern with how flight was controlled was a crucial element

in the eventual success of the brothers. Unlike earlier would-be airmen striving for powered flight, the Wrights thought about control from the beginning.

Sir George Cayley — "The Father of Aerial Navigation" — established the basic requirements for successful manned flight in a series of articles published in 1809 and 1810, but it was over sixty years later before anyone claimed to have flown in a powered aircraft. In 1874, the French naval commander Felix du Temple accelerated his hot-air–engined craft down a ramp and left the ground in what is thought to be the first man-carrying "hop." A Russian naval officer, Alexander Mozhaiski, managed a similar feat near St. Petersburg ten years later. The French engineer Clement Ader's bat-winged *Eole* rose briefly into the air from level ground in 1890. Four years after that, the American-born Hiram Maxim's gigantic biplane, 110 feet across the wing and driven by two 180-horsepower steam engines, lifted its bulk from a track in England and strained against the inadequate restraint of prudently positioned guardrails, to the considerable alarm of its owner, who immediately abandoned his experiments. In 1903, a German civil servant, Karl Jatho, managed a *Flugsprung* (leap into the air) or two in what was hardly more than a powered kite, one of which covered 60 meters.

In the United States, Samuel Pierpont Langley, a distinguished physicist and astronomer who became Secretary of the Smithsonian Institution, was another who believed that power and lift came first in the development of a flying machine. He began aeronautical research in 1886 and, by 1891, had begun construction of a series of large steam-powered models that he rather oddly called "Aerodromes." In 1896 he had some success. Two machines built with two wings in tandem, and with a one-horsepower steam engine and twin propellers amidships, were launched from a houseboat on the Potomac and flew considerable distances, the second managing three-quarters of a mile. President McKinley appointed a committee to investigate these achievements, and the War Department later gave Langley a $50,000 subsidy to build a "man-carrying aeroplane." The full-size Aerodrome was completed in 1903. It resembled its small relations in having tandem wings closely followed by a large vertical tail. It was 48 feet across the wing and 52 feet long. To provide power for a machine of this size he proposed a gasoline engine which would weigh about 100 pounds and produce 12 horsepower. His assistant, C.M. Manly, designed and built an engine from scratch, and the finished article was an astonishing achievement. Weighing only 136 pounds when dry, the five-cylinder radial produced 52 horsepower, figures hardly matched by any other engine before WWI.

Attempts were made to fly Langley's creation, with Manly as the pilot, on October 7 and December 8, 1903. On both occasions it was intended to launch the Aerodrome from a catapult mounted on the Potomac houseboat, but each time the hoped-for flight became a plunge into the river. As a reporter for the *Washington Post* wrote: "A mechanic stooped, cut the cable holding the catapult; there was a roaring grinding noise, and the Langley airship tumbled over the edge of the house-boat and disappeared into the river sixteen feet below. It simply slid into the water like a handful of mortar." The chorus of jeers in Congress and the press that greeted the failures of the Aerodrome forced the withdrawal of government support and crushed Langley's spirit. He died a sadly disillusioned man less than three years later.

None of these would-be airmen had really thought about what would happen if they became truly airborne. They concerned themselves only with providing sufficient thrust and overcoming gravity, making only rudimentary arrangements, if any, to deal with the problem of control. Their brave efforts deserve recognition as milestones in the history of aviation, but it cannot be claimed that they achieved powered flight. The Wright brothers, on the other hand, recognized from the start that without adequate control the provision of sufficient lift and power to get them off the ground would be meaningless.

THE WRIGHT APPROACH

Circumstances had denied Wilbur and Orville Wright the benefit of a college education, but there was no doubt about their intelligence or inventive flair. They were methodical and self-sufficient by nature, and moderately successful. Their bicycle shop in Dayton, Ohio, gave them a solid background as light engineers and businessmen. When they turned their attention to flying, they did so with predictable thoroughness, writing to ask the Smithsonian Institution for a list of the relevant literature. They read voraciously, noting the results of previous researches before moving on to experiments of their own. Included in their reading was

"It simply slid into the water like a handful of mortar." Langley's Aerodrome on its way to an ignominious end in the Potomac River.

Octave Chanute's *Progress in Flying Machines*. This was the first reliable account of man's attempts to fly and one of the classics of aviation history. It included a simple summary of the science of aeronautics as it stood in 1894:

"The mechanical difficulties are very great, but…none of them can now be said to be insuperable. The resistance and supporting power of air are approximately known, the motor and the propelling instrument are probably sufficiently worked out to make a beginning; we know in a general way the kind of apparatus to adopt, its approximate extent and required texture of sustaining surfaces, and there remain to solve the problems of the *maintenance of the equilibrium, the guidance,* the starting up, and the alighting, as well as the final combination of these several solutions into one homogeneous design…. *A flying machine must at all times be under intelligent control.* [Italics added]."

This shows that Chanute understood the importance of creating an aeronautical triumvirate, with lift, thrust and control combined as equal partners. His words so impressed Wilbur that he wrote to Chanute in 1900, thus beginning a correspondence that marked a close and often fruitful friendship. Chanute's consistent encouragement of the Wrights in his letters was no small factor in their eventual success.

Although the accumulated wisdom of earlier pioneers often provided a basis for the Wrights' work, they took nothing for granted. Figures recorded by others might be used by them as a starting point, as were those of Lilienthal for wing area and camber, but the results they realized in trials were closely scrutinized and the figures corrected when they varied from what had been achieved. These systematic methods went hand-in-hand with a frugal practicality when it came to building a flying machine.

ABOVE *Wilbur Wright flying the 1901 glider at Kittyhawk.* LEFT *A Wright wind tunnel replica, a 6-foot-long, 16-inch-square box with a glass viewing window on top. The metal honeycomb straightened out air flowing into the tunnel from a large belt-driven fan. Balances measured the lift and drag of model wings. Scraps of paper are covered with the Wright brothers' calculations.*

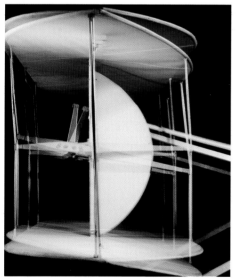

TOP *The third Wright glider in flight from Kill Devil Hill. The sheds built by the Wrights to offer some protection from the sometimes severe Outer Banks weather can be seen in the background.* LEFT *The 1909 Wright Military Flyer at the USAF Museum in Dayton, Ohio, is an exact replica. In front of the pilots were small vertical stabilizers and what the Wrights called horizontal rudders (elevators), here shown deflected in the up and down positions.* MIDDLE *Wing-warping was the method used by the Wrights to achieve control in the air, an essential element of the aerodynamic triumvirate (lift, thrust and control) ignored by so many others. The extent of the warping can be seen in this multiple exposure.* RIGHT *Vertical rudders to the rear of the Flyer were the answer to the problem of sideslipping in turns.*

The brothers used timber, fabric and wire readily available in local stores, and they shaped spars, stitched seams and rigged wings with their own hands. By the time they needed propulsive power, internal combustion engines had been developed to a point where their power/weight ratios made them just about suitable for aircraft. With the help of their able assistant, Charlie Taylor, they designed and made an engine themselves. Since there was then no propeller theory, they developed one, and built remarkably efficient propellers, too. As each problem arose, they confronted it with logic and worked their way to a solution. It sounds simple, yet not until the Wrights had anyone drawn all the elements of the flying puzzle together and made them into a comprehensible whole. Starting from basic principles and building steadily toward their goal, the Wrights changed the world from the bench of a home workshop.

When the brothers built their first glider in 1900, they avoided the inherent stability pursued by others and sought to make the machine as responsive as possible to pilot control. As Wilbur put it, "We therefore resolved to try a fundamentally different principle. We would arrange the machine so that it would *not* tend to right itself." The 1900 glider also featured what the Wrights called "helical twisting of the wings," a system that they had tried on a biplane kite in 1899. It was a method of control later described by Chanute as "wing-warping," a term that became the common usage. By introducing a capacity to alter the shape of the wings, twisting the trailing edge of one wingtip up and the other down, the brothers correctly interpreted the flight of soaring birds and at one stroke overcame the problem of controlling an aircraft in the rolling plane.

Three gliders were built, in 1900, 1901 and 1902. All were flown at Kill Devil Hill, near Kitty Hawk, on North Carolina's windswept Outer Banks. The site was chosen for its lively breezes, but it had the added advantage of being remote and away from the public's prying eye. With their first two gliders, biplanes with no tails and a forward control surface that they called a "horizontal rudder," they felt their way toward the daring conclusion that Lilienthal's figures for wing area and camber were wrong. As Wilbur wrote, "Having set out with absolute faith in the existing scientific data, we were driven to doubt one thing after another, till finally, after two years of experiment, we cast it all aside and decided to rely entirely upon our own investigations."

The investigations included designing and building their own wind tunnel, capable of providing a steady wind of 30 mph or so, in which they tested a great many differently shaped wings. Their researches led them to rework Lilienthal's aerodynamic tables and gave them a firm basis on which to build. In 1902, using their own figures, they constructed their third glider, adding vertical tail surfaces to the design. They had already discovered that, although wing-warping gave them the control in roll they were looking for, it introduced another problem. The wing that was warped down rose as it should, but it also swung back, causing a nasty sideslip toward the down-going wing. The twin vertical tail surfaces were an attempt to stop that happening.

Once they started flying the third glider, it was quickly apparent from its sharply improved performance that they had been right to doubt Lilienthal. In September and October 1902, it completed over 1,000 glides and flew splendidly, although to begin with the side-slipping problem was still there. The brothers eventually worked out that when a wing was warped down, its drag increased markedly. The solution they devised was to convert the fixed tail surfaces into a single movable rudder interconnected with the wing-warping control. Whenever a banked turn was initiated, rudder was automatically applied to counter the "warp drag" on the rising wing. (On later aircraft, the term became aileron drag.)

Now sure that they had a practical flying machine, the Wrights turned their attention to adding power. The water-cooled engine they built with the help of Charlie Taylor weighed, with its accessories, about 200 pounds and produced 12 horsepower. It turned over at 1,090 rpm and was

> "Let us hope that the advent of a successful flying machine, now only dimly foreseen and nevertheless thought to be possible, will bring nothing but good to the world; that it shall abridge distance, make all parts of the globe accessible, bring men into closer relationship with each other, advance civilization, and hasten the promised era in which there shall be nothing but peace and good-will among all men."
>
> FROM *PROGRESS IN FLYING MACHINES* BY OCTAVE CHANUTE, 1894.

The 1903 Wright Flyer seen from Wilbur's point of view as Orville rose into the air and opened the door to the first century of aviation on December 17, 1903. This Flyer is in the National Air & Space Museum Collection, Washington, D.C.

geared down through simple bicycle-style chains and sprockets to drive twin propellers. If the engine was a triumph of do-it-yourself light engineering, the propellers were works of art. They were 8 feet across and made of laminated spruce, carefully shaped with a gentle twist. In the absence of any useful information on propellers other than marine, the brothers determined their form by viewing them as wings moving through the air along a helical path in the vertical plane. The concept was difficult to grasp but the finished propellers proved to be remarkably efficient, offering further evidence of the thoughtful logic that was characteristic of the Wrights' work. They were "pushers" because it was thought that the airflow over the wings should not be unnecessarily disturbed, and they were made to counter-rotate to avoid any possible difficulties from gyroscopic effect.

The first Wright "Flyer," built in the summer of 1903, was taken to Kill Devil Hill in September. By the time the preparatory work had been completed, it was December and the weather was both cold and unexpectedly calm. For a while, the Wrights waited for a stiff breeze, but by December 14 they could wait no longer. The Flyer was taken to the crest of a gentle rise and its portable "runway" laid so that it ran down the slope into what little wind there was. To ease its landings on the Kitty Hawk sands, the Flyer was fitted with gracefully curved skids, but they would not do for takeoff. The skids, therefore, rested on a wooden plank that was itself lying on another board fitted with two modified bicycle wheel hubs one behind the other. These tiny wheels ran along the runway, a 60-foot-long track made out of two-by-four planks standing on edge and covered with thin metal sheet.

1903 FLYER

In the 1903 Flyer and other early Wright biplanes, the pilot flew lying down, resting on his elbows while controlling the "horizontal rudder" (elevator) with his hands and warping the wings by moving his hips against a cradle. As can be imagined, the prone position was not comfortable. Orville admitted that the longer test flights of 1904 and 1905 over Huffman's Prairie were a challenge: "I used to think the back of my neck would break if I endured one more turn around the field." The simplicity inherent in the design of the 1903 Flyer is evident in these photographs, as is the bicycle engineering background of the Wright brothers. Bicycle-type chains of industrial strength are used on the engine and to drive the twin propellers. Store-bought wood, fabric and wire are combined in the airframe.

Success at Kitty Hawk

The memorial atop Kill Devil Hill along North Carolina's Outer Banks celebrates the accomplishments that changed the world. The inscription reads: "In commemoration of the conquest of the air by the brothers Wilbur and Orville Wright / Conceived by genius, achieved by dauntless resolution and unconquerable faith."

By a coin toss, Wilbur was chosen as pilot for the first try with the Flyer. Once the engine had been warmed up, he settled himself in the prone position on the lower wing and slipped the restraining cable. The Flyer surged down the slope and rose into the air, but too sharply. The large "horizontal rudders" proved extremely sensitive, and Wilbur underestimated their effect. The Flyer stalled and came down after being in the air for less than four seconds, doing some minor damage on impact. Wilbur was disappointed, but also sure that success was now certain. In writing to his family that night, he admitted his mistake, saying, "the real trouble was an error in judgement in turning up too suddenly after leaving the track," but then he added, "The machinery all worked in entirely satisfactory manner, and seems reliable. The power is ample, and but for a trifling error due to lack of experience with this machine and this method of starting, the machine would undoubtedly have flown beautifully."

As the damage to the Flyer was being repaired, the wind rose and the temperature fell. On the morning of December 17, there was a cutting northerly breeze of about 25 mph, almost too strong, but the brothers decided to try again.

This time the track was laid on level, hard-packed sand, and it was Orville's turn at the controls. At about 10:35 A.M. he slipped the restraint and moved forward, with Wilbur running alongside steadying a wingtip. After traveling along the rail for some 40 feet, the Flyer rose into the air.

Orville recorded his impressions in his diary: "I found the control of the front rudder quite difficult on account of its being balanced too near the center and thus had a tendency to turn itself when started so that the rudder was turned too far on one side and then too far on the other. As a result the machine would rise suddenly to about 10 feet and then as suddenly, on turning the rudder, dart for the ground. A sudden dart when out about 100 feet from the end of the track ended the flight. Time about 12 seconds (not known exactly as watch was not promptly stopped)."

Apart from Wilbur, the audience on the beach was just five local men. Standing there in the icy wind, it may not have occurred to them that they were witnesses to an event that was a turning point in history. In a mere 12 seconds of undulating progress, the realization of the dream of human flight had begun and the door had cracked open on the aviation century. By the end of the day, the door was significantly further open. Alternating as pilots, the brothers made four flights in all, improving with each one. On the last, Wilbur remained airborne for 59 seconds and traveled 852 feet. Given the strength of the wind, the actual distance through the air was about half a mile. There was no longer any question that the Flyer really could fly.

The Flyer's place in aviation history is assured, for its performance on December 17, 1903, but it never flew again after that. Before it could be returned to its shed, it was caught by a strong gust of wind and turned over. The damage was substantial and the Wrights left Kitty Hawk to spend Christmas in Dayton without attempting repairs. The career of one of the world's most famous flying machines was over after it had been in the air for a total of little more than a minute and a half.

There were times between 1899 and 1903 when the Wrights had become depressed at what they felt to be the crawling pace of their progress. In later years Wilbur wrote that, after suffering some disappointments with the 1901 glider, he had confided to Orville his opinion that "man would sometime fly, but that it would not be within our lifetime." Looking back at what was accomplished in those four years, however, a dispassionate observer must surely be astonished that the Wrights solved a problem of the ages in so short a time. The significance of their achievement was immense, and yet it passed almost unnoticed. The withdrawn nature of the brothers and the remoteness of Kitty Hawk combined to ensure that their activities were not well reported, whereas the public failures of Samuel Pierpont Langley in the heart of the nation's capital were covered by some very influential newspapers. Few people got to hear a true account of the events at Kitty Hawk, and to most who did it seemed unlikely that an obscure pair of bicycle mechanics would succeed where a distinguished scientist such as Langley had failed. The claims of the Wrights were therefore either ignored or viewed with great skepticism.

Developments at Dayton

The lack of public interest had little effect on the Wrights. They knew that their first Flyer was an imperfect flying machine and they set out to make it better. By the spring of 1904, a second Flyer was ready. Very similar in design to its predecessor, it was sturdier and had an engine capable of producing up to 16 horsepower. Now that they were engaged in powered flying, the Wrights were no longer so needful of the breezes of the Outer Banks, so they made arrangements with a farmer to carry out their trials in an 80-acre field near Dayton known as Huffman Prairie. To make up for the relative lack of wind in Ohio, they erected a derrick in the field and hung 600 pounds of metal weights from a rope inside it. The rope ran from the top of the derrick, under the launching rail, to the front of the Flyer II's trolley.

Orville Wright completing a 33-minute flight over Huffman Prairie on October 4, 1905.

When ready, the pilot tripped a catch restraining the weights and their fall considerably augmented the thrust of the twin propellers as the Flyer II surged forward to take off.

During 1904, the brothers made over 100 flights in the Flyer II. None of them was very long but a great deal was learned and, by the end of the year, both Wilbur and Orville had managed circling flights of more than five minutes.

1905 FLYER

The 1905 Flyer was the world's first practical aeroplane. Restored by Orville Wright himself, it is now housed in the Carillon Historical Park, Dayton, Ohio.
BELOW Since the 1905 Flyer can never return to the scene of its triumphs, photographer Dan Patterson conceived the idea of setting an image of the aircraft down on Huffman Prairie. A reconstructed launching derrick can be seen in the background.

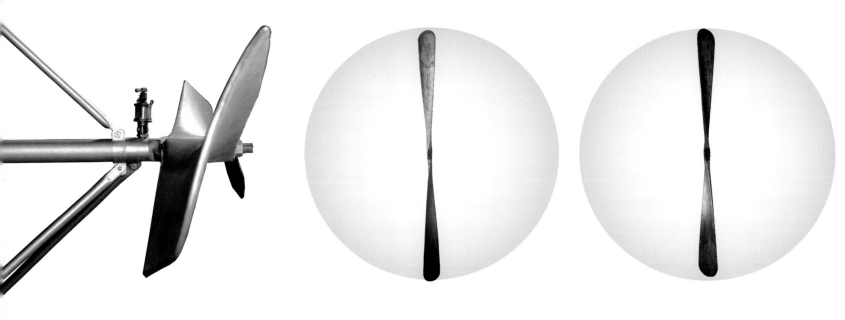

WRIGHT ENGINES AND PROPELLERS

ABOVE The Wright propeller was a masterpiece, designed from first principles by the brothers. As Orville described it, "With the machine moving forward, the air flying backward, the propellers turning sidewise, and nothing standing still, it seemed impossible to find a starting point from which to trace the various simultaneous reactions." Lubrication was supplied from the small receptacle above the shaft, which was filled before flight.

BELOW AND RIGHT On display at the National Air & Space Museum, a Wright engine, bolted to the lower wing of the 1903 flying machine, off center to counterbalance the weight of the pilots, Orville and Wilbur Wright. Also visible are the few basic instruments used to measure their efforts and the first cockpit. This engine developed 12 horsepower. The chains and sprockets suggest the bicycle engineering background of the designers.

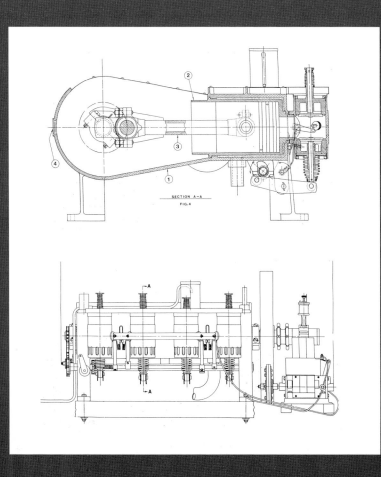

Top Wright engine No. 3, built by Charlie Taylor in 1904 and seen in the large photograph, is now held by the Engineers' Club in Dayton, of which the Wrights were members. It never flew, but served as a test-bed, providing valuable experience in engine design and building. It eventually achieved 25 horsepower, over twice that of the first motor of the same size.

Left Charlie Taylor, seen here in a photo from 1905, has been called by his biographer, Howard DuFour, the Wright brothers' "mechanician." This talented toolmaker was able to translate the concept of a lightweight internal combustion engine into metal. The engine was built from castings and tooled on a lathe and a drill press.

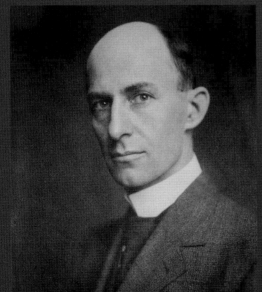

FIVE GENERATIONS OF WRIGHTS

OPPOSITE PAGE

TOP The Wright family in 2002, gathered on Huffman Prairie, the field near Dayton, Ohio, used by the Wright brothers for the flying trials of 1904 and 1905: Marion Wright, Wick's wife; Stephen Wright; Amanda Wright Lane; and her daughter Meredith. The locust trees in the center of the field are descendants of a group of trees with which Orville had a nearly disastrous flying incident. BOTTOM The studio portraits of the brothers reveal something of their personalities. Wilbur's strong features hid a relatively withdrawn character; he was a steady, thoughtful man described as being kind and tender. Orville's softer face suggested the more outgoing of the two; he was talkative and less reserved than his brother and careful about his appearance. These differences notwithstanding, theirs was an inseparable partnership. Wilbur wrote that they "lived together, played together, worked together, and in fact thought together."

THIS PAGE

TOP Wilkinson "Wick" Wright, grandnephew of Orville and Wilbur Wright, a kind and gentle man, died in 1999. His passion was the accurate remembrance of his uncles and their accomplishments. RIGHT The wingtip of the 1905 Flyer. Wick described the elegant simplicity typical of the Wright brothers' work and so evident in the anchor for the strut; the genesis for this fitting was the screen door hinge from the back door of their home on Hawthorn Street. BOTTOM LEFT Ivonette Wright Miller and Horace Wright, niece and nephew of the Wright brothers. Ivonette flew with Orville in August of 1911 and was the family spokesperson until her death at the age of ninety-three. Horace recalled "fishing with Uncle Orv" as a young boy while visiting the brothers at Kitty Hawk. BOTTOM RIGHT Ivonette sits behind her Uncle Wilbur at the 1909 celebration in Dayton.

In 1905, the Wrights poured their experience into designing and building a third aircraft. In its final form, Flyer III was a more aesthetically pleasing and effective machine than either of its forebears. The front and rear control surfaces were mounted further from the wings, and the link between the rudder and the wing-warping mechanism was disconnected to improve controllability. The result was an aircraft that was both graceful and maneuverable. By the end of the year, Flyer III had proved capable of completing tight figure-eight patterns and flying for as long as its fuel lasted, which on October 5 had been for more than 38 minutes. It was the world's first practical flying machine. All this was accomplished at a time when no other would-be aviator had achieved any kind of controlled powered flight, and when most people refused to accept that such a thing was possible. (In 1902, Simon Newcomb, a Harvard graduate and a professor of mathematics and astronomy, said, "Flight by machines heavier than air is unpractical…if not utterly impossible.")

The Wrights had decided as early as 1902 to seek patent protection. While that was pending, they did not want anyone to get close to their Flyers or watch their trials. Apart from local farmers, few people realized what was happening at Huffman Prairie. Nevertheless, the brothers began to feel that they should look for some return on their investment, and it had occurred to them that their aircraft had military potential, principally for reconnaissance. They therefore approached both the American and British governments, stating that they had produced a flying machine and offering to supply similar machines for a contracted price. The British government appeared to accept the Wrights' claims, but refused to go further without a practical demonstration, something the brothers were not prepared to give without promise of a contract. The U.S. government's rejection was even firmer. Three separate approaches were made to Washington, but the responses from the Board of Ordnance and Fortification in October 1905 represented the official blind eye at its most

The first man to achieve powered flight in Europe was the Brazilian Alberto Santos-Dumont. His machine, the 14 bis, was a bizarre collection of box kites strung together in a canard configuration. It was of no significance in the development of aviation, but it did fly in a straight line for 198 feet on October 23, 1906. The first rudimentary tests were conducted in June 1906, when the 14 bis was suspended from cables and towed across a clearing by a donkey!

opaque. The third letter concluded: "The Board does not care to…take any further action until a machine is produced which by actual operation is shown to be able to produce horizontal flight and to carry an operator." The bureaucratic indifference encapsulated in that sentence is hard to understand. No American official thought it worthwhile to visit Dayton, or even to examine the Wright brothers' claims. It is hardly surprising that the Wrights were discouraged. Since there was little likelihood of a government contract, they elected to keep the Flyers from prying eyes until their patents had finally been approved and governments had become more amenable. They stopped all flying and did not take to the air again for two and a half years.

In the course of their self-imposed period of abstinence, the Wrights refined their engine design and continued to build aircraft. Promise of a French contract led them to ship one to France in 1907, but the deal fell through and the Flyer sat in its crate at Le Havre until the following year. French aviation enthusiasts, alarmed by stories of the Wrights' success and the thought that France might be left behind, were working on a variety of machines, but there was no real appreciation of the problems to be confronted in making human flight practicable. The secrets of the Wrights had been hinted at in a 1903 lecture by Chanute in Paris, and by the publication of the Wrights' patent in 1906, but such clues were misinterpreted by Europeans who should have known better. No methodical program of research was undertaken and the critical problem of three-dimensional control in the air was not even considered. The Wrights took note and rightly concluded that there were no serious rivals on the horizon.

Small successes there were, however. In September and October of 1906, a Paris-based Brazilian, Santos-Dumont, managed a few barely controlled flights of up to 250 yards in a tail-first creation known as No. 14 bis, which was little more than a few large box-kites strung together. It was impractical and contributed nothing to the advance of aeronautics, but it was applauded with wild enthusiasm by a French population ignorant of what the Wrights had done.

> *"Success four flights Thursday morning all against twenty one mile wind started from Level with engine power alone average speed through air thirty one miles longest 57 seconds inform Press home Christmas. Orevelle Wright"*
>
> TELEGRAM, AS RECEIVED BY BISHOP WRIGHT, DECEMBER 17, 1903.

(The box kite was developed in 1893 by Lawrence Hargrave, an Australian. It was a stable device, with considerable lifting power, and was later adopted by many aircraft designers, particularly in Europe. In September 1906, the Danish engineer Jacob Ellehammer managed a circular "hop" of some 140 feet in his semi-biplane. It was tethered to a post and lacked controls, so was incapable of free flight.)

Although Santos-Dumont's success posed no real technological threat to the Wrights, it did sound an alarm about the prospects for aircraft contracts. There was little understanding of what the Flyers represented in terms of research and development, and the suggestion that the secrets of flight were about to become common property might be enough to make contract negotiation difficult. In 1907, therefore, the Wrights renewed their efforts to attract customers. They had talks with a company interested in selling Flyers to the French government, and sent a new proposal to the U.S. Board of Ordnance and Fortification after President Theodore Roosevelt, his attention drawn to the Wrights by the Aero Club of America, nudged his administration into finding out more about what they were up to in Dayton.

The U.S. Army Stirs

At the same time, the U.S. Army felt the tremors of growing aviation fever in Europe and decided to revive its moribund interest in the third dimension. On August 1, 1907, an Aeronautical Division of the Signal Corps was established under Captain Charles Chandler to "have charge of all matters pertaining to military ballooning, air machines, and all kindred subjects." Within months, the new Aeronautical Division had issued Signal Corps Specification No. 486 for "the construction of a flying machine supported entirely by the dynamic reaction of the atmosphere and having no gas bag." It was based on the Wrights' performance estimates and was issued for competitive bids on December 23, 1907. The aircraft was required to carry two persons weighing a combined 350 pounds, reach a minimum speed of 40 mph, and fly for 125 miles. A 10 percent bonus or penalty on the agreed price was included for each mile per hour achieved

Piloted by Orville Wright, the Flyer lifts away from its launching rail at Fort Myer in September 1908.

above or below 40, and it was stipulated that the machine should be easily disassembled for transporting in army wagons, with reassembly taking no more than an hour. Other provisions were that the aircraft should be able to land on an unprepared field without damage, and that it should be capable of safe descent if the propulsion unit broke down. Most particularly, it had to be "sufficiently simple in its construction and operation to permit an intelligent man to become proficient in its use within a reasonable length of time." Such was the general ignorance of what the Wrights had achieved that the American press ridiculed the specification, claiming that it asked for the impossible. Surprisingly, forty-one bidders responded, but only three bids were thought to be worth accepting, including the bid from the Wrights, who set their price for meeting the contract at $25,000. As it turned out, only the Wrights proved capable of providing a machine for trial.

Public Demonstrations

After doing some refresher flying at Kitty Hawk in the modified 1905 Flyer III, Wilbur set off for France in May 1908 to collect the Flyer stored at Le Havre, reassemble it at a racecourse near Le Mans, and demonstrate it publicly for the first time. A skeptical French audience gathered to view Wilbur's first flights on August 8, 1908. The reaction to his mastery of the air was dramatic. The Flyer's easy maneuverability and soaring flight put the struggling efforts of European pioneers into perspective, and people were at last forced to recognize the magnitude of the Wright brothers' achievement. The European press lionized Wilbur, calling his performances "Marvelous! Glorious! Sensational!" One commentator remarked, "We are as children compared with the Wrights." Francois Peyrey expressed French repentance when he said: "For too long a time the Wright brothers have been accused of bluffing.... Today they are hallowed by France." In Britain, Major Baden-Powell of the Aeronautical Society reached beyond the collective European astonishments to offer the somber comment: "That Wilbur Wright is in possession of a power which controls the fate of nations is beyond dispute."

While Wilbur widened the eyes of the Europeans, Orville arranged for the trials of the Type A Military Flyer, which were to be carried out at Fort Myer, near Washington, D.C. Like the Flyer in France, this new biplane had upright seats for a pilot and a passenger. Orville began flying on September 3, 1908, and electrified onlookers with the sureness of his control in the air. Within the next two weeks he achieved an endurance record of more than an hour, set an altitude record of 310 feet, and carried the first military observer, Lieutenant Frank Lahm of the Aeronautical Division. The Army was impressed and the spectators wild with enthusiasm. The trials could not have gone better — until the last day. On September 17, Orville took off with Lieutenant Thomas Selfridge as his passenger. They were circling Fort Myer when a crack developed in a blade of the starboard propeller. It became unbalanced enough to strike and tear loose one of the bracing wires supporting the rudder. Control of the Flyer was lost and it dived steeply into the ground, severely injuring Orville and killing Lieutenant Selfridge, who thus gained the morbid distinction of being powered flight's first aerial fatality.

The First Military Aircraft

The accident did not discourage the U.S. Army. Observers were convinced that the Wrights had a machine that was more than capable of meeting the contract specifications. An extension of the contract gave Orville time to recover from his injuries, and in July 1909 he was back at Fort Myer.

After a few days of false starts, Orville got into his stride and showed that the Flyer did indeed meet the specifications. On July 27, with President Taft looking on, Orville and Lieutenant Lahm were airborne for 1 hour, 12 minutes, 40 seconds — a new record for a flight with a passenger. Three days later, Orville flew with Lieutenant Benjamin Foulois as navigator on a cross-country speed trial between Fort Myer and Alexandria. The average speed achieved was 42.583 mph, which was enough to secure the $25,000 contract price, plus a $5,000 bonus. On August 2, the U.S. Army accepted the Flyer as the world's first heavier-than-air flying machine. Officially designated Signal Corps Aeroplane No. 1, it was said by the Washington *Evening Star* to be "Aeroplane No 1, Heavier-than-air Division, United States Aerial Fleet." The exploitation of warfare's third dimension had begun to gather momentum.

On September 17, 1908, Orville took off from Fort Myer with Lieutenant Thomas Selfridge as passenger. He had completed four circuits of the field when a cracked propeller gave way, leading to a series of structural failures and a crash. Amid the mass of wreckage, Orville lay badly injured, having broken a thigh and several ribs. Selfridge also had multiple injuries, including a fractured skull. He died after surgery, so gaining the morbid distinction of becoming the world's first fatality in an aircraft accident.

CREEDS MARTIAL AND MESSIANIC

It is a sobering thought that the majority of technological advances in human history have been almost immediately exploited for their military potential. Heavier-than-air flight was no exception, and it is a sad commentary on the nature of mankind that an achievement so long dreamed of as offering liberation from earthly restraints and the heavenly bliss of birdlike three-dimensional freedom should first be promoted, doubtless for practical commercial considerations, as an instrument of war.

Of course, the Wrights were not the first to think that any nation adding the ability to fly to its military capacity would gain significant advantages. Airborne military development had been foreseen and, to a limited extent, practiced for a very long time. Man-carrying kites had been used for reconnaissance in the Far East for centuries, and tethered balloons had been similarly employed by the French army as early as 1794, and by both sides in the American Civil War. Offensive action was predicted as far back as 2000 B.C. in a Hindu legend about a battle between an aerial city and a flying chariot. In 1670 the Jesuit priest Francesco de Lana suggested that an airship could be borne aloft by large evacuated copper balls, and he offered a dire warning: "Who sees not that no city can be secure against attack, since our ship may at any time be placed directly over it…that the same it would happen to ships on the sea, for our ship may overset them, kill their men, burn their ships by artificial fire-works and fire-balls. And this they may do not only to ships but to great buildings, castles, cities."

After witnessing Professor J.A.C. Charles' balloon ascent in 1783, Benjamin Franklin was equally discouraging about being attacked from the air: "Convincing sovereigns of the folly of wars may perhaps be one effect of it, since it will be impracticable for the most potent of them to guard his dominions. Five thousand balloons, capable of raising two

men each, could not cost more than five ships of the line; and where is the prince who could afford so to cover his country with troops for its defence as that ten thousand men descending from the clouds might not in many places do an infinite deal of mischief before a force could be brought together to repel them?"

Franklin was not the only one to meditate along those lines. Engravings exist that show a Napoleonic project for a French invasion of England by troops carried in balloons, and there are also sketches of English soldier-bearing kites intended to meet and defeat the aerial threat. One French poet, exasperated by the sea-borne truculence of the islanders, wrote: "At sea let the British their neighbors defy; The French shall have frigates to traverse the sky."

Conceived in the early years of the 19th century, these ideas for airborne confrontation may have been premature, but they foresaw the nature of future air defense problems and foreshadowed a very real 20th-century Battle of Britain.

Ominous predictions notwithstanding, the most powerful ideas usually associated with human flight, both before 1903 and for some time after, were those that assumed it would somehow establish links with the divine or the supernatural, and that its effects would be wholly benevolent. There is ample evidence that a reverence for the heavens and a recognition of the powers flight could bestow appeared at a very early stage in human development. Eyes seemed naturally drawn upward to search the skies for deities. Gods, angels and other immortals were often imagined as having wings. In the evolution of religions everywhere, wings were used to enhance the supernatural qualities of such divine figures as the Egyptian Isis, the Hindu Garuda, and the Greek Hermes and Eros, who became the Roman Mercury and Cupid. Christian artists have almost invariably depicted angels with the wings thought necessary to carry them between Heaven and Earth.

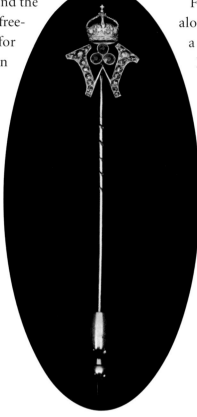

In 1909, when Orville was demonstrating the Flyer in Berlin, one of the spectators was Crown Prince Wilhelm. He wore this gold stickpin on his uniform, decorated with diamonds and rubies in the letter W. He removed the pin and presented it to Orville, commenting that the letter W was appropriate for both Wilhelm and Wright.

For many people who were present during the public flying demonstrations by Wilbur and Orville in 1908 and the months that followed, the experience was almost religious. Words such as "miraculous," "divinely inspired," and "spiritually uplifting" were used in describing reactions to the phenomenon of flight. Predominant among the predictions made at the time were those emphasizing the peace and prosperity manned aircraft would bring to the world. Some believed that historic international rivalries would disappear as people flew from place to place unhindered by land frontiers rendered irrelevant by air travel. Even such a distinguished U.S. statesman as Philander Knox, formerly President Taft's Secretary of State, expressed the opinion in 1910 that aircraft would actually eliminate war by bringing nations closer together.

Others less confident of human nature, and more conscious of martial traditions, nevertheless thought that the threat of airborne weapons being carried to a nation's heartland, so placing in jeopardy political leaders who might otherwise have felt themselves secure, would be a considerable deterrent to war. As early as 1899, during an international conference to discuss armament reduction at The Hague, delegates heard that the air weapon could "decrease the length of combat and consequently the evils of war." It was even suggested that soldiers under attack by aircraft would lay down their weapons and leave the battlefield, so making old-fashioned warfare pointless. Since an effective defense against aerial attack was then inconceivable, and aircraft were seen to be relatively cheap and easy to build, it was believed that nations large and small could be equally well equipped, so rendering international bullying less than sensible.

Whether views of an aerial future were based on looked-for benefits of worldwide travel and trade, on the threat of intolerable international strife, or on trust in the essential godliness of aircraft, most of those expressed in the early part of the 20th century reflected the hope that the world was about to become a better place, led to a brighter future by the disciples of a new faith — aviation. Even before the Wrights flew, such sentiments were well established. In 1894, Octave Chanute wrote: "So may it be; let us hope that the advent of a successful flying machine, now only dimly foreseen and nevertheless thought to be possible, will bring nothing but good into the world; that it shall abridge distance, make all parts of the globe accessible, bring men into closer relationship with each other, advance civilization, and hasten the promised era in which there shall be nothing but peace and goodwill among all men."

In taking mankind's first steps along the road to this social revolution, the Wright brothers' inspiration was perhaps more practical than spiritual. They solved the aerodynamic problems; others spoke the eulogies and spread the gospel of flight. Kindred spirits of the Wrights set out to explore the world revealed by the brothers' genius.

Louis Blériot contemplates the wintry scene from his Type IX on January 27, 1909.

RIVALS IN FLIGHT

The Wrights and their aircraft dominated the aviation world during the first decade of the century, but a number of rivals did eventually appear. Wilbur's performance in France initially chastened the Europeans, but as the shock wore off they were inspired by his brilliant flying. Great airmen such as Henri Farman, the Voisin brothers, Hubert Latham, Louis Blériot, S.F. Cody and J.T.C. Moore-Brabazon soon stepped forward, showing themselves eager to learn, adapt and develop the Wrights' methods and ideas. As they grasped the essential nature of the Wrights' system of three-axis control, they also saw value in retaining the inherent stability that was a feature of the largely unsuccessful European machines. Reaching for sensible compromise between the two, they made rapid progress and before long were producing aircraft that could outperform the Wright Flyers.

In the United States, too, the Wrights faced competition from the Aerial Experiment Association (AEA), a group under the leadership of Alexander Graham Bell. Among the original members, known as "Bell's Boys," were Lieutenant

> *"In matters of defence, we live on an island no longer. The day that Blériot flew the Channel marked the end of our insular safety, and the beginning of a time when Britain must seek another form of defence beside ships."*
>
> SIR ALAN COBHAM

Thomas Selfridge, who died in Orville's crash at Fort Myer, and Glenn Curtiss, a young motorcycle engineer and racer who turned to aviation because it combined new engineering challenges with an adventure promising excitement and speed. He was involved with the AEA's construction of four biplanes in 1908, the third of which (*June Bug*) he designed and flew with considerable success. On July 4, 1908, with the Wrights otherwise occupied, Curtiss and the *June Bug* won the *Scientific American* magazine's prize for the first public flight in the United States of more than a kilometer by staying in the air for almost a mile in front of several hundred people at Hammondsport, New York. By the Wrights' standards that was not much to shout about, but it was done in public and was given far more acclaim than anything the secretive Wrights had done up to that time.

European Beginnings

For Europeans, and for the French especially, the thought that someone from elsewhere might be the first to unlock the secrets of flight was intolerable. France was at the heart of European aeronautics in the early days of the century, with men dedicated to seeing that a French machine would become the first powered aircraft to fly. In April 1903, Octave Chanute gave a lecture to the Aero Club de France in which he described the Wright's progress with gliders, mentioned the methods of control used, and forecast the imminent building of a powered flying machine in America. The information spurred the French to react, reviving an interest in powered flight that had become almost moribund. A rich lawyer named Ernest Archdeacon founded an Aviation Committee to promote heavier-than-air flying, with the

Hats, coats and ties were accepted dress for workers at the Farman aircraft factory near Chalons, France.

avowed intention of beating the Wrights into the air. Leading figures in the efforts to be made were Captain Ferdinand Ferber, Robert Esnault-Pelterie, and Gabriel Voisin. "Will the homeland of the Montgolfiers have the shame of allowing the ultimate discovery of aerial science to be realized abroad?" trumpeted Archdeacon, while Ferber was even more direct, saying, "The aeroplane must not be allowed to be perfected in America." (In 1783, the Montgolfier brothers constructed the first balloons capable of carrying human beings. Over Paris, on November 21 of that year, François Pilatre de Rozier and the Marquis d'Arlandes made the first untethered flight in a Montgolfier balloon.)

Despite these passionate declarations and the incentive of upholding national pride, the achievements were disappointing. Taking Chanute's revelations as a starting point, Archdeacon, Ferber and Esnault-Pelterie all produced gliders that set out to copy the Wrights' designs. However, the significance of the control systems escaped them, so the gliders were inadequate copies and notably unsuccessful. Furthermore, there was no appreciation of the need for methodical research or the value of intensive testing. Far from inspiring a careful examination of the reasons for their repeated disappointments, the failures reinforced a belief that reports of the Wrights' success were exaggerated. Even the publication of the Wright patents in 1906, which included accurate details of their flying controls, was ignored. French aviators remained mired in ignorance

and blind over-confidence, Archdeacon remarking that the problem of "equilibrium and actual control of the machine is unfortunately far from being solved."

The situation in Britain was far worse. With no achievements at all to brag about, one pompous columnist for the *Daily Mail* stated, "We know more about aeronautics than any other country in the world. As yet, we have not attempted to apply our knowledge, but…our scientists may claim to have conquered the air on paper. To achieve the victory in practice will not be a difficult matter." This extraordinary state of affairs persisted until Wilbur Wright finally shocked the Europeans out of their complacency with his demonstration flights at Le Mans in 1908.

Although France had some claim to being the leading aeronautical nation in Europe in the early years, two of the first men to make a significant impression on powered flight in that country were not French. Besides the Brazilian Santos-Dumont, and even before he flew his 14 bis in 1906, a Romanian, Trajan Vuia, who also lived in Paris, achieved a few short leaps in a machine resembling a shopping cart shaded by a fragile parasol. Pulled along by a carbonic-acid engine of 25 horsepower, it rose no higher than a few feet during its brief and uncontrolled upward lunges. In its basic form, however, it foreshadowed the monoplane configuration that was to be a major part of early European efforts.

It was 1907 before Frenchmen began to make a real impact on the flying world, the most important advances being made first by Louis Blériot and the Voisin brothers. Blériot spent the year building, flying and crashing a number of designs, impatiently abandoning each in turn without

benefit of testing and modification, but in the process establishing the classic monoplane configuration, with the engine and propeller in the nose, the wings well forward, and a long fuselage ending in a tail unit, the whole resting on an undercarriage of two main wheels and a tail-wheel. The Voisins, held back by European apprehensions about instability, produced machines combining a biplane form with a box-kite tail unit containing a rudder; no control was provided in roll. On most Voisins, the wings were joined together by fabric curtains, effectively converting them into large box-kites too, evidence of a determination to achieve lateral stability. At this stage, the idea of freedom of maneuver in three dimensions was so novel that European airmen flew as though they were driving an airborne car, striving to keep the horizon in its proper horizontal place. Intentional rolling was an unnatural act.

ABOVE *Wilbur demonstrates his mastery of flight at Pau in 1909 before a crowd including King Edward VII, Charles Rolls and Louis Blériot.* TOP RIGHT *Orville stands by as Wilbur checks the wind with their homemade anemometer at Pau, France, 1909.*

Voisin Farman 1 bis. The aircraft on display at the Musée de l'Air et de l'Espace, Le Bourget, is an accurate replica of the aircraft flown on January 13, 1908, by Henry Farman when he became the first man in Europe to fly round an officially observed closed circuit of one kilometer. The awkward box-kite tail is a prominent feature. In modified form, the Voisin Farman 1 bis made the first cross-country flight in Europe, covering 17 miles from Bouy to Reims on October 30, 1908.

One Voisin was sold to Henri Farman, who had the sense to learn from his mistakes and make a series of modifications to his machine as he grew in experience. In November 1907, he succeeded in flying the modified aircraft in a rough circle and remaining airborne for 1 minute and 14 seconds. At a time when the Wrights were capable of staying in the air for as long as their fuel lasted, this was the first European flight to last for more than a single minute. Henri Farman went on, in January 1908, to be awarded the Grand Prix d'Aviation, established for the first man in Europe to fly an officially observed circle of a kilometer, awkwardly ruddering his biplane round a course near Issy-les-Moulineaux in France to win the prize.

The period between January and Wilbur's dramatic demonstrations in August was marked by a series of minor achievements. Farman managed a flight as long as 20 minutes, and on May 29 gave Ernest Archdeacon the privilege of being the first European passenger in an aircraft. (Two weeks earlier, C.W. Furnas had flown with both Wilbur and Orville Wright in the U.S. to become the world's first airborne passenger.) On July 8, another pioneer, Léon Delagrange, having shown off his Voisin in the first flights seen in Italy, persuaded Madame Thérèse Peltier to become the first woman to leave the ground in a heavier-than-air flying machine. (Inspired by the experience, Madame Peltier later went on to become also the first woman to fly solo.)

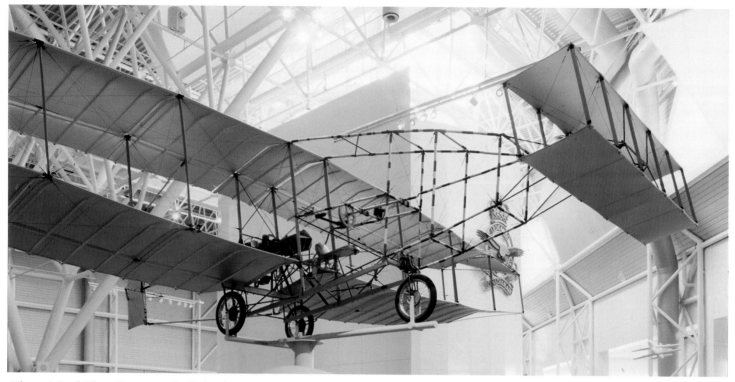

The original Silver Dart *was built by the Aerial Experiment Association formed by Alexander Graham Bell. Powered by a 65-horsepower Continental engine, it had a wingspan of 49 feet and was capable of reaching 43 mph, but its service ceiling was only 70 feet. The first controlled powered flight in Canada occurred on February 23, 1909, when it was flown off the ice at Baddeck, Nova Scotia, by designer J.A.D. McCurdy. The* Silver Dart *is a canard, or "elevator in front," design. Like most aircraft of the time, it had poor control characteristics. It was made of steel tube, bamboo, friction tape, wire, wood, had no brakes, and was covered with rubberized silk balloon-cloth. The example in the Canadian National Aviation Museum is a replica made between 1956 and 1958 by RCAF volunteers.*

Once these several tiny steps had been overtaken in one bound by Wilbur at Le Mans, progress was more rapid. Farman and Blériot both made cross-country flights of 17 miles or so in October, and Farman showed that the roll-control message had been received when he fitted four large, aileron-like controls to his aircraft, thereby moving toward a more effective system than wing-warping. By the end of the year, however, the Wrights were still the masters of aviation. Orville's unfortunate crash at Fort Myer apart, 1908 saw the brothers triumphant, with Wilbur posting most of aviation's records. Operating from Camp d'Auvours just east of Le Mans between August 21 and December 31, he made over 100 flights, accumulating more than 25 hours in the air. In his hands, the Flyer III, now modified and called the Type A, had regularly flown at speeds above 40 mph, maneuvered freely with two people aboard, stayed aloft for 2 hours, 20 minutes on one flight, and climbed to a height of 360 feet.

The Baton Passes

Poised by themselves at the pinnacle of the aviation world when 1909 began, the Wrights were no longer so lonely when the year ended. European aviators (mainly French) and Glenn Curtiss in the U.S. made rapid progress, and the number of would-be aviators and designers rose sharply. Several lines of development pointed the way to the future, but many impractical forms also took shape. Multi-winged and underpowered monstrosities, some looked more like birdcages or Venetian blinds than flying machines. Most were destined never to fly, but they at least provided amusement as curiosities and gave evidence of the imaginative flair inspired by the promise of aviation's new world.

Once converted to the benefits of pilots having positive control of their aircraft, French designers were still reluctant to abandon the concept of inherent stability. They sought a compromise between the two, aiming to produce a stable aircraft that could nevertheless be easily controlled.

This broke away from the Wright brothers' principle of inherent instability, which meant that an aircraft had to be mastered like a fractious horse for every second it was in the air. It was correctly believed that, once achieved, the stable, simply controllable aircraft would be a safer, more forgiving machine, requiring a less demanding level of skill from a pilot and therefore offering a greater number of potential airmen the chance to fly. The French approach soon proved successful, wresting the leadership in aviation development from the Wright brothers, who seemed content to rest on their laurels. Having shown themselves to be so innovative and determined only a few years before, they now appeared to be wedded to the basic design of their Flyer, stubbornly retaining the features of a rail-launched, unstable, wing-warping biplane with a forward elevator long after they might have used their extraordinary gifts to move on. In time the Wrights' company did fit wheels instead of skids, relinquish wing-warping in favor of ailerons, and design an airframe to accept a tractor propeller instead of a pusher, but only after Wilbur had died and Orville was no longer with the organization. The Wrights had shown the world how to fly, but from 1909 onward the baton of aviation leadership was grasped ever more firmly by others, while the brothers spent far too much of their time on lawsuits.

Perhaps piqued by all the attention given to Glenn Curtiss for his achievements, in 1909, Orville wrote to Curtiss claiming that since the *June Bug* had "movable surfaces at the tips of the wings, adjustable to different angles on the right and left sides for maintaining lateral balance," the Wright patents were infringed. The brothers thereafter embarked on a long, bitter lawsuit against Curtiss that set out not only to punish him but also to prove that their patents should apply to all forms of lateral control on aircraft worldwide. Sadly, the implacability of the Wrights on this matter diminished their reputation. They were widely viewed as standing in the way of aeronautical progress, and the strictures of their patents were largely ignored or circumvented. Rightly recognized as men of genius who had once pointed the way to the future for the world, after 1909 they were often attacked for defending the achievements of the past as their personal property. While they expended their energies in trying to hang on to what they had, others overtook them and went on to greater things. (When Wilbur died of typhoid in 1912, Orville believed that his inability to resist the disease was due to exhaustion brought on by the stress of dealing with the patent lawsuits.)

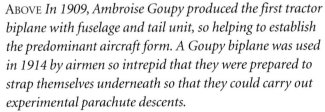

ABOVE *In 1909, Ambroise Goupy produced the first tractor biplane with fuselage and tail unit, so helping to establish the predominant aircraft form. A Goupy biplane was used in 1914 by airmen so intrepid that they were prepared to strap themselves underneath so that they could carry out experimental parachute descents.*

LEFT *By 1912, the aeroplane had become something of a status symbol, taking its place alongside other treasures in displays of opulence by the rich — an estate with a great house, the latest motorcars, horses, trophies of the chase, a well-dressed family, servants and a Farman biplane.*

By 1911, European designs had taken the lead, notably Blériot monoplanes, but Santos-Dumont, too, was among those who found some reward for his efforts. Although somewhat overshadowed by others in 1909, he did produce a popular version of his little Demoiselle, which can be said to have been the first successful light aircraft. Also notable were the biplanes produced by Breguet and Goupy. While not very successful in themselves, they established the standard form of the biplane — tractor airscrew, long fuselage, and tailplane with elevator — that dominated aviation for years to come. If anything served to illustrate the lead French designers held in aviation at this stage, it was the fact that so many of their designs were being built under license in the United States. Blériots were sold complete for $1,000, carrying the proud boast: "All assembled machines guaranteed to fly!"

POWERED FLIGHT ESTABLISHED

It was in 1909 that the heavier-than-air flying machine gained public acceptance as a practical airborne vehicle. Biplanes remained the dominant form, but monoplanes gained some prominence. Leon Levavasseur produced several elegant Antoinettes, and Blériot had his Type XI, the latest of his fragile line. These aircraft fired the public imagination as they took center stage in the competition to see who would be the first to fly across the English Channel. The London *Daily Mail* newspaper offered a prize of £1,000 as encouragement. The dashingly handsome figure of Hubert Latham was the first away in his Antoinette IV. Powered by a 50-horsepower engine, its long, slim fuselage was reminiscent of a canoe, which proved fortunate. It seemed entirely appropriate that Latham, born of French and English parents, should be the one to complete the aerial bridge. He took off full of confidence from Sangatte, near Calais, on July 19, only to have his engine fail in mid-Channel. His aircraft's boat shape and its broad wings kept him afloat until he could be rescued by the French navy. Latham

ABOVE *Santos-Dumont Demoiselle 20, on display at the Musée de l'Air et de l'Espace, Le Bourget. This tiny monoplane made its debut at St. Cyr in March 1909. Powered by a 35-horsepower two-cylinder engine, it could achieve 56 mph.*

BELOW *Alberto Santos-Dumont, a rich Brazilian living in Paris, recorded the first powered flight in Europe in 1906 in his 14 bis. He later turned to monoplane designs such as the little Demoiselle, the first successful ultralight aircraft.*

remained nonchalant throughout. As he described it: "I settled on the water in a horizontal position. I swung my feet up on to a cross-bar to prevent them getting wet. Then I took out my cigarette case, lit a cigarette, and waited."

Latham determined to repeat the attempt and had Antoinette VII made ready at Sangatte. Meanwhile, not far away at Les Baraques, Blériot was ready to go with his tiny Type XI. The weather intervened, however, and strong winds kept both airmen grounded for several days. Finally, in the early hours of July 25, Blériot, awake because of a troublesome burn on his foot suffered in an accident a few days before, noticed that the wind had dropped. At 3:30 A.M., he air-tested the Type XI. Satisfied that all was well, he refueled and took off at 4:41 A.M., heading out into a mist over the gray waters of the Channel. Ten minutes later, without a compass or a watch, and with the 25-horsepower Anzani engine already showing signs of over-heating, Blériot had outpaced the escorting French destroyer. In a later account, he said: "For ten minutes I was on my own, isolated, lost in the middle of the foaming sea, seeing no point on the horizon, perceiving no boat." He flew between 150 and 300 feet above the sea and "let the aeroplane take its own course. Then, twenty minutes after I have left the French coast, I see the cliffs of Dover, the castle, and away to the west the spot where I had intended to land.... It is evident that the wind has taken me out of my course." It had indeed, and Blériot had further difficulties when he tried to reach his planned landing place. The freshening wind threatened to prevent him from crossing the cliffs, but he managed to coax the Type XI through a gap and make a rough landing near Dover Castle. With a flight of a little less than 37 minutes, Louis Blériot had written his name large on the pages of aviation history, and people everywhere began to consider the proposition that aircraft could be much more than a mere sportsman's plaything.

The statue of Hubert Latham is on the French coast at Sangatte, near Calais, the place from which he launched his unsuccessful attempts to cross the English Channel in his Antoinette monoplane.

British commentators were among the first to register some concern. As H.G. Wells said, "In spite of our fleet, this is no longer, from the military point of view, an inaccessible island."

Alan Cobham agreed: "In matters of defence, we live on an island no longer. The day that Blériot flew the Channel marked the end of our insular safety, and the beginning of a time when Britain must seek another form of defence beside ships." Although the frail little Type XI could hardly be seen as endangering national security, it would not be long before events showed the potential airborne threat to be very real.

Blériot had won the *Daily Mail's* prize, but Hubert Latham persisted with his Antoinette. He tackled the Channel again on July 27, and once more his engine stopped, this time forcing him into the water within a mile of the English coast. (The Honorable C. S. Rolls used a Wright Type A to complete the first double crossing of the Channel on June 2, 1910. He was killed in a crash of this aircraft only a month later, but his name lives on in Rolls-Royce cars and aircraft engines.)

Latham's two ditchings served to emphasize a problem that now bedeviled airmen more than any other. The basics of lift and control might be largely understood, but engines that provided sufficient power and did so reliably were hard to come by. Engine failure was a common occurrence, and there was no such thing as a surplus of power. This was a difficulty that would diminish but persist in one way or another over the decades to come. Indeed, many aviators would claim that, despite the extraordinary thrust-to-weight ratios and trouble-free hours recorded by engines of all kinds during the later part of the 20th century, the problem has never been completely solved. Small as it has become, the risk of engine failure has always been present.

A head-on view of the Antoinette clearly shows the paddle-bladed propeller and the V-shaped eight-cylinder in-line engine, which produced 50 horsepower.

Hubert Latham tried to coax his Antoinette across the Channel twice, on July 19 and 27, 1909, but both times ended in the Channel. On July 25, Louis Blériot ended Britain's isolation for ever by flying from Les Baraques to Dover in 37 minutes.

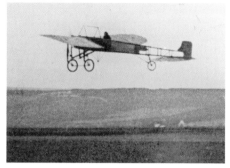

BELOW The Blériot XI at Le Bourget is the same type as the aircraft used by Louis Blériot for his crossing of the English Channel on July 25, 1909. It relied on wing-warping for lateral control, and its 25-horsepower three-cylinder Anzani engine gave it a top speed of 47 mph. The Type XI established the conventional monoplane form and was the foundation of Blériot's subsequent commercial success.

Suspended below the Blériot XI is an Antoinette VII, designed by Leon Levavasseur. This is the type flown by Hubert Latham on his second attempt to cross the English Channel on July 27, 1909. Latham had it repaired after its soaking in sea water, and went on to use it to win the Prix d'Altitude at Reims, climbing to a record height of 508 feet.

Following the French Lead

After Blériot's Channel crossing there was a slow public awakening in Britain to the facts of the dawning air age. There was little official enthusiasm, however. A government committee on aerial navigation reported in February 1909 that, with regard to "aeroplanes," it had not been possible "to obtain any trustworthy evidence to show whether great improvements may be expected in the immediate future, or whether the limit of practical utility may have already been nearly attained." The committee members interviewed no one who might have had firsthand knowledge of heavier-than-air flying, and they were strongly biased in favor of airships. They therefore recommended providing funds for airships and canceling proposed expenditure on other flying machines.

In the face of such inept behavior, it was left to a few private enthusiasts to carry aviation's flag in Britain. Leading the field was an American, Samuel F. Cody, who made the first powered flight in Britain on October 16, 1908, and a year later was flying up to 40 miles at a time. The first British-born airman to fly in Britain was J.T.C. Moore-Brabazon (later Lord Brabazon of Tara). He learned to fly in France in 1908, bought a Voisin and flew it from the Isle of Sheppey in the Thames Estuary in the spring of 1909. Admirable though that was, he garnered far more publicity later in the year by getting airborne with a pig as a passenger, so challenging the sarcastic cliché "and pigs might fly!"

Among British manufacturers in 1909, Alliott Verdon Roe built, flew and crashed an ungainly aircraft that had both the main wings and the tail as triplanes. His determination to succeed made up for his lack of funds, a situation that led him to cover the wings in brown paper instead of fabric. The Short brothers designed their own aircraft and built Wright biplanes, and Robert Blackburn, Geoffrey de Havilland and Frederick Handley Page were working on their first flying machines. Late starters though they were, Short, Blackburn, de Havilland and Handley Page would be at the forefront of the British aircraft industry for the next half century, and most British aviators would fly aircraft from at least one of their factories at some time or other.

Showman extraordinary and aviation pioneer, Samuel Cody built an ungainly looking flying machine and in 1908 became the first man to fly an aeroplane in England.

SHUTTLEWORTH

The home of the Shuttleworth Collection is a grass airfield in the heart of Bedfordshire, England. Several hangars house the collection, which is comprised of aircraft built between 1909 and 1955. Military aircraft include a Sopwith Triplane, a Gloster Gladiator and a Hawker Sea Hurricane. Most are kept in flying condition and regularly flown during air shows each summer. Among the earliest aircraft types at Shuttleworth are a Blériot and an A.V. Roe Triplane.

Basically similar to the machine used for the Channel crossing, the Shuttleworth Blériot (constructor's No. XIV) was one of the original aircraft used by the Blériot School at Hendon in 1910. It crashed in 1912, and was stored under Blackfriars Railway Bridge in London before being acquired by A.E. Grimmer, who rebuilt and flew it. Richard Shuttleworth obtained it in 1935 as his first historic aeroplane. Today, the Blériot is restricted to straight hops across the airfield, but it remains the world's oldest aeroplane/engine combination still in flying condition.

TOP RIGHT Shuttleworth's Roe Triplane IV is a replica built for the film *Those Magnificent Men in their Flying Machines*. The original was powered by a 35-horsepower Green four-cylinder engine that was barely adequate for overcoming the considerable drag of the airframe. Nevertheless, it was flown at the Avro flying school in 1910. The replica is fitted with a 1927 Cirrus Hermes II, which proved more robust. The center and upper wings use Roe's sophisticated wing-warping system, in which the wings are hinged at the rear spars so that warping does not bend the spars. By the standards of the day, the controls were considered to be reasonably light.

OPPOSITE PAGE AND RIGHT Dan Patterson's photographs emphasize the complex elegance of early aircraft construction. Light streams through the translucent fabric, revealing curving spars, while gleaming metal shapes fill out the fragile fuselage, and taut wires brace the aircraft for flight.

The Antoinette Latham Monobloc of 1911 sought to introduce the concept of streamlining to reduce drag. It was a three-seat monoplane with a completely enclosed fuselage. Control cables were internal and the undercarriage was fitted with fairings. Much of the skin was aluminum. Unfortunately, it was an idea before its time; the 50-horsepower engine could not cope with the overall weight of a ton and a half.

Slow to follow the American and French leads though the British were, the rest of the world was generally even slower, although a widening ripple of aviation awareness was spreading. Wilbur Wright established the world's first flying school in France, and the number of qualified pilots began to grow. Most aspiring pilots, however, still learned about flying by listening to helpful hints from those who had gone before and then trying it for themselves. Germany's first native pilot got airborne in January 1909, and the Canadian J.A.D. McCurdy flew an aircraft of his own design over Nova Scotia in February. Blériot and others took the gospel of flight wherever they could, and first flights were recorded during the year in Austria, Denmark, Sweden, Rumania, Russia, Turkey, Portugal, the Netherlands and Australia.

Intrepid Birdmen

If 1909 was the year when powered aircraft came of age, 1910 saw a notable rise in flying's popularity with the general public. Competitions, races, meetings and air shows proliferated in response to a growing demand from people who wanted to see aircraft being flown by the heroic figures lionized in the newspapers. Some brave souls even wanted to fly in those aircraft capable of carrying a passenger or two. The year 1910 was also when the accidents that had been waiting in the wings began to exact payment for aeronautical lessons learned the hard way. Thirty-two flyers died during the year, and many more survived accidents, including two fortunate enough to live through the first

mid-air collision, between an Antoinette and a Farman near Milan. Such statistics tended only to enhance the public perception that aviators must be exceptional individuals, courageous adventurers who braved the unknown and were in some way especially gifted. It seemed unlikely that they could be normal human beings. In magazine and newspaper articles, pilots were often referred to as supermen or "intrepid birdmen." They were "a breed apart," a phrase taken literally by at least one author who maintained that natural selection had been at work in producing pilots. Most humans were descended from fish, he insisted, whereas the remote ancestors of pilots were birds.

Whether that curious argument was taken seriously or not, pilots were regarded with considerable awe. People wanted to see or hear about them because they were doing exciting, risky things that the majority could not imagine doing themselves. Flying was fascinating because it was either inaccessible or terrifying, and pilots were heroic, larger-than-life figures who reached for the skies and overcame impossible odds. Between 1910 and the beginning of WWI, many flights were undertaken that helped to support this public view of aviators, as flyers faced and overcame one new challenge after another.

From Here to There

In April 1910, Louis Paulhan and Claude Grahame-White competed to become the first to fly from London to Manchester, a distance of almost 200 miles, in less than 24 hours. A prize of £10,000 for this achievement had been offered by the London *Daily Mail* as early as 1906. Both airmen flew Farman biplanes, and both braved turbulent winds and icy cold in their flights north. Grahame-White had damaged his aircraft in strong winds during an earlier attempt, and by the time he was ready to try again, Paulhan had appeared on the scene, fresh from his triumph at an air meet in Los Angeles, where he had set a new altitude record of 4,165 feet. (In 1906, flying from London to Manchester in 24 hours was thought to be so impossible that a rival newspaper sarcastically countered the *Daily Mail*'s challenge with another that offered £10,000 to the first person who could fly to Mars and back within a week.)

The race to Manchester caught the attention of the wider world, with bulletins being posted as far away as New York and Berlin. Paulhan was the first away and was 57 miles ahead when nightfall forced both pilots to land. Desperate to close the gap, Grahame-White did something unheard of by getting airborne again at 2:30 A.M. and rumbling off into the darkness, where he faced the alarming novelty of night flying. As he said: "A great difficulty presented itself in not knowing whether I was ascending or not…. The weirdness of the sensation can scarcely be described. I was alone in the darkness with the roar of the engine in my ears." Paulhan went on to win the race, but Grahame-White had the distinction of surviving the first night flight in Europe. In a frail biplane, buffeted by the weather and without instruments, that in itself was a considerable achievement. Tongue in cheek, he came to the conclusion that, really, "there is hardly any difference between day and night flying, only at night you can't see." Grahame-White's disappointment was diminished by his subsequent success in the 1910 Gordon Bennett Cup race at Belmont Park on Long Island, a triumph he celebrated in exuberant manner by going on to land in Pennsylvania Avenue near the White House in Washington, D.C. (The first night flights anywhere were made near Buenos Aires on March 10, 1910, by Emil Aubrun in a Blériot.)

Unlike the 1911 Monobloc, Louis Paulhan's ethereal triplane of the same year appeared to have been constructed as an exercise in flimsiness, its bathlike cockpit seemingly added as an afterthought to the aircraft's spindly timber and floating draperies.

LEFT *The business end of the Morane-Saulnier Type H from the collection of the Amicale Jean Baptiste Salis at La Ferte Alais near Paris. In an aircraft similar to this, Roland Garros became the first aviator to fly across the Mediterranean on September 23, 1913. The AJBS machine is fitted with a Le Rhône rotary, whereas Garros used a very similar 80-horsepower Gnôme, which kept running (albeit roughly) for most of the almost eight hours of the flight.*

RIGHT *Roland Garros had intended to become a concert pianist, but then he attended the Reims aviation meet in 1909. Within a year, he was a member of the Moisant International Aviators display team in the United States, and by 1913 he affirmed his position as one of France's leading airmen with his astonishing 450-mile flight across the Mediterranean. In 1915, he had metal deflector plates attached to his propeller so that he could fire a machine gun through the propeller's arc. On April 1, 1915, he shot down an Albatros two-seater, then destroyed two more and forced two others down in the next two weeks. He was called an "ace" by his countrymen, and the term was adopted by the press as a way to describe a pilot with five aerial victories. Brought down by ground fire on April 18 of that year, Garros was a prisoner of war for three years. He escaped in 1918 and returned to flying combat in SPADs, only to be shot down and killed just a month before the war ended.*

Later that year, another triumph ended in tragedy when the Peruvian Georges Chavez succeeded in crossing the Alps in a Blériot via the Simplon Pass at nearly 7,000 feet, only to be killed while trying to land at Domodossola in Italy. Undeterred, pilots flew point-to-point over longer and longer distances. In January 1911, McCurdy braved crossing 90 miles of water to take a Curtiss from Key West to Havana, and in August, H.N. Atwood flew a Wright from St. Louis to New York via Chicago. In Europe, there were long-distance races, including two 1,000-mile circuits, one from Paris that circled via Brussels and London, and the other, an event again sponsored by the *Daily Mail*, round Britain. Both were won by André Conneau (pseudonym Beaumont) flying a Blériot.

Recording his experiences in a book that became a bestseller (*Mes Trois Grandes Courses*), Conneau stressed the feeling of liberation and the invigorating challenge the aviator finds in flight: "He follows a path free of any limitation. At his pleasure, he can ascend, descend, maneuver; he meets no obstacle. He is truly free…the victorious machine that he has created obeys his every movement with the lightness of a bird. The danger? But danger is one of the attractions of flight. If man loves flying so much, it is because every leap forward he makes toward the conquest of space threatens his existence."

Coming only three years after Wilbur's demonstrations at Le Mans, these were remarkable European flights, and they were matched by a real epic of determination and endurance in the United States.

William Randolph Hearst was offering $50,000 for the first coast-to-coast flight across the United States in less than 30 days. On September 17, 1911, Calbraith P. Rodgers set off from New York, flying a Wright EX biplane named *Vin Fiz* after a sponsor's soft drink. A rugged, six-foot-four, cigar-chewing motorcycle racer, he fitted the image of the dashing aerial adventurer perfectly. After a tumultuous send-off from Sheepshead Bay, his erratic progress across the continent was followed avidly by an American public desperate for him to succeed. He finally reached Pasadena, California, on November 5, nineteen days too late to qualify for the prize, but his achievement staggered the imagination. During his forty-nine-day journey, Cal Rodgers spent just over 82 hours in the air while covering 4,321 tortuous miles, following railway lines and avoiding mountains wherever he could. Of the sixty-nine landings, many unplanned, nineteen resulted in crashes. Neither Rodgers nor the *Vin Fiz* were in very good shape when they reached California. The aircraft had been effectively rebuilt more than once, and its pilot had suffered a wrenched knee, a broken leg and collarbone, an arm torn by steel splinters from an exploding engine, and other smaller abrasions. Failing in his bid to cross America in thirty days, he nevertheless became the first to fly from coast to coast. There was no arguing with his blunt comment: "I made it, didn't I?" Four months later, the indestructible Cal Rodgers was dead, killed when his aircraft crashed into the sea off Long Beach, California.

On the other side of the Atlantic, French pilots covered almost inconceivable distances in their efforts to outdo each other. In 1913, first Jules Védrines in a Blériot, and then a pairing named Bonnier and Barnier in a Nieuport monoplane, flew from France to Cairo via the Middle East. Even more impressive was the first crossing of the Mediterranean, from St. Raphael in the south of France to Bizerta, Tunisia, by Roland Garros in a Morane-Saulnier H monoplane. It was not without incident. Somewhere off Corsica, he heard "a sinister sound of breaking metal. The whole plane shook. I thought I was lost. Yet the motor

> *"Until now I have never really lived! Life on earth is a creeping, crawling affair. It is in the air that one feels the glory of being a man and of conquering the elements. There is an exquisite smoothness of motion and the joy of gliding through space — it is wonderful!"*
>
> GABRIELE D'ANNUNZIO, 1909

continued to turn with a knock that reverberated through my body…. On the hood a hump appeared; the metal was punctured and drops of oil seeped through…obviously one of the motor parts had come off." Reluctant to abandon the flight, Garros pressed on, trying to convince himself that, since the engine was still running, it would be sensible to keep going, at least until he reached Sardinia. As that island came and went, he could not bring himself to stop. "A mysterious force, stronger than my reason and my will power, carried me along towards the sea." Seven hours and 53 minutes after leaving France, a relieved Roland Garros landed safely in Tunisia, his face covered in oil blown back from his disintegrating engine.

Stunts

News of long-distance flights was eagerly devoured, but flying of another kind excited the crowds at air shows and meetings. As machines improved and pilots grew more proficient, demonstrating an aircraft came to be more than a mere flyby for the spectators. Stunt pilots, who were prepared to take planes to their limits and sometimes beyond, were much in demand. Glenn Curtiss, the Wrights, and a Texan named John Moissant formed exhibition teams that toured the United States, introducing small-town America to flying. At fairgrounds and farms people gathered to be thrilled by daredevils in their flying machines. Among the most celebrated was Lincoln Beachey, who joined the Curtiss team in 1910. He raised pulse rates by snatching handkerchiefs from the ground with his wingtip, racing against automobiles, and pulling out at the last second from steep dives. In 1911, he set an altitude record of 11,600 foot, and electrified huge crowds by flying over Niagara Falls and under the Niagara Falls bridge. In his obsession with speed, Beachey almost seemed to want to justify his cynical belief that people "only come to see me die." In 1915, during a display at the San Francisco International Exposition, he fell to his death after vastly exceeding the limiting speed of his aircraft and collapsing its wings.

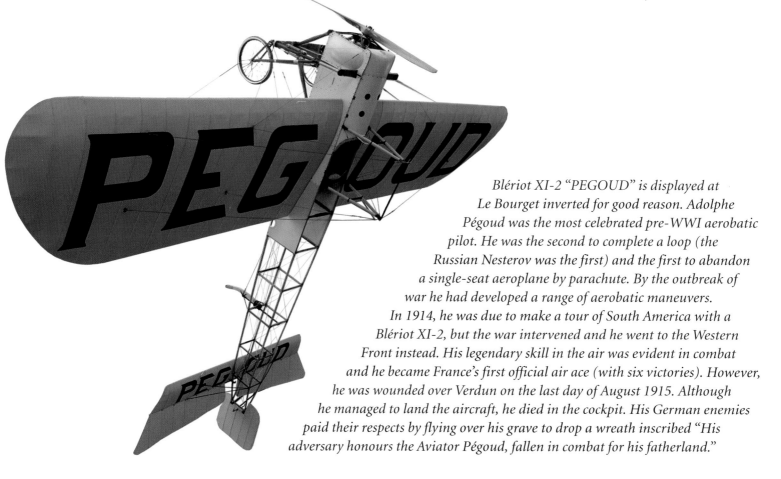

Blériot XI-2 "PEGOUD" is displayed at Le Bourget inverted for good reason. Adolphe Pégoud was the most celebrated pre-WWI aerobatic pilot. He was the second to complete a loop (the Russian Nesterov was the first) and the first to abandon a single-seat aeroplane by parachute. By the outbreak of war he had developed a range of aerobatic maneuvers. In 1914, he was due to make a tour of South America with a Blériot XI-2, but the war intervened and he went to the Western Front instead. His legendary skill in the air was evident in combat and he became France's first official air ace (with six victories). However, he was wounded over Verdun on the last day of August 1915. Although he managed to land the aircraft, he died in the cockpit. His German enemies paid their respects by flying over his grave to drop a wreath inscribed "His adversary honours the Aviator Pégoud, fallen in combat for his fatherland."

The first man to perform a full loop in an aircraft was a Russian, Lieutenant P.N. Nesterov, flying a Nieuport Type IV monoplane over Kiev on August 27, 1913, a feat for which he was promptly arrested on the grounds that he had endangered government property. The distinction of having developed more complex aerobatics goes to a Frenchman, Adolphe Pégoud. In September 1913, he used a Blériot to demonstrate sustained inverted flight, and later went on to perform a loop, a bunt, and a tail-slide. (A bunt is done with the cockpit on the outside of the maneuver rather than on the inside, the pilot experiencing negative "G" throughout.) That year, he also made the first emergency parachute jump in Europe. It is reputed that Pégoud had his Blériot mounted upside down on trestles and strapped himself into the cockpit for 20 minutes at a time, so determined was he to become accustomed to the discomforts of inverted flight.

Women with Wings

Although the popular image of a typical pilot in the early days of flying was that of a dashingly handsome young man, there were women ready to show that aviation was not exclusively for males. Those who became involved devised costumes shocking to the sensibilities of the time, in order to cope with the challenges of being exposed to the elements in rudimentary and fragile machines. The impracticality of voluminous skirts had been a particular problem for ladies who flew with the Wrights, overcome by tying string round below the knees. The first women pilots, such as Bessica Raiche and Harriet Quimby in the United States, and Hilda Hewlett, Hélène Dutrieu and Melli Beese in Europe, soon abandoned skirts and frilly blouses in favor of more sensible, if outrageous, garments — padded long-sleeved jackets with hoods, and trousers tucked into boots. Belgium's Hélène Dutrieu even took off her corsets to fly because they were too confining.

This liberation from confinement was not only a matter of clothing. Women pilots found that flying gave them a sense of freedom from social restriction unlike any other activity. Once off the ground, their fate rested in their hands alone, and that, for women normally bound by post-Victorian society's burdensome conventions, was a heady experience. It gave them a tremendous boost when they matched the performances of the "heroic supermen" of public adulation, and their achievements helped to break down barriers facing women generally in their struggle for emancipation, showing conclusively that they were more than capable of taking on something thought to be appropriate only for the bravest of the brave. As the French pilot known as Baroness Raymonde de Laroche pointedly remarked: "Flying does not rely so much on strength as on physical and mental coordination." (On March 8, 1910, the Aero Club de France issued Raymonde de Laroche her pilot's license, making her the world's first formally licensed woman aviator.)

Unfortunately, flying is no respecter of persons, male or female. In 1912, America's first licensed woman pilot, Harriet Quimby, became the toast of the aviation world when she flew her Blériot monoplane across the English Channel. Just months later, she added her name to the growing list of flying fatalities, crashing during a display near Boston, Massachusetts. The conservative *Boston Post*, searching for a way to report the shocking news that a woman had been killed while facing the hazards of flying — a privilege normally reserved for heroes rather than heroines — was moved to give her honorary male status, saying: "She took her chances like a man and died like one." Undeterred, women continued to pursue the independence and self-confidence that flying offered. Ruth Law Oliver and the Stinson sisters, Katherine and Margaret, were among those in the U.S. who went on performing at air meets, racing against automobiles, and running their own flying schools. Ruth Law Oliver once flew her Curtiss the 512 miles from Chicago to Hornell, New York, to capture the American

long-distance record. Following a night's rest, she flew on to Governor's Island, arriving 27 hours after leaving Chicago. The New York Central Railroad made a point of being unimpressed, drawing attention to the rail time between the two cities of 22 hours.

Spinning Lesson

Many of the increasingly frequent flying accidents were the result of pilots having only vague ideas about the aerodynamic limits of their aircraft. The whys and wherefores of stalling and spinning were not common knowledge. The first pilot to survive an unintentional spin and describe the recovery action was a British naval officer, Lieutenant Wilfred Parke. On August 25, 1912, his Avro Type G cabin biplane entered a spin after Parke had tried to tighten a gliding turn at 600 feet. With the aircraft descending rapidly, he initially pulled the stick back and applied rudder *into* the direction of rotation. Noting that these actions only caused the spin to speed up, he consciously reversed the controls, putting the stick forward and applying rudder against the spin. The Avro recovered instantly, only 50 feet from the ground. Parke's detailed explanation of the incident was instrumental in saving many lives. It was Parke's accurate description of his recovery that made his spin memorable. (The first pilot to enter a spin unintentionally and recover was F.P. Raynham, who survived the experience on September 11, 1911, but may have been unclear as to how or why.)

In August 1911, Harriet Quimby became the first American woman to gain a pilot's license. After spending some time touring with Moisant's International Aviators, she decided that she should be the first woman to fly across the English Channel. This she did flying her Blériot on April 16, 1912, taking off from Dover and landing on the coast of Normandy. On July 1, 1912, she got airborne with a passenger at the Harvard-Boston air meet. Over Boston Harbor, the machine suddenly became uncontrollable, and the flyers, who were not wearing seat belts, were thrown out. Both were dead when pulled from the water.

CAPRONI

The Caproni Museum at Trento, Italy, is full of aviation history treasures, including a unique collection of aircraft, nine of which are the only ones in existence. There is also a reconstruction of Gianni Caproni's study and an example of an aeronautical workshop as it was in 1912.

PREVIOUS PAGE
TOP LEFT Dr. Gianni Caproni, Conte di Taliedo, is one of aviation's great pioneers. He turned his attention to aviation after Wilbur Wright's demonstrations in France during 1908. In 1910 he produced his first powered aircraft, and by 1913 he was pioneering the construction of large bombers. American airmen got their first experience of strategic bombing in Caproni bombers operating from Italy in WWI.
TOP RIGHT Maria Fede Caproni, Contessa di Taliedo, is Gianni Caproni's daughter and president of the Caproni Museum in Trento. Enthusiastic about aviation and knowledgeable about aeronautical subjects, she is a leading figure in the aviation history world and a passionate exponent of preserving its treasures.
BOTTOM Among the aircraft on display is the Caproni Ca.9, a small monoplane inspired by Blériot's successful Type XI. The Ca.9 at Trento is preserved in original condition. Its 35-horsepower Anzani engine could pull it along at 56 mph, and on January 20, 1912, Enrico Cobioni flew a Ca.9 to claim the world speed record for aircraft powered by an engine of less than 40 horsepower.

THIS PAGE
TOP Perhaps inspired by the shape of the Copernican sphere that modeled a three-dimensional solar system, Caproni's elegantly integrated controls offered a solution to the problem of achieving smoothly coordinated three-dimensional flight.
BOTTOM The propeller store at the Caproni Museum, filled with the sculpted, laminated artistry of Italian airscrew craftsmen.

As is evident from the example at Le Bourget, the Deperdussin Monocoque of 1912 was a remarkable advance in aircraft design and construction. Beautifully sleek, it made use of the monocoque technique in which the aircraft's skin bears much of the structural load. It was the first aircraft in the world to exceed 100 mph.

LEFT *Igor Sikorsky's Il'ya Mourometz aircraft were the first successful four-engined flying machines ever produced. A mere decade after Kittyhawk, Sikorsky's monsters were flying for hours and carrying undreamed-of loads over vast distances, sometimes with passengers taking a walk outside!* RIGHT *A cloud of smoke billows from the Gnôme rotary as it bursts into life during a competition in Britain in 1913.*

Technical Developments

Often aerial mishaps were due to the flimsy nature of the machines and an imperfect understanding of the stresses an airframe could be expected to stand without coming apart. Given the urgent need to solve problems of structural weakness, the business of designing and building an aircraft made great strides, even though it proceeded in a largely haphazard manner, driven for the most part by individuals working and experimenting alone.

From 1911 onward, metal was more frequently introduced into aircraft structures, although most machines were still constructed principally of ash and spruce with wire bracing, and covered with silk or linen. The inadequately powered Levavasseur Latham monoplane of 1911 was a failure as a flying machine, but it was remarkably prophetic. A three-seater with cantilevered wings, a completely enclosed and streamlined fuselage and a spatted undercarriage, it was a generation removed from the skeletal biplanes seen at aviation meets. It was followed in 1912 by a more successful streamlined monoplane, the Monocoque Deperdussin. The invention of the monocoque construction technique, in which the aircraft's skin carries much of the structural load, was a significant step forward. Despite the Deperdussin's demonstrated success, however, the method was not widely used until several years later. Flown by Jules Védrines, the Deperdussin soon made its mark. Powered by a cowled 140-horsepower Gnôme, it became the first aircraft to exceed 100 mph in February 1912, and set the world's speed record of 108.18 mph while winning the Gordon Bennett Cup at Chicago in September. An improved version, with a 160-horsepower Gnôme, was flown to victory and another record by Maurice Prévost in the 1913 Gordon Bennett at 126.67 mph.

Other pre-WWI novelties were the first enclosed cabin aircraft produced by Avro, a tail-less biplane developed by J.W. Dunne in Scotland, and the world's first four-engined aircraft, built and flown in Russia. Igor Sikorsky's *Bolshoi Baltiskiy* appeared in 1913. With a wingspan of more than 92 feet and powered in its final form by four 100-horsepower German Argus engines, Sikorsky's monster boasted a glazed cabin containing four armchairs, a sofa and a table. The cockpit was fitted with dual controls. Within a year, Sikorsky had moved on to greater things with the *Il'ya Mourometz*, the Type A version of which was an even larger machine with a span of 113 feet and a gross weight of 10,580 pounds. A washroom had been added to the sixteen-passenger cabin and a wind-driven generator gave electric light after dark. For the exceptionally intrepid traveler, there was even a passenger promenade deck on top of the fuselage for use in flight! Less than ten years after Kitty Hawk, it was a far cry from the Wright Flyer.

OFF TO SEA

The first tentative floatplane flights were made by Henri Fabre as early as March 1910, but it was Glenn Curtiss in the United States who soon led the world in seaplane development. In January 1911, Curtiss mounted a large float beneath the fuselage of one of his standard land-planes, and placed two small outriggers under the wings. The following month, he carried a passenger in the machine, and also fitted it with wheels, so creating the first amphibian. By the end of 1912, Curtiss had fitted the floatplane with an enclosed cockpit, and then went on to build a genuine flying boat. Evolving into the "F-boat," this was the ancestor of a long line of Curtiss flying boats. Following the Curtiss lead, Benoist and European companies such as Short Brothers, Sopwith, Farman and Voisin all developed practical marine aircraft.

Competition

The competitive spirit came early to aviation, with races and challenges springing up wherever flyers came together. Newspaper owners soon saw advantages in becoming patrons of this exciting new sport. Lord Northcliffe of the London *Daily Mail* was one of the first, and his American counterpart was James Gordon Bennett, eccentric owner of the *New York Herald* and the man who had sent H.M. Stanley into Africa to find Dr. Livingstone. Victory in the annual Gordon Bennett Cup was vigorously pursued, since it brought the lucky aviator considerable financial reward and a greatly enhanced reputation.

The first hydro-aeroplane contest was held at Monaco in March 1912. The tests included one that required aircraft to take off from water with a passenger, then fly a selected course and return to harbor, landing both pilot and passenger without getting their feet wet. Since most of the contestants either crashed or could not take off, it came close to farce, but the Belgian pilot, Jules Fischer, was judged to have won with a Henri Farman biplane.

A second, more elaborate hydro-aeroplane contest was held at Monaco in April 1913. The last day introduced a competition sponsored by Jacques Schneider, a rich French aviation enthusiast. He was also an idealist who saw marine aircraft as the best hope for spanning oceans and bringing nations closer together. His *Coupe d'Aviation Maritime Jacques Schneider* (the Schneider Trophy) was intended to promote the development of practical aircraft, fast but with reasonable range, and capable of operating from the open sea with a useful payload. The trophy was a magnificent silver creation, topped by a winged feminine figure, later popularly called "The Flying Flirt." Surprisingly, since it featured only marine aircraft, no competition grew to have more prestige than the Schneider Trophy.

The French Albessard was an early attempt to provide an enclosed cabin for pilot and passengers.

GLENN CURTISS

The Wright brothers opened the door to powered flight in 1903, but Glenn Hammond Curtiss, pictured at left, was close behind and was responsible for many of the significant developments in American aviation during the years that followed. The list of his aeronautical achievements is unmatched by any other aviation pioneer — among them the 1908 *June Bug*; the ubiquitous Jenny; the first operations from ships; the first flying boats and the NC-4, which recorded the first transatlantic flight; the series of Curtiss record-breakers and Schneider Trophy winners; and the D-12 engine, the design of which later influenced Rolls-Royce as they began development of their series of in-line engines. When the Curtiss Aeroplane and Motor Company went public in 1916, it was the world's largest aviation company, producing over 10,000 aircraft during WWI.

OPPOSITE PAGE
TOP LEFT Historical images of early Curtiss flying boats.
BOTTOM The 1911 Curtiss A1 at the Museo Storico del'Aeronautica Militare Italiana near Rome is a beautifully built and accurate replica of the first Italian military aircraft.

THIS PAGE
TOP RIGHT Prominent on the Curtiss biplanes were the ailerons, placed midway between the wings. An effective and more efficient alternative to wing-warping, they were the cause of the long-running feud between the Wrights and Glenn Curtiss.
BOTTOM RIGHT The Curtiss A1 at the National Aviation Museum, Pensacola, Florida.
BELOW The 1911 Curtiss A-1 was powered by an eight-cylinder, V-form in-line water-cooled Curtiss engine of 75 horsepower. It was the ancestor of the great D-12 engine of the 1920s, which exerted a powerful influence on all subsequent in-line engine design. This example is at the USAFM.

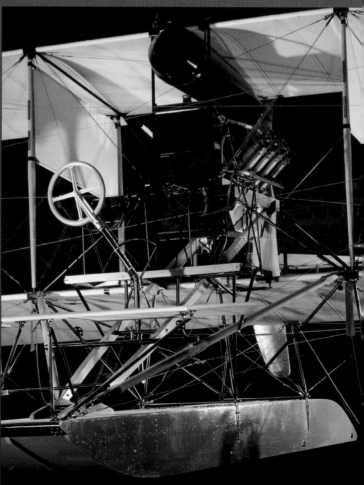

In its later years particularly, the buildup to the contest was followed eagerly by people of the competing countries, with daily newspapers carrying detailed reports on the aircraft and the pilots. Governments involved themselves in the preparations and the event itself became an occasion of unbridled nationalism, with excited crowds cheering on their heroes and banner headlines lauding the victorious team. Alas for Schneider's ideals; by the 1920s, the international fervor surrounding his competition had distorted his guiding principles. The idea of developing aircraft that combined speed, range and payload was forgotten and the contest became an outright pursuit of speed. With national pride at stake, it seemed that the thrill of the chase was all that really mattered.

The Schneider Trophy was established as an international challenge, with a team of up to three pilots allowed from each competing nation. Any nation winning the trophy three times in succession won the right to keep it in perpetuity. In 1913, there were only four contestants, three French and one American, with all four flying French aircraft. It was not an auspicious beginning and gave no hint of what the event would later become. The rules demanded that an aircraft must be taxied on the surface for the first 5 kilometers to demonstrate seaworthiness, before flying a further 280 kilometers at speed. Various misadventures eliminated two of the Frenchmen, leaving the race between Maurice Prévost and Charlie Weymann. The circuits were flown independently after a staggered start, and Prévost was the

first to finish, but he made the mistake of landing short and taxiing across the finishing line, which was against the rules. With Weymann apparently on the way to recording a faster time, the visibly upset Prévost declined an invitation to take off again and fly over the line to post an official finish. When Weymann was forced out by a broken oil-line, Prévost changed his mind. His final time for the race included his sulking period of nearly an hour, reducing his actual average speed of 61 mph to 45 mph for the record books. (Charles Weymann, born in Haiti, brought up in France, and flying a Nieuport, claimed to represent the U.S. Weymann had won the 1911 Gordon Bennett Cup, flown in the U.K.)

The 1913 Schneider Trophy may have been more fizzle than fireworks, but the entries for April 1914 promised better things. Pilots representing France, Germany, Switzerland, the U.S. and the U.K. arrived to compete at Monaco. Only two aircraft finished the contest. A small flying boat entered by Switzerland finished second; the winner was a tiny British biplane called the Sopwith Tabloid. Flown by Australian Howard Pixton, the Tabloid covered the 280-kilometer course at an average of nearly 87 mph. Although they took heart from knowing that the Tabloid was powered by a 100-horsepower Gnôme rotary, the French were deeply disappointed. Their sleek monoplane Deperdussins and Nieuports had struggled even to get off the water, despite having more powerful engines, whereas Sopwith's biplane had jumped off and shown that it was fast, maneuverable and had a good rate of climb.

Reservations

Splendid though the victory was for Britain, the Tabloid's success had a disturbing effect on aeronautical progress. For some time, questions had been raised about the advisability of continuing with the monoplane form. From 1912, a number of fatal accidents involving structural failure of monoplanes in flight alarmed authorities and aviators alike. Given the methods of construction and the materials available before WWI, and the limited knowledge of aerodynamic loading, it is hardly surprising that the safe solution to the problem seemed to be to prefer biplanes. The performance of the Tabloid served to accelerate the process. Here was a biplane matching the monoplanes for speed,

outclimbing and outmaneuvering them, yet having all the benefits of lifting power, low landing speed and sturdy construction inherent in the biplane form.

The monoplane's fall from favor might have been temporary had not authorities in Britain and France concluded that monoplanes were essentially dangerous. In France monoplanes were prohibited from flying until modified to more stringent structural standards, and in Britain the War Office banned monoplanes from military use. Improvements in design and manufacture were to no avail. The psychological damage was done, and the bias in favor of the biplane took root. Growing military interest in aviation, strengthened by European instability and the imminence of war, cemented that bias in Britain and France, where conservative soldiers were not keen to equip their air arms with machines of doubtful reliability. Aircraft generally were unknown military quantities, believed by many to be of limited use, but the proven qualities of biplanes at least made them the preferred form. With some notable exceptions, particularly in Germany, the monoplane retired to the shadows until the fighting was over.

At the 1913 Paris Exposition, Morane-Saulniers shared a prominent position with the remarkable Dunne No. 8 tail-less biplane, which had flown from Eastchurch in England to Paris. John Dunne was the first to develop powered flying wings, and they proved to be astonishingly stable. More than once, Dunne showed just how stable they were by abandoning the controls and climbing out onto a wing during a flying demonstration.

FLYING AND THE MILITARY

In the period immediately after the U.S. Army acquired the 1909 Wright Type A, American airmen eagerly embraced the idea that the third dimension could be exploited in war. In 1910, Glenn Curtiss tried dropping dummy bombs on a target shaped like a battleship, and in 1911, live bombing trials were carried out by Lieutenant Myron Crissy and Philip Parmalee. USN Lieutenant Riley Scott devised a rudimentary bombsight that markedly improved aiming accuracy. The possibilities of airborne combat were examined as early as 1910, when Lieutenant Jacob Fickel shot at targets with a rifle from a Curtiss pusher, and in 1912, when Captain Chandler fired a machine gun, developed by Colonel Isaac Lewis, from the right seat of a Wright Type B. Important naval advances were made, too. On November 14, 1910, Eugene Ely flew a standard Curtiss biplane off the deck of the cruiser USS *Birmingham* in Hampton Roads. Two months later, he landed on the USS *Pennsylvania* off San Francisco. Then Glenn Curtiss flew out to the USS *Pennsylvania* in San Diego Bay, landed alongside and was hoisted aboard by derrick, proving that there was more than one way for ships to handle aircraft.

Alas for individual enterprise, few of these efforts were welcomed at an official level. The U.S. War Department's lack of interest often forced Americans with bright ideas to cross the Atlantic, where they were warmly received. Scott won a competition in France with his bomb-aiming device, and Lewis was able to set up a company in Belgium to manufacture his machine gun. It later became a significant weapon in the aerial battles of WWI. Having been first in the field of military aviation, the United States failed to build on its lead and fell behind the Europeans, some of whom applied themselves seriously to thinking about war in the air. By contrast, the potential of military aviation was not rated highly in the United States. In the eyes of the American public, flying was a great new adventure, in which daredevils broke records or entertained the crowds at the fair. The United States was protected by oceans and vast distances, and it seemed inconceivable that flimsy aerial machines could ever be more than marginally useful to either the army or the navy. In Europe, the picture was quite different. The smaller, more densely populated European countries were traditionally on guard against each other across notoriously porous land frontiers. Only

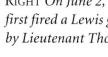

ABOVE *On November 14, 1910, Eugene Ely flew a Curtiss biplane off the deck of the cruiser USS* Birmingham *in Hampton Roads.*
RIGHT *On June 2, 1912, Captain Charles Chandler first fired a Lewis gun from a Wright B Flyer piloted by Lieutenant Thomas de Witt Milling.*

Designed by an Austrian, Igor Etrich, the birdlike Taube (Dove) was built under license by Rumpler in Germany. Here a Mercedes-powered Taube gets ready to leave on the Circuit of Berlin in 1913.

the British had the luxury of a water barrier, and the effectiveness of that was questioned as soon as Louis Blériot flew his monoplane across the English Channel.

It was true that many officers in the older European armed services sneered at the manned aircraft. Britain's most senior soldier regarded aviation as "A useless and expensive fad, advocated by a few individuals whose ideas are unworthy of attention." Marshal Foch of France later added: "It is good sport, but for the army the aeroplane is useless." Nevertheless, there were other Europeans who saw the military potential of flying machines. Air Leagues were formed in France and Germany to promote the need for national readiness in the air, and in Britain the Aerial League of the British Empire proclaimed "the vital importance to the British Empire of aerial supremacy, upon which its commerce, communications, defence, and its very existence must largely depend."

To put the relative attitudes of the U.S. and Europe into perspective it is useful to examine the total amounts spent on military aviation and the numbers of pilots trained by various countries before WWI. Between 1908 and 1913, both France and Germany spent the equivalent of well over $20 million each; Russia, $12 million; and even Belgium, $2 million. Campaigns for aviation in Britain, France, Germany, Italy, Austria, Switzerland, Russia and Greece were able to raise funds from the public, the Greek campaign even benefiting from money collected in the United States. In the same period, the U.S. allocated less than $500,000 to military aviation. In terms of certified pilots, both civilian and military, the disparity was startling; in 1913 there were some 2,400 pilots in the world, and of those fewer than 100 were American.

Airmen Go to War

It was in 1911 that manned aircraft first took part in military operations, when the Italians went to war in North Africa to loosen the Ottoman Empire's shaky grip on Tripolitania. They took with them an air force of nine aircraft — two Blériots, three Nieuports, two Farmans and two Etrich Taubes. On October 22, Captain Piazza flew the first operational sortie, reconnoitering Turkish positions near Tripoli from his Blériot. His exploits inspired the Italian poet Marinetti to draw an idealized pen portrait of the military airman, foreshadowing the creation of the "ace" in World War I: "Higher, more handsome than the sun…his bold, sharp-edged face chiseled by the wind, his little mustache crazy with will."

Little more than a week after Piazza's reconnaissance, on November 1, Lieutenant Gavotti was flying an Etrich Taube when he dropped the first bombs in anger on Turkish encampments at Ain Zara and Taguira. In a leather bag he carried four bombs, each weighing 4.5 pounds, and he kept the detonators in his pocket. Approaching a target, he took a bomb on his knees, fitted a detonator and then heaved the weapon overboard. Afterward, in bravura style, he claimed that his attacks had produced "disastrous results." If the Turks were taken aback by this bolt from the blue, they were quick to grasp the propaganda opportunity, protesting the attack on what they insisted was a hospital.

Dispassionate observers reported that the damage done by the tiny Italian bombs was minimal and of little value, but noted that the aerial reconnaissance carried out, including both still and motion-picture photography, had a significant effect on the struggle. Not everyone was content with such dismissive judgments on offensive operations. An Italian officer and budding air-power prophet named Guilio Douhet predicted that greater things would follow from these small beginnings. "A new weapon has come forth," he said. "The sky has become a new battlefield."

The air weapon appeared again in the Balkan Wars of 1912–13. Both sides had a few aircraft, but they were seldom used offensively. As in North Africa, most operations were undertaken for reconnaissance, seeking information about the disposition of enemy forces. If any lesson was learned, it was that ground forces were becoming intolerant of being spied on from the air. Sorties flown below about 3,000 feet ran the risk of being hit by small-arms fire. These events were duly noted elsewhere and, by 1914, most European armies recognized the dangers of allowing enemy aircraft free use of the air above their forces. Training manuals began to include instructions on shooting at aircraft, and there was talk of providing specialized anti-aircraft guns. For their part, airmen considered the possibility of developing armored aircraft.

The Europeans Get Organized

Although many senior officers still had doubts about the usefulness of manned aircraft, by 1912 most military forces felt the need to organize air services that were growing, slowly but inexorably. The British Royal Flying Corps was formed in April 1912, and its Naval Wing, encouraged by Winston Churchill to go its own way, was separated to become the Royal Naval Air Service in June 1914. A German Air Arm was inaugurated in October 1912, and equipped with more than 200 aircraft. The French formed the Direction de l'Aeronautique Militaire in April 1914, and the Italians followed with the Corpo Aeronautico Militare in January 1915. All of these air services busied themselves not only with acquiring aircraft and training the men to operate them, but also with creating air bases capable of supporting operations.

Before WWI, most aircraft operated by the fledgling air services were entirely unsuitable for war. However, a standard form of combat aircraft — nose, cockpit, wings, fuselage, tail — was beginning to appear. At the first military aviation exhibition, the 1911 Concours Militaire at Reims, French manufacturers dominated the show, both in airframes and in engines. At this stage, France was the world's leading aeronautical nation and was acquiring military aircraft and training pilots at a faster rate than any other country. Among the aircraft at the Concours, a two-seater Nieuport was shown with a machine gun, an indication that, to some aircraft builders at least, not all aircraft were destined to be unarmed reconnaissance machines. Aware of being left behind, the Germans hastily organized their aircraft industry. Initially it owed a great deal to French designs, with only the outdated birdlike Etrich Taube made at home, although even that was created by an Austrian. In 1913, the German Army issued regulations for its future aircraft, including one stating that they must "henceforth be entirely of national manufacture." Apparently they were prepared to stretch a point for Anthony Fokker of Holland, who opened a factory in Berlin in 1912.

In Britain, the Royal Aircraft Factory at Farnborough was established to produce military aircraft. Its first designer and test pilot was Geoffrey de Havilland, who soon made his mark with several influential designs. His B.E.1 of 1911 was the forerunner of a line of reconnaissance aircraft flown throughout WWI. Developed into the B.E.2c, it was both controllable and very stable, if slow. While the B.E.2c's stability was admirable for reconnaissance duties, that quality reduced its maneuverability and, since it lacked the speed to run, it was easy meat for German fighters. It gained the tragic distinction of carrying more airmen to their deaths than any other type of aircraft during the war.

(The designation B.E. stood for Blériot Experimental, denoting the Blériot tractor airscrew form. F.E.s were pushers, therefore Farman Experimental. Later initials included B.S. [Blériot Scout], S.E. [Scout Experimental] and R.E. [Reconnaissance Experimental]. Although many of the aircraft soon ceased to be experimental and became operational, they retained their initials, as in the S.E.5 and R.E.8, for example.)

De Havilland's other aircraft was the B.S.1, a single-seat biplane first flown in 1912. Conceived from the outset as an aircraft intended for combat, it can be regarded as the ancestor of all subsequent scout and fighter aircraft. The remarkable Tabloid and its Sopwith successors owed a great deal to the B.S.1, and among its direct British descendants was the outstanding S.E.5a, flown by many of the RFC's top-scoring aces. Other significant prewar aircraft included the F.E.2a pusher biplane fighter prototype, fitted with a Maxim gun in the nose, and

The AGO (Aerowerke Gustav Otto) company began building pusher-engined airplanes in 1912. Two enthusiastic airmen, encased in a bath-shaped AGO cockpit, smile for the camera before taking part in the 1913 Circuit of Berlin.

Among the treasures held by the Caproni Museum in Trento are a number of aviation posters. This one, advertising the International Circuit of Milan in 1910, shows a daring aviator flying his Antoinette perilously close to the spires of Milan's splendid cathedral. A Farman biplane floats by at a more discreet distance.

the Avro 504, a biplane with staggered wings that became one of the most celebrated aircraft in history. Used principally as a two-seat trainer, it was versatile enough to suit more warlike roles and was built by the thousand.

Anxious not to be left behind, the Royal Navy's airmen noted what Ely and Curtiss had accomplished with the U.S. Navy and did some trials of their own. In January 1912, a Short 27, piloted by Lieutenant Charles Samson, was flown from a bow platform on the moored battleship HMS *Africa*. Too flimsy and primitive to be modified for floats, the S.27 had cylindrical air bags fitted to its undercarriage in case of a splashdown. On May 8, during a Royal Review of the Fleet, S.27s demonstrated bombing from 500 feet, and located a submarine submerged at periscope depth. The following day, an S.27 took off from HMS *Hibernia* while the ship was steaming at 10.5 knots. These successes encouraged the Admiralty to convert a light cruiser, HMS *Hermes*, into a carrier for two seaplanes. Shorts eased the problem of storage aboard ship by fitting the aircraft with folding wings. The seeds planted by these small beginnings took time to germinate, but in time they bore fruit in a new era of naval warfare.

Storm on the Horizon

With each month that went by during the prewar years, the expanding horizons of aviation brought new flying experiments. Thinking that pilots needing to fly straight and level for long periods might prefer to be able to fly "hands off," Lawrence Sperry of the United States installed a gyroscopic stabilizer in a Curtiss flying boat. In August 1910, James McCurdy managed to both send and receive radio messages from a Curtiss while flying at Sheepshead Bay, New York. Theodore Ellyson used a compressed-air catapult to get a 1912 Curtiss airborne at Annapolis, and in July 1914, Commander Arthur Longmore, RN, launched a torpedo from a Short seaplane. Daring pilots everywhere tried flying at night in the belief that airmen could find the cover of darkness comforting. The business of flying was rapidly becoming a complex art, and, more often than not, military airmen found themselves at the forefront of its development.

By 1914, the aeronautical foundations had been laid. Aircraft of increasing capability were being designed, the number of pilots was rising, small aircraft factories were in

On May 2, 1912, Lieutenant Charles Rumney Samson of the Royal Navy became the first to fly from a moving ship when he took off in a Short "pusher" biplane from a platform mounted on HMS Hibernia *as it steamed into wind at 10.5 knots off the south coast of England.*

production, and organizations, both civil and military, were in place to promote and control aerial activity. As the political situation in Europe deteriorated, and war became ever more likely, it was generally recognized that aircraft would have something to contribute to the conflict. The question was —what? Strategists and tacticians, with few real precedents to fall back on, were confined to theory, and without experience that did not convert easily into policy and doctrine. With vague ideas that aircraft would be useful in extending the range of army and navy eyes, and might also find some undefined roles requiring the use of weapons, the European nations prepared for the coming confrontation. At this stage, not many people expected air power to be a significant force in battle. The next four years would begin to show them just how terrible the airborne weapon could be.

CHAPTER 2

Aerial Warfare: 1914 to 1918

*"Everything presently serves war,
there is no invention whose military use
the military does not contemplate,
no single invention that it will not endeavor
to use for military ends."*

NICHOLAS FEDOROV, 1906

ON JUNE 28, 1914, the Archduke Ferdinand of Austria was assassinated in Sarajevo by a Serbian fanatic. Ignited by that spark, the flames of international conflict spread rapidly during July and August, declarations of war following one after another in a headlong rush. The summer of 1914's madness saw Austria, Serbia, Russia, Germany, France, Belgium, Britain, Montenegro and Japan tumbling into a maelstrom that would grow in the next four years to engulf many more countries, destroying the lives of people on every continent.

In Western Europe, hostilities began on August 4, 1914, when German troops crossed into Belgium. To army commanders on both sides it was essentially a confrontation between massive ground forces. For them air power was an unknown quantity, and a minor one at that. The opposing European nations in August 1914 mobilized more than six million men for battle, but the air services of all the countries concerned mustered fewer than 2,000 pilots and 1,000 aircraft between them. Even at the war's end, the numbers of aircraft held on strength, though greatly magnified, were not large when set against the awesome dimensions of the land war. By November 1918, the combatants had raised the total number of men and women placed under military orders in the course of the war to a staggering 63 million, and had kept them provided with a matching flood of vehicles and armaments of every kind. In the closing weeks of the war, the German Air Service (Luftstreitkräfte) could field some 2,500 aircraft, and they were faced by the French and British, with about 3,700 and 2,600 respectively.

To airmen, these were impressive figures, representing as they did the forces remaining from the production of more than 150,000 aircraft by the three major combatants. After all, only five years before the war there had been no military aircraft of any kind anywhere. The transformation in the first decade of military aviation had been dramatic. Of those produced, well over 100,000 aircraft had been lost in combat

OPPOSITE PAGE
World War I memorabilia, from the collection of Hawker Restorations, UK.

The Airco D.H.4 was typical of the aircraft reaching Allied squadrons in the latter stages of WWI. It was introduced to combat by the RFC in 1917, and more than 6,000 were produced, over two-thirds of them under licence in the U.S. The American version (seen here) was powered by the 400-horsepower Liberty engine. Although the U.S. production of the type was impressive, fewer than 500 Liberty DH-4s had reached front-line squadrons by the end of the war.

or in training accidents, or had been written off through obsolescence. Germany lost nearly 6,000 airmen killed in action, France almost 3,000, and Britain more than 6,000. With missing, wounded and captured figures added, the casualty totals were over 16,000 each for Britain and Germany, and more than 7,000 for France. American airmen were at the front only during the last few months of the war, and the American Air Service had 569 battle casualties. To those involved, the casualties suffered in the aerial struggle were devastating, but in terms of the war as a whole the numbers were small, air combat accounting for less than one-third of one percent of the total military fatalities.

Viewed in the light of such bald statistics, it might be thought that the air war barely rated a mention outside its own esoteric circle. That may have been so in the beginning, but as the war progressed, and the awful impersonal nature of the trench-bound carnage was recognized, the opposite became true. The novelty of aviation as a whole, the public perception of aviators as a special breed, and the apparent separation of aerial combat from the horrors confronting the average infantryman — these were all factors that contributed to the romantic image of the airborne warrior, seen by many as the inheritor of chivalry's ancient

traditions. The pitiless slaughter of faceless soldiers en masse was too much for most people to grasp, and they reached out for individual heroes, men who could become the stuff of legend. In consequence, airmen and their exploits became newsworthy, with some pilots assuming the stature of Arthurian knights, complete with the trappings of personal battle emblems. One recruiting poster for the Royal Flying Corps went so far as to say: "War in the air recalls the olden times, when knights rode forth to battle and won honour and glory by their deeds of personal heroism." It promised prospective airmen "romance, action, adventure, and opportunities for glorious achievement."

The facade of rakish glamour and devil-may-care gallantry created offered a life in sharp contrast to the nightmare of the trenches and was useful in developing some morale-raising heroics for public consumption, but it also helped to mask the harsh realities of air fighting. Commentators, safe behind their desks, were often misled by their own flights of fancy. As one American writer enthused in 1916, "Aviators are freed from much of the ruck and reek of war by their easy poise above it." He thought this allowed them to "take time and pains to be gentlemen-warriors." In his postwar book *Fighting the Flying Circus,* the American ace Eddie Rickenbacker put it more bluntly: "Fighting in the air is not sport. It is scientific murder."

Rickenbacker, an ex-chauffeur and racing car driver with a working-class background, was not everyone's idea of what a military airman should be. It was popularly assumed that pilots must be daring and courageous, born risk-takers who enjoyed testing themselves to their limits. These characteristics, however evident in men such as Rickenbacker, were thought to be most easily found in men of good education, and therefore more than likely from a privileged background. It was felt that "good hands" would be important, and that suggested experienced horsemen, often another indication of privilege. In Germany, France and Britain, it was believed that cavalrymen and the sons of landed gentry, eminently suitable on all counts, would make ideal pilots.

Some commentators looked for more obvious physical evidence of the typical airman. A reporter for the *Morning Post* believed he could identify one on sight: "They are curiously alike in type — quiet, keen, interested faces, foreheads narrow rather than wide, and eyes set somewhat close together.... Their heads may well be the new fighting type, as unlike the old bullet face as possible, tenacious and determined rather than aggressive and obtrusive." The ample brows of airmen such as Oswald Boelcke, Albert Ball and Raoul Lufbery suggested that such exclusive classification was to be found only in a writer's imagination.

At the outset, most pilots probably did come from the upper and middle classes of society. In time, however, the demands of the expanding front-line, together with the development of practical selection procedures, swept away

Designed before WWI, the Caproni Ca.20 can claim to be the world's first fighter aircraft. Built as a derivative of the Ca.18 reconnaissance machine, the Ca.20 had a larger engine covered by a streamlined cowling and wings clipped to allow greater speed. Capable of over 100 mph, the Ca.20 was fitted with a forward-firing machine gun, mounted so that it fired over the top of the propeller arc. The Italian military preferred that Caproni concentrated his efforts on producing heavy bombers, so only one Ca.20 was ever built. The little fighter was stored by the Caproni family in Italy for eighty-five years before being sent to the Museum of Flight, Seattle, in 1999. The Ca.20 is particularly remarkable in being entirely original and unrestored. It wears the clothes it wore in 1914, and can be seen today bearing the scars and stains of almost a century.

arbitrary classifications and made it possible for men with varying backgrounds to climb into cockpits. Even so, it was found after the war that most pilots had come from urban rather than rural families, perhaps because they were then more likely to be familiar with aviation and its attractions, or with machines in general, than were the country boys of 1914–18. Wherever they came from, a high proportion of the men who qualified as pilots were also commissioned as officers, and so helped the fledgling air services to stand military tradition on its head. For the first time in warfare, the junior officers would not always be in company with a strong force of enlisted men as they went into battle. In the air war, it would become common practice for the officers to form a majority of the fighting men. NCOs did fly as pilots, especially in the early days when the pilot was regarded as little more than a chauffeur for the observer, and they acted as gunners or observers too, but most enlisted men of the air services did technical or administrative work well away from the chaos of the front lines.

Besides its effects on the social order, the experience of war usually leads to changes in military thinking (too often after the fact) and spurs technological progress. The four years after 1914 saw air power advance rapidly in doctrine, training and technique. Looked at superficially, the improvement in aircraft performance was not so obvious. In 1914, the best of the high-performance types in service, such the Sopwith Tabloid, could manage 90 mph, but the Royal Aircraft Factory's experimental S.E.4 was capable of 135 mph and had a sea-level rate of climb of 1,600 feet per minute. Engine problems prevented its development, and it never flew burdened by armament, but surprisingly, the S.E.4's figures were rarely matched by the best operational aircraft even four years later. Rickenbacker's SPAD XIII, for instance, achieved very similar figures to the S.E.4, but neither the Fokker D VII nor the Sopwith Snipe were as fast.

Nor had there been much significant change in fundamental aircraft design. The widespread bias against monoplanes and a general apprehension over high wing-loading tended to restrict the possibilities for designers, but even basic aircraft structures remained much the same

> "I hope none of you gentlemen is so foolish as to think that aeroplanes will be usefully employed for reconnaissance from the air. There is only one way for a commander to get information by reconnaissance and that is by the use of cavalry."
>
> GENERAL SIR DOUGLAS HAIG, ADDRESSING THE BRITISH ARMY STAFF COLLEGE, 1914

throughout the war. Simple fabric-covered frameworks of wood or metal tubing still predominated in 1918. Such efforts as were made to improve airframe construction came in the German aircraft industry. Less hampered by the inhibitions prevalent in France and Britain, German designers produced some excellent scouts (notably Albatros and Pfalz) that used wooden monocoque fuselages rather than simple frameworks, and Junkers pioneered a number of far-reaching aeronautical innovations, including several all-metal, cantilever-winged monoplanes. The most significant of these, the Junkers J 7 and J 9, not only made use of duralumin in their structures but were also the world's first practical low-wing monoplanes, a shape that would become the dominant aircraft form in later years.

The most apparent change brought about by four years of war was in the number and the capabilities of the aircraft being flown. When the war began, the Royal Flying Corps had about 100 aircraft of all types available in the front line and for training. In November 1918, the Royal Air Force (as it had become) was the largest air force in the world, with more than 20,000 aircraft on strength in various parts of the globe. Other air services experienced similar, if not quite such imperial, expansions. The aircraft in the operational squadrons were not only more numerous, they were more robust, more specialized, and often much larger. The occasional handheld bomb dropped from a reconnaissance machine in 1914 was nothing compared to the ton of bombs carried in giant four-engined Russian, Italian, German and British bombers later on. Aircraft technology extended its advance to cockpits, too, which now boasted a few helpful instruments. Private venture handguns and rifles were replaced by machine guns that, controlled by interrupter gear or synchronizing mechanisms, could be fired through propeller arcs. Engines quadrupled in power and became more reliable, allowing both better power-to-weight ratios and greater peace of mind. Aircraft controls were more responsive. Even safety features were becoming acceptable, as airmen overcame their fear of being seen as less than manly if they used seat belts and parachutes.

Instruments were an unheard-of luxury in most early aircraft, and the Blériot XI, seen at left, was no exception, a watch and a map of the flight route rolled onto a scroll the only aids for the pilot. Such things as airspeed and altitude were left to the pilot's judgment. Basic though they were, Blériots were reportedly "quite easy to handle," although the controls were not well balanced. The rate of roll with wing-warping was poor, and rudder control was weak, but the elevators were powerful. Blériots were widely used by the military at the outbreak of war in 1914, equipping eight French and seven British squadrons. There were also six Italian squadrons of Blériots when that country entered the war. This example, warming up its whirling Gnôme rotary, has been beautifully restored at Le Bourget.

RECONNAISSANCE ROOTS

Sailors at mastheads and soldiers on high ground or in balloons had always known the value of having a lofty perch from which to observe the enemy. It was therefore no great surprise that the airplane should first be thought of by most military men merely as a convenient means of widening their horizons to gain intelligence of enemy strength and deployment. It was believed in 1914 that the ideal aircraft should be a slow and stable two-seater that would provide the observer with a steady platform. Speed and maneuverability were thought to be unnecessary, even undesirable, qualities for aircraft engaged in the business of gathering information. Commanders did not envisage any likelihood of aerial combat. Airplanes were to observe and report, not fight. To begin with, even the airmen themselves thought it unsporting to shoot at other aviators. Lieutenant Sholto Douglas, RFC (later Air Chief Marshal Sir Sholto Douglas, RAF), described passing opposing reconnaissance aircraft: "We waved a hand at the enemy and proceeded with our task. The enemy did likewise. At the time this did not appear to me in any way ridiculous. There is a bond of sympathy between all who fly — even enemies."

Such gentlemanly behavior did not last long. It became apparent that aerial reconnaissance could influence the land battle profoundly and aircraft could not be allowed to wander freely wherever they wished. On August 22, 1914, a Royal Flying Corps aircraft operating near Mons detected the far right wing of the German Army's sweeping advance through Belgium and alerted the British Expeditionary Force to the danger of being outflanked. The news gave the British just enough time to prepare a defensive line and check the advance. This was probably the one occasion during the war when the Germans had an opportunity to secure outright victory by racing through to Paris before the Allies were properly organized, so the aerial intervention by the RFC proved to be of vital importance. The British commander, Field Marshal Sir John French, went so far as to admit: "[Aerial reconnaissance] has been of incalculable value in the conduct of operations."

The Allied Commander-in-Chief, Marshal Joffre, joined in after other airmen revealed the Germans wheeling to the southeast, exposing their flank and allowing a successful Allied counterattack along the Marne, saying: "Please express most particularly my thanks for the services rendered to us every day by the Royal Flying Corps. The precision, exactitude and regularity of the news brought in by them are evidence of their perfect organization and also of the perfect training of pilots and observers." Such flowery language may have overstated the case, but it nevertheless revealed a dawning realization in an old soldier's mind that flying machines had something of value to offer from their vantage point above the battlefield.

The French success on the Marne also drew attention to the dangers of being without "eyes in the sky." The German commander did not have aircraft available and so was unaware until too late of the French Army's move against his flank. (The first report of the German Army's turn to the southeast, made on September 2, 1914, came from French designer Louis Breguet himself, flying one of his own aircraft.)

> "The aeroplane's first duty was reconnaissance. All its other uses were consequences of this central purpose, and were forced on it by the hard logic of events."
>
> RALEIGH AND JONES, THE WAR IN THE AIR

At almost the same time, on the Eastern Front, the Germans had reason to be grateful to their air service. The German Army's victory at the Battle of Tannenberg depended on being able to defeat two equally strong Russian armies separately, holding one in place with a screening force, while fighting the other. Without a continuous flow of aerial intelligence about the movements of Russian forces, this would have been a formidable task. Field Marshal von Hindenburg probably went too far in reporting that his victory was "totally due to air power," but it was undeniably true that aircraft had played a crucial part in the German success. The Russian General Danilov admitted that because of German superiority in the air: "[The German Army] could maneuver as they wished...and be certain that their plans would not be discovered." The few Russian airmen who did fly often did so under fire from their own troops. A Russian cavalry commander explained that most of his soldiers "seriously believed that such a cunning idea as an aeroplane could only emanate from, and be used by, a German."

Events such as Mons and Tannenberg changed attitudes toward enemy aviators. Tolerance was replaced by resentment and a determination to discourage their activities. This was particularly true once the stalemate of trench warfare froze the Western Front into immobility. The cavalry's traditional reconnaissance role was no longer possible, so commanders became almost wholly dependent on aircraft. It was increasingly important not only to occupy airspace over the front but also to deny it to the enemy. This situation had been foreseen by a number of military men before the war. Following maneuvers in 1912, one British general commented: "Warfare will be impossible until we have mastery of the air." In 1913, Major Frederick Sykes, then commander of the RFC's Military Wing, said that command of the air would be essential "in order to obtain information ourselves and to prevent enemy air reconnaissance from doing so." Flying aircraft generally unarmed and ill-suited for combat, aircrew began to carry pistols and rifles to persuade their enemies to leave particular blocks of airspace. Some went so far as to devise grapnels that might be entangled in enemy machines, and even ramming was not considered unthinkable. On September 8, 1914, the Russian Captain Nesterov, celebrated for being the first to loop an aircraft, deliberately rammed an Austrian intruder, having said, "sooner or later one has to fall all the same, and to sacrifice one's life is the duty of every soldier." In keeping with that sentiment, Nesterov's first aerial victory also proved to be his last.

More effective means of destroying or driving off the enemy were not long in coming. Various methods of mounting machine guns were proposed and tried. The first RFC aircraft to be reasonably well armed for air fighting were the Maurice Farman Shorthorns of No. 4 Squadron. They were "pushers," with the engine in the rear, and the absence of a propeller at the front allowed a machine gun to be mounted in the nose. However, they were so slow, with a maximum speed of less than 70 mph, that it was almost impossible for them to bring another aircraft to combat. In aircraft with the propeller in front, desperate measures were sometimes tried. Lieutenant Strange of No. 5 Squadron, RFC, rigged a pulley on his Avro 504 so that his observer could hoist a Lewis gun to his shoulder on a rope. After the fruitless chase of an enemy two-seater on August 22, 1914,

The Shuttleworth Collection's Avro (H5199) was originally a 504N. Discovered abandoned on the top of the old Airspeed stores building at Portsmouth Airport in 1951, it was restored as a 504K by Avro apprentices and flown in the movie Reach for the Sky. *Renowned as a gentle, forgiving airplane, the 504 was celebrated by generations of British pilots in many songs, one of which ended: "My good old Avro can loop, roll or spin; and there isn't a field that I can't put her in." H5199 still flies regularly in the summer air shows held at Old Warden airfield, near Bedford in the U.K.*

Strange was ordered not to carry the gun again, as its weight restricted the Avro's already minimal performance. Success nevertheless crowned this crew's efforts on November 22, 1914, when they defied orders and used a Lewis gun to damage a German aircraft and force it down on the British side of the front. The German pilot's capitulation apparently did not meet with the officer observer's approval. Once on the ground, he dragged his non-commissioned "chauffeur" from the cockpit in a fury and was seen by Strange to punch and kick the man until British soldiers arrived to take them both prisoner.

A simpler solution to the weapon problem was to mount a gun on the edge of the observer's cockpit, but most reconnaissance aircraft were "tractors" (with the propeller pulling rather than pushing) and had the observer in the front seat. In this configuration, firing the gun through the network of surrounding struts and wires, and with the propeller directly in front, could be more of a hazard to the home team than to the opposition. The obvious answer had been proposed more than once before the war. It was to arm the faster and more maneuverable single-seat scouts with guns that could be fired directly forward, preferably through the propeller arc, so that the pilot could aim the guns by aiming the whole aircraft. With this in mind, propeller deflector plates and both interrupter and synchronizer gearing systems had been examined by 1914, but none had

been perfected. (Interrupter gears were operated by the propeller; synchronizers by the engine.) Until they were, success in aerial combat remained largely a matter of luck aided by considerable skill and ingenuity in the use of rudimentary equipment.

Eyes for the Guns

As the land war dragged on, becoming less based on maneuvers and more on entrenched confrontation, with the opposing armies dug in along a line stretching from the Swiss border to the Belgian coast, the static nature of the battlefield brought a change of emphasis in the primary duties of the air services. The principal task became spotting for the guns of the artillery, WWI's most deadly weapons. To do this successfully, communication had to be established

The B.E.2a was easy to fly and very stable, but very slow. While a high degree of stability seemed at first to be just what was needed for reconnaissance duties, that quality reduced its maneuverability and, since it lacked the speed to run, it was easy meat for German fighters. More airmen went to their deaths in B.E.2s than in any other type during WWI.

between the aircraft and the guns. Many means were tried, including landing the observer near his associated battery, dropping message bags, and flashing signaling lamps, but transmitting Morse code by wireless was the best method. To begin with, the wireless sets available were both heavy and cumbersome. The first RFC sets weighed 75 pounds and could be carried in the lumbering B.E.2 only in the absence of the observer, thus complicating the pilot's task and making him more vulnerable than ever to enemy action. Matters improved in 1915, with the introduction of the 20-pound Sterling set, although reconnaissance in the B.E.2 and its successors remained a hazardous occupation.

At the same time, systems were devised for passing information from air to ground. Standardized maps using a lettered grid eased the problem of identifying positions. The fall of shot was reported by clock code, where 12 o'clock was due north. Circles round a chosen target were imagined at distances of 10, 25, 50, and then 100 to 500 yards at 100-yard intervals. The letters Y, Z, and then A to F were used to represent these distances. To tell a battery that its shells had fallen to the south of a target by 100 yards, the

observer would send "B6." A "Z9" indicated 25 yards west, while direct hits drew a congratulatory "OK." Throughout the war it remained almost impossible to receive a wireless response in the cockpit from the battery, but visual signals, using such things as flares, signal lamps, or large fabric panels laid out on the ground, usually proved adequate.

Photographic Evidence

Useful though the human eye was in observing the fall of shot, it proved to be less reliable for gathering more detailed information. Photography was the answer. The camera provided a permanent record that could be carefully studied by interpreters, and the product, with enemy deployments and defensive positions identified, could be duplicated and distributed to field commanders. Before the end of 1914, the French air service, which, together with its Italian counterpart, had automatic cameras for taking sequential photographs at the outbreak of war, produced maps outlining the growing German trench system. The Germans, supported by their excellent optical industry, were at least as well prepared, with some 100 aerial cameras in service. The

British, on the other hand, had none initially, and some RFC observers made do with large folding plate cameras they supplied themselves. This amateur approach was overtaken in February 1915 with the introduction of the "A" camera, a rugged conical box with brass handles that the observer gripped as firmly as he could with frozen fingers while pointing the camera over the side in the blast of the slipstream. Eleven distinct operations were necessary before taking the first exposure, and ten more for each one after that. An improved semi-automatic version, the "C" type, appeared in the summer of 1915, and cameras were then fixed to the aircraft's fuselage or in the floor to ensure accurate mapping of enemy positions. By the end of the war, reconnaissance aircraft were taking photographs from 15,000 feet with cameras that revealed details as small as footprints. Vertical, oblique and stereoscopic photographs were being regularly supplied in large numbers, with important areas, such as concentrations of enemy artillery, being covered daily.

Other Duties

Most aerial reconnaissance work was done within sight of the front lines on the ground, but some aircraft probed deeper, discovering such activities as the buildup of supply depots, the laying of new rail lines, or the massing of forces. A few aircraft even undertook the hazardous work of depositing agents behind enemy lines. This was usually done at night and added the risk of the crew being shot as spies if they were caught. That danger could be avoided if the agent was dropped in by parachute, a mission that

LEFT *The Caudron G.IV (C1720) at the Musée de l'Air at Le Bourget hovers above the world's finest exhibition of WWI aircraft. From in front and below, it is seen as a large aircraft, spanning some 56 feet. Behind the broad wings, however, it appears impossibly fragile, with four small fins mounted on a distant tailplane tenuously connected to the rest of the aircraft by a spidery arrangement of wires and thin wooden booms.*
ABOVE *Later versions of the G.IV often had an additional machine gun placed so that the observer could fire to the rear over the top wing, a hazardous operation for which he had to stand up, battered by the slipstream and enduring the pilot's maneuvers, having no parachute and with his unsecured body well outside the confines of his cockpit.*

occasionally led to drastic aircraft modifications. Clandestine operations flown from Italy sometimes used aircraft adapted to overcome the problem of the reluctant or apprehensive agent. Both his seat and the cockpit floor were hinged so that the pilot could guarantee the timely departure of his passenger over the appropriate place.

In the war's later years, observers were required to work closely with troops on the ground in the infantry contact patrol. This was to ensure that commanders were kept informed of the progress of their forward units during an offensive, or of their positions if cut off by the enemy. Occasions when artillery fire was brought down on the heads of luckless friendly troops were all too frequent, so patrols were flown with the express intention of eliminating such incidents. Soldiers were supposed to mark the positions of their units with strips of fabric, smoke candles or flashing lights. Often they were too heavily engaged to comply, or were reluctant to do so for fear of revealing themselves to the enemy. Contact patrols, therefore, flown at relatively low level over the battlefield, were not popular with airmen, since the business of finding elusive units while operating within range of the enemy could be both frustrating and unduly dangerous. Quite often, "friendly" artillery fire could be an equal threat. During the battle of the Somme in 1916, airmen of the RFC's IX Squadron reported that: "The amount of ammunition passing through the air posed a safety problem for the aviators, who could frequently see salvoes pass near them. In fact more crews were lost by being hit by our own shells than were lost to enemy action."

Reconnaissance Evolution

As the war went on, the three principal aviation powers developed differing attitudes to air power, and this was reflected in the balance of their air force front lines. Both France and Germany, with their long history of reliance on large land armies, maintained their early conviction that the most valuable service aircraft could provide was that of observing the enemy. In the closing months of the war, at least half of their respective air forces were still dedicated to

> *"To fly in a straight line, taking photos of the enemy trenches, an easy Archie [anti-aircraft] target, within range of the ground machine-guns, bumped by the eddies of passing shells and pestered by enemy scouts, that required nerve. And it would have to be done twice a day, day after day, until you were hit or went home."*
>
> CECIL LEWIS, B.E.2c PILOT,
> IX SQUADRON, RFC

reconnaissance. The British, on the other hand, adopted a more offensive policy, and reconnaissance units formed less than a quarter of the RFC's front line. Since the demands for their services increasing steadily year by year, the wisdom of this often eluded the RFC's reconnaissance crews. Their observation reports proved so valuable that army commanders inevitably wanted more, and their patrols, flown in all weathers, always attracted determined opposition from both ground fire and enemy fighters. Still flying slow, cumbersome machines, they suffered losses at a crippling rate, and the job of reconnaissance did not even have the compensation of being considered particularly glamorous. With all that, it remained essential to the conduct of the war. Even the RAF's postwar official historians said of the aircraft's contribution to operations: "Its first duty was reconnaissance. All its other and later uses were consequences of this central purpose, and were forced on it by the hard logic of events."

THE WAY OF THE FIGHTER

During the first months of the war, the absence of a solution to the problem of firing a machine gun forward through the propeller did not prevent airmen claiming the occasional aerial victory, sometimes without the aid of weapons. On August 25, 1914, three B.E.2s of No. 2 Squadron, RFC, were on patrol when they came across a German Taube, a birdlike airplane even slower than they were. Their mock attacks convinced the enemy pilot that he should land in a field. One B.E.2 landed alongside and its crew chased their opponents into a wood before setting fire to the Taube. Similar incidents occurred elsewhere, increasingly involving the use of pistols, rifles and a rare machine gun. The difficulties of aiming handheld weapons while exposed to slipstream and the gyrations of an aircraft were such that little damage was caused, but it was only a question of time before more effective measures were tried.

The first aerial combat in which a machine gun was used to shoot down an enemy took place on October 5, 1914. A French Voisin Type III pusher biplane, newly fitted with a Hotchkiss machine gun mounted on the edge of the

Norman Prince, a founding member of the Lafayette Escadrille and a five-victory ace, is seen in the bizarre Voisin Avion Canon, fitted with a huge 47 mm gun. Firing so fearsome a weapon from such a slow and seemingly fragile biplane might well have had more effect on the Voisin's crew than on their targets.

observer's cockpit in the nose, crossed paths with a German Aviatik near Reims. The Voisin was so ungainly it was nick-named the "chicken coop," but the pilot, Sergeant Joseph Frantz, managed to maneuver so that his observer, Corporal Louis Quénault, could use his gun. A few bursts of fire were sufficient to send the Aviatik down in flames, and to change the character of war in the air irrevocably.

The first serious attempts to develop a method of achieving air superiority were made by the French. Toward the end of 1914, the celebrated aviator Roland Garros resuscitated the work done before the war by Raymond Saulnier on a system for firing a machine gun through the disc of the propeller. He had steel deflector plates fitted to the propeller of his Morane-Saulnier Parasol monoplane. A Hotchkiss machine gun was mounted on the fuselage directly in front of the cockpit. On April 1, 1915, he inter-cepted a formation of Albatros two-seaters and shot one down in flames. The remaining Germans fled to report on the terrifying phenomenon of a single-seat aircraft that could fire a machine gun straight forward.

Garros was as shocked as they were at what he had

done. He later recalled what happened when he stopped firing: "It was tragic, frightful. At the end of perhaps twenty-five seconds of falling, which seemed long, the machine dashed into the ground in a great cloud of smoke. I went by car to see the wreck. Those first on the scene had pilfered souvenirs — sidearms, insignia and the like. I took energetic steps to retrieve them. The two corpses were in a horrible state, naked and bloody. The observer had been shot through the head. The pilot was too horribly muti-lated to be examined. The remains of the aeroplane were pierced everywhere with bullet holes."

The horrified reaction of Garros was to prove typical of pilots confronted by the stark realities of aerial combat. Their general distaste for the end result did not, however, prevent the vast majority from doing their duty and contin-uing to fight. Garros himself shot down a second German aircraft on April 15 and a third three days later. Flying again on the day of his third victory, Garros had his aircraft dam-aged by ground fire and was forced to land near Courtrai. A single rifle bullet had severed a fuel line and delivered the secret of the French success to the Germans.

Gunners in WWI two-seaters occupied open cockpits and had to stay alert in the mind-numbing cold at altitude. Most were armed with the standard Lewis gun, which fired at 550 rounds per minute, and they had to cope with the problem of needing to reload after firing each drum of 97 rounds. The drums were heavy and not easy to change with freezing hands while in combat. RIGHT *The gunner's position in the Nieuport 12 at the National Aviation Museum, Ottawa.*

The Fokker Scourge

Given the task of producing a forward firing system to match that of the Allies, the young Dutch engineer, Anthony Fokker, went one better. Within five weeks, his team designed and built an engine-driven cam mechanism that effectively stopped a gun firing whenever a propeller blade was in front of the muzzle. By July 1915, Fokker monoplanes (Eindeckers) were flying with synchronizing gear fitted, and the period of the air war known to the Allies as the "Fokker Scourge" began. In retrospect, it seems extraordinary that such a limited aircraft should have become the first real fighter and that it remained dominant for as long as it did. The Eindecker was an unremarkable performer even for its day. Its maximum speed was 87 mph and it took over half an hour to climb to 10,000 feet. It was still controlled by wing-warping and it was not easy to fly. After several fatal accidents, confidence in the aircraft was lost and the Fokker training unit was disbanded. Production was slowed so that only some eighty-six Eindeckers were produced in 1915. The German authorities thereby unwittingly penalized themselves and limited the Eindecker's impact on the air war. In 1915, that must have been less than obvious to the Allies, who saw only that their losses were mounting alarmingly. Imperfect though it was, in the hands of pilots such as Max Immelman and Oswald Boelcke, the Eindecker gave the Germans a decided edge in the air.

Given the opportunity to operate the Fokker Eindecker, Oswald Boelcke could see the possibilities it offered and so he set about developing a system of fighter tactics. Whenever possible, the advantages of height and of being into sun were to be gained. Two-seaters were to be attacked from below and behind, and all attacks were to be pressed in to close range before opening fire. Fighters operating in pairs would be able to cover each other. When attacked themselves, pilots should turn into the attack, making the enemy's shot as difficult as possible. Boelcke also recommended the establishment of specialized pursuit units, rather than placing pairs of fighters in squadrons with mixed responsibilities. Max Immelman added the benefits of vertical maneuvering to allow repeated attacks while retaining positional advantage, giving his name to the "Immelman turn," a half loop or steep climbing turn with a roll-out at the top. Boelcke and Immelman flew Eindeckers together to prove these tactics and were eminently successful. Both officers were awarded the coveted Pour le Mérite (Blue Max) for their exploits. Immelman shot down fifteen Allied aircraft before himself falling on June 15, 1916, during a combat with F.E.2bs of No. 25 Squadron, RFC. Boelcke survived until October 28, 1916, when he was killed in an Albatros scout after colliding with a wingman, Erwin Bohme, during an attack on British reconnaissance aircraft.

His score of victories had risen to forty. In a manual written in 1916, he established principles for aerial combat that formed the basis for fighter tactics adopted by air forces everywhere. His ideas have stood the test of time and remain essentially sound as military aviation enters the 21st century.

In the absence of a synchronizing system to match that of the Eindeckers, both the French and the British tried other ways of countering the threat. On January 14, 1916, the RFC issued an order establishing reconnaissance policy: "Until the Royal Flying Corps are in possession of a machine as good as or better than the German Fokker it seems that a change in the tactics employed is necessary…. In the meantime, it must be laid down as a hard and fast rule that a machine proceeding on reconnaissance must be escorted by at least three other fighting machines. These machines must fly in close formation and a reconnaissance should not be continued if any of the machines becomes detached…. Flying in close formation must be practised by all pilots."

Effective escorts were not available, so this meant that a number of two-seaters had to fly together, offering covering fire as best they could. Close formation flying having become a matter of policy, it soon became common practice. It was noticed that Eindeckers tended to shy away from large formations, fearing the potentially formidable barrage of defensive fire. Unfortunately, this beneficial effect had a downside. Assigning several aircraft to each task effectively cut the available Allied front-line strength and reduced the number of reconnaissance sorties possible. This in turn led to more insistent calls from commanders for more squadrons, increasing the demands placed on the training system and on aircraft industries struggling to develop while competing for materials with every other facet of the war effort.

French efforts to reclaim aerial supremacy included seeking improvements both in equipment and organization that would allow them to conduct the air war more efficiently. Units were established according to their increasing

Henri Farré's painting of a Breguet-Michelin bomber pursued by a Fokker Eindecker shows that French bomber crews were sometimes driven to desperate measures to defend themselves. The B-Ms were clumsy and slow, and had to be withdrawn from daylight operations soon after reaching front-line squadrons in 1916.

specialization — reconnaissance, artillery cooperation, bombing, and pursuit or *escadrilles de chasse* (hunting squadrons). Among the hunters, the first French aircraft to challenge the Fokker's supremacy was the Nieuport 11, nicknamed the Bébé. Introduced operationally in January 1916, this small, highly maneuverable biplane had a machine gun mounted on the top wing, firing over the propeller. It could outfly the Eindecker, but it was difficult to aim the gun, usually a Lewis, which was itself limited in being able to fire only forty-seven rounds before reloading with a new drum, whereas the German Spandau was fed by a 500-round belt.

Reloading the Lewis gun in flight was difficult. The pilot had to wrestle with a heavy drum in the slipstream while holding the stick between his knees. In combat, such a chore could be a far greater challenge, as Louis Strange, now with No. 6 Squadron, RFC, found out on May 10, 1915. Flying a Martinsyde Scout with a Lewis gun on the top wing, he had emptied the contents of one drum at an Aviatik two-seater and needed to replace it. The drum resisted his efforts, so he undid his lap belt to stand up and get a better grip. As he struggled to loosen a crossed thread, the Martinsyde flicked onto its back, throwing Strange out of the cockpit. He gripped the drum desperately as the aircraft descended upside down. He later wrote: "Only a few seconds previously, I had been cursing because I could not get that drum off. Now I prayed fervently that it would stay on for ever. It dawned on me

LEFT *The first Fokker E.III Eindeckers appeared on the Western Front in August 1915. Fairly unimpressive performers, they nevertheless proved dominant in the air, allowing the Germans to achieve and maintain air superiority throughout the winter months, a period known to the Allies as the "Fokker Scourge." This success was built upon an interrupter gear, designed by Fokker, which for the first time allowed a pilot to aim his whole aircraft at his enemy and fire a machine gun through the propeller arc. The principal prey of the E.III was the RFC's unwieldy B.E.2, which was helpless against such direct attacks.*

RIGHT *Charles Nungesser was a glamorous adventurer with a reckless disregard for his own safety. A rancher in Argentina when WWI started, he returned to France and joined the cavalry, transferring to the air service in 1915. Operating first as a bomber pilot, he joined Escadrille 65 in November 1915, flying Nieuports. In a fiery combat career, Nungesser was shot down and was wounded, or crashed and was injured, seventeen times, breaking many bones and spending months in hospital. Crippled so that he had to be helped into his aircraft, he nevertheless became the third-ranking French ace, with forty-five aerial victories. With characteristic flamboyance, he adopted a personal emblem of a black heart decorated with skull and crossbones, two candles and a coffin. His was a casual attitude to the dangers of combat: "Before firing my gun I shut my eyes. When I open them, sometimes the Boche is going down, sometimes I am in hospital."*

that my only chance of righting the machine lay in getting my feet into the cockpit. I kept on kicking upwards behind me until I got first one foot and then the other hooked inside. Somehow I got the stick between my legs again and jammed on full aileron and elevator. The machine came over the right way up and I fell into my seat with a bump."

Despite the difficulties associated with an over-wing gun, the Nieuport 11, when flown by men such as the French aces Georges Guynemer and Charles Nungesser, was one of the aircraft that brought the era of Eindecker supremacy to an end. During the Battle of Verdun, which opened in February 1916, the Bébé inflicted heavy losses on the enemy and forced the Germans to recognize that the pendulum of air supremacy was swinging in favor of the Allies.

Meanwhile, the British ran round the problem of firing through the propeller by producing a new generation of "pushers." Until they arrived in 1916, the RFC did the best they could with what they had. Lanoe Hawker of No. 6 Squadron, RFC, described being hit by ground fire while on reconnaissance: "Picked up fifty bullet holes through my plane…one chipped the propeller, one a strut, one through my exhaust pipe, one through my tailskid and one into my leg. It fell out when I took my sock off and I have sent it home as a souvenir."

Hawker gained a reputation as a sharpshooter while using a rifle in the air, but, frustrated by his lack of firepower, he had a Lewis gun fixed beside the cockpit of his Bristol Scout, set to fire forward at an angle that ensured that the bullets would clear the propeller. This offset arrangement posed a difficult aiming problem and promised to be effective only in the hands of an exceptional marksman.

On July 25, 1915, Hawker was on patrol at 10,000 feet when he saw two enemy aircraft. The combat report

Georges Guynemer standing by his SPAD VII Vieux Charles. Reckless in combat, Guynemer became a popular hero in France and was credited with fifty-four victories by the time he failed to return from patrol on September 11, 1917. No trace of him or his aircraft was ever found.

records the subsequent action: "The Bristol attacked two machines behind the lines, one at Passchendale about 6 pm and one over Houthulst Forest about 6:20 pm. Both machines dived and the Bristol loosed a drum at each at about 400 yards before returning." [One of these aircraft then made a forced landing.] "The Bristol climbed to 11,000 ft and about 7 pm saw a hostile machine being fired at by anti-aircraft guns over Hooge. The Bristol approached down-sun and opened fire at about 100 yards. The hostile machine burst into flames, turned upside down, and crashed East of Zillebeke."

For this and his determined aggression in all the previous actions he had fought, Lanoe Hawker was awarded the Victoria Cross, the first ever given for air combat.

Spirited men such as Lanoe Hawker were just what Major General Hugh "Boom" Trenchard (so called because of his resonant voice), appointed Commander of the RFC in August 1915, wanted in his front-line squadrons. For him, maintaining the offensive was paramount. It did not matter that, at this stage of the war, the RFC's aircraft were generally inferior to those of the Germans, that the return to base was almost invariably a struggle for slow aircraft against the prevailing wind, that losses were heavy and that those who survived being brought down generally became prisoners. In the face of these unpalatable facts, Trenchard insisted that the RFC must continue to penetrate enemy airspace and bring German aircraft to battle as often as possible.

The Pendulum Swings

In 1915, a British aircraft that at least held the promise of being able to measure up to the Fokker menace appeared in the shape of the first of the "pusher" fighters. The Vickers F.B.5 Gunbus arrived to equip No. 11 Squadron, RFC, in

July 1915, making that unit the first of any air service formed specifically to operate a single aircraft type in the air combat role. The Gunbus was a two-seat pusher biplane powered by a 100-horsepower Gnôme Monosoupape rotary engine. With a maximum speed of only 70 mph, it was not a stellar performer and it was beset by engine problems, but it was very maneuverable and the observer, positioned in the nose, had a Lewis gun with an uninterrupted field of fire. It was followed in 1916 by two more "pushers," both designed by Geoffrey de Havilland, the Royal Aircraft Factory F.E.2 and the Airco D.H.2. The F.E.2 was a two-seater in the style of the F.B.5, but faster and more capable. A large aircraft with a wingspan of over 48 feet, it became a jack-of-all-trades and saw action in a number of roles. Later versions often had an additional Lewis gun placed so that the observer could fire to the rear over the top wing, but he had to stand up until his body from mid-calf up was outside his cockpit.

The D.H.2 was the RFC's first single-seat fighter. With a top speed of 93 mph, it was noticeably faster than the Eindecker, and it was both easy to fly and extremely agile.

Armament was a free-mounted Lewis gun in the nose, which most pilots found was more effective if fixed to fire straight ahead, when aiming the gun became a matter of aiming the aircraft.

The first squadron to reach France equipped with D.H.2s in February 1916 was No. 24, commanded by Major Lanoe Hawker. His confidence in the new aircraft, and in his young pilots, was reflected in his letters: "It's a school I run and not a squadron…the majority are not yet of age. They are a splendid lot though and I am very fond of them."

This was followed by: "One of my chickens so terrified one of these monsters [Eindeckers] that he dived straight into the middle of a town."

Hawker's feelings were shared by General Sir Henry Rawlinson, Commander of the 4th Army: "I cannot speak too highly of the work of these young pilots, most of whom have recently come out from England, and the de Havilland machine has unquestionably proved itself superior to the Fokker in speed, maneuverability, climbing and general fighting efficiency."

Together with the Nieuport 11, the "pushers" had found the counter to the Fokker Scourge and were beginning to do some scourging of their own.

Verdun and the Somme

From the earliest days of air combat, the fighter pilot had generally been a lone hunter, but in 1916 that began to change. That was also the year that marked the true beginning of aerial warfare, as both sides began to develop air arms capable of gaining air superiority over the battlefield. In the winter of 1915/16, during preparations for their Verdun offensive, the Germans concentrated aircraft opposite that part of the front and flew constant patrols, principally formations of two-seaters, with the aim of setting up an aerial barrier to prevent the French from observing the German Army's buildup. The few Eindeckers available tackled any French aircraft that managed to break through the barrier.

The 100-horsepower Gnôme Monosoupape rotary of the Gunbus is mounted at the rear of the crew's nacelle. The fuel tank and the pilot's cockpit can be seen beyond.

LAFAYETTE ESCADRILLE

Southwest of Paris, near Versailles, is an impressive memorial to the members of the Lafayette Escadrille who died in combat. The high central arch is flanked by colonnades bearing the names of the squadron's American and French pilots, and a poetic tribute that ends with the words "Their golden youth they gave, and here are laid — Deep in the arms of France for whom they died." Beneath the memorial is a curving crypt containing sixty-eight named sarcophagi. Some sixty still hold remains. Several bodies were later moved to burial places in the U.S. Among the Americans lie two of their French commanders. On a sunny day, the crypt is bathed in colored light streaming through stained-glass windows commemorating the Lafayette Escadrille's aerial battlefields.

BELOW Five members of the Lafayette Escadrille, the squadron of American volunteers that flew with the French Air Service before the U.S. entered WWI. At the center is the French CO, Georges Thibault. From left to right, the Americans are James McConnell, Kiffen Rockwell, Norman Prince and Victor Chapman.

NIEUPORT

Designed by Gustave Delage for the Establissement Nieuport, the tiny Nieuport 11 was a significant step forward in the evolution of fighter aircraft. Known as the Bébé, the Nieuport 11 was an instrument of great destruction in the hands of many Allied aces, including Ball, Bishop, Deullin, Navarre, Nungesser and Guynemer.

OPPOSITE PAGE
TOP The example suspended above the Grande Galerie of the Musée de l'Air is in the colors of Commandant Tricornot de Rose, the fighter leader who transformed French fighter tactics during the air battles over Verdun.
BOTTOM If there was a problem with Nieuport's fighters, it was that they tended to be a little fragile. In the Bébé, the lower wing occasionally twisted and broke under stress, and the upper wing fabric of the later Nieuport 28 could be stripped off at high speed, sometimes leading to the aircraft shedding the wing altogether. Here, airframe riggers begin repairs on one shredded 28 that managed to make it back to base.

THIS PAGE
In the Nieuport 28, designer Gustave Delage abandoned the sesquiplane form of his earlier fighters. It was armed with two Vickers machine guns offset to the left and firing through the propeller. The use of a basketwork seat helped to keep the weight as low as possible. Elegant in appearance and clean in design though it was, the 28 was not a great success. It was not adopted by the French Air Service, but was bought for the U.S. forces, which took delivery of 297. However, the Nieuport 28 proved to be no match for the Fokker D.VII and was withdrawn from front-line service after only four months. The Nieuport 28 featured here is from the USAFM Collection.

LEFT *Raoul Lufbery was a French-born American who flew with the Lafayette Escadrille and the 94th Aero Squadron. He was credited with seventeen aerial victories before his death in combat on May 19, 1918. He lies with his former comrades in the crypt of the Lafayette Memorial outside Paris.* BELOW *A detail from the Lafayette Memorial arch.*

This policy was reasonably successful, and when the storm broke with a massive artillery barrage on February 21, 1916, the French were caught unprepared and initially overwhelmed, both on the ground and in the air. It is also true, however, that those reconnaissance flights that did report German preparations were discounted by French Army commanders reluctant to trust the eyes of their airmen.

As the French absorbed the shock and began a defense that would threaten to bleed their nation to death, the local air establishment was increased from four escadrilles (squadrons) to sixteen, of which six were to be fighters under Commandant Tricornot de Rose. He formed a force of Nieuport 11s and brought together all the experienced pilots he could find, French aces such as Jean Navarre, Georges Guynemer and Charles Nungesser among them. This group of escadrilles became celebrated as "Les Cigognes" (the storks) and carried a stork emblem on their aircraft. Added to their strength in May was a squadron of American volunteers who had joined the French Air Service. Initially identified only by a squadron number (N124), they were also known as the Lafayette Escadrille, a name adopted after Germany complained that their original title of Escadrille Americaine was inappropriate for airmen from a supposedly neutral country. Formed at least in part for the political benefits it would bring, the Lafayette Escadrille was blooded in combat during 1916 and in time became an effective fighter squadron, counting several aces among its members, including Raoul Lufbery, whose seventeen victories made him the eighth-ranking American ace of the war. As an American unit operating with the French, the Lafayettes naturally attracted considerable publicity,

but they were not the only U.S. citizens flying on the Western Front. Many more Americans flew elsewhere, either in squadrons of the French Air Service under the umbrella title of the Lafayette Flying Corps, or with the British in the RFC or RNAS. Indeed, ten of the thirteen American pilots who scored more than twelve kills in WWI did so while flying only with French or British squadrons.

The orders issued to the French fighter squadrons at Verdun included instructions that were specific about aim and method: "The mission of the escadrilles is to seek out the enemy, to fight him and destroy him. They will patrol by escadrille or demi-escadrille. They will adopt a formation that will place them in echelon in three dimensions."

Officially, the days of the lone hunter were over. Commanders were beginning to recognize that success in the air war would follow only if individual initiative and brilliance could be made subservient to unit discipline. Nevertheless, until the techniques of fighting as a team were worked out, meetings of opposing formations quickly broke up into duels between individuals. It was also true that some pilots still actively sought opportunities to fight alone, unencumbered by the responsibilities that went with formation flying and driven by the need to prove themselves as solitary warriors.

As the land battle of attrition at Verdun raged on, the Allied policy of pursuing an unrelenting offensive in the air began to have its effect. The French Air Service added to their number and gained the upper hand, forcing the Germans onto the defensive and making reconnaissance difficult. Even so, it became apparent that air superiority was a transient affair, dependent not only on having better machines and tactics, but also on the capacity of one side or the other to concentrate its forces in time and space to win a temporary advantage where needed.

> *"Here's a toast to the dead already;*
> *Hurrah for the next man who dies."*
> FROM A WWI ROYAL FLYING CORPS TOAST

For the longer term, 1916 offered the first indication that success in aerial warfare would depend as much on industrial strength and technological competence as on military prowess. On the industrial front, Germany was losing ground. Although German aircraft production outpaced the French in 1916 (8,182 to 7,549), British factories added another 5,716 aircraft during the year. Even more significant was the French lead in aero-engines, the result of an enlightened policy that brought the automotive industry into aero-engine production at an early stage of the war. In 1916, French industry produced 16,875 engines to Germany's 7,823, with Britain adding 5,363. From the German point of view, such imbalances held ominous implications for the future, suggesting the probability of their being materially overwhelmed and forced to adopt an increasingly defensive posture in the air.

By the time the Allies launched their attack on the Somme on July 1, 1916, the French Army's commitment to Verdun had turned what was intended to be a shared offensive into a predominantly British Army affair. In the air, the situation was more evenly balanced between the Allies, and much in their joint favor, with nearly 500 British and French aircraft facing less than 200 German. As the mincing machine of the land battle consumed human lives at an appalling rate and Allied hopes for a convincing victory were dashed on seemingly impregnable defenses, the aerial struggle continued to go against the Germans. Outnumbered and facing aircraft that could outperform their own, German airmen sometimes seemed reluctant to fight. Lanoe Hawker reported that when Allied planes crossed the lines, a few Eindeckers would appear and then they would "hang like minnows in a stream, but they would not

fight." German soldiers composed an uncomplimentary saying that was commonly heard in the trenches: *Gott strafe England, Frankreich und unsere Flieger*. (God smite England, France and our own airmen.)

Even as the individual pilot was being rendered officially less important, so the reputations of a few extraordinary men grew. No pilot of 1916 exploited the capabilities of the Nieuport 11 (and the later Nieuport 17) better than the RFC's Albert Ball. Only nineteen years old when he joined his first squadron, Ball was a sensitive loner who would rather relax by listening to the gramophone or playing the violin in his room than by joining in the riotous escapades of his brother officers. In the air, too, he preferred to operate alone, and the roving commission he was given when he reached No. 60 Squadron suited him ideally. He seemed never to be concerned about unfavorable odds and frequently attacked enemy formations regardless of numbers. Between July and the end of

Albert Ball *by Jim Dietz*

September 1916, Ball destroyed thirty enemy aircraft and was, at that time, the world's most successful fighter pilot. This was not accomplished without cost. As with many airmen, the stress of daily combat took its toll. His courageous behavior in the air contrasted with his often nervous introspection on the ground.

Phrases from Ball's letters home are revealing: "I only scrap because it is my duty, but I do not think anything bad about the Hun. Nothing makes me feel more rotten than to see them go down, but you can see it is either them or me, so I must do my best to make it a case of them…. At night I was feeling rotten and my nerves were quite poo-poo…. I went to see the CO and ask him if I could have a short rest…. I do so want to leave all this beastly killing for a time."

At a time when Allied propaganda was fostering the image of "the Hun" as an inhuman monster, and Albert Ball was being seen as an aerial knight, a fearless and unstoppable destroyer of his nation's enemies, the young pilot's words point to a truth more easily recognized by airmen of either side.

Black Cross Resurgent

Faced with the unpalatable fact of Allied air superiority over the Somme, the Germans made strenuous efforts to put their house in order. Fighter organization was changed to group fighter aircraft into Jagdstaffeln (Jastas, or hunting units) of fourteen machines each. Two Jastas were operating by September and four by October. They were equipped with new aircraft, and it was not long before the

ABOVE Boelcke's Last Combat *by Jim Dietz* LEFT *The L.V.G. C.VI, seen here in the Shuttleworth Collection, was a capable light bomber and reconnaissance machine, the last and most prolifically produced of a series of similar L.V.G. types. It was armed with a single forward-firing Spandau and a Parabellum LMG 14 machine gun ring-mounted on the observer's cockpit. The LMG 14 could sustain its fire far longer than its Allied adversaries. The usual aircraft Lewis gun could take only 97-round drums, but the LMG 14's drums held 250 rounds.*

pendulum of air superiority swung back in their direction. The streamlined D series Albatros was a more advanced design than anything it faced in 1916. Less agile than the Nieuports, it was faster and had a better rate of climb. It was also a sturdier aircraft and more heavily armed, with two forward-firing machine guns placed directly ahead of the pilot. Used properly, in Jastas, the Albatros was more than sufficient to wrest control of the skies away from the Allies.

Oswald Boelcke, fresh from a rest spell in the rear, returned to the front in August as commander of Jasta 2. Under his leadership, the unit converted to the Albatros D.I and D.II and became proficient in the new art of operating as a squadron. On its first patrol over the lines in mid-September, Boelcke led Jasta 2 against a formation of eight B.E.2cs and six F.E.2bs, shooting down four without loss. Over the following two weeks, the pilots of Jasta 2 shot down twenty-five of their enemies, of which Boelcke accounted for ten. The squadron suffered only seven losses while raising its victory total to seventy-six by the end of October. German enthusiasm at such conspicuous success withered at the news that one of the seven lost was Oswald Boelcke, killed after a midair collision with another Albatros during combat with RFC D.H.2s of No. 24 Squadron. In a gesture typical of the noble sentiments that lingered on in 1916, the RFC dropped a wreath over their dead enemy's airfield. The attached message read: "To the memory of Captain Boelcke, our brave and chivalrous opponent."

As one leader falls, so another rises. With Boelcke when Jasta 2 flew its first operational sortie was the young Manfred von Richthofen. He scored his first victory on that day and quickly added others. Less than a month after Boelcke's fatal crash, Richthofen exacted stinging retribution for his leader's death. On November 23, 1916, flying his Albatros D.III on the German side of the lines, he engaged a D.H.2. They fought for over half an hour, the D.H.2's maneuverability unable to overcome the speed and climbing power of the Albatros. At last, his fuel running low, the D.H.2 pilot made a break for friendly airspace, but Richthofen caught his quarry and fired a killing burst. Hit in the head, Major Lanoe Hawker, VC, commander of No. 24 Squadron, RFC, fell just 50 yards inside German-held territory. Richthofen fired more than 900 rounds in claiming his eleventh, and most illustrious, victim.

Given the intensity of the air war, it is hardly surprising that even the most talented pilots, recognized by their peers as exceptional, should eventually find their way on to the casualty lists. Immelman, Boelcke and Hawker were among the earliest of the aces to die but they were by no means the last. A seemingly endless parade of heroic figures, greatly mourned by their respective nations, was overtaken by the harsh realities of aerial combat. Luck, judgment and fate all played their part in deciding who would survive on a given day. Inferior aircraft were facts of life and had to be flown until better ones arrived, but even a superior aircraft could be a liability if it had an engine problem or its guns jammed. A pilot might fly when not fully fit, he might make a fatal error of judgment in the heat of combat, or he might simply be in the wrong piece of sky at a bad time.

Oswald Boelcke established the basic principles for aerial combat adopted by air forces everywhere. By the time of his death in combat on October 28, 1916, he had accumulated forty aerial victories, many of them while flying the Fokker E.III Eindecker.

Added to these factors for the RFC was the Trenchard policy of carrying the fight to the enemy no matter what the cost. Lanoe Hawker was caught deep in enemy airspace, driven by orders to give combat at every opportunity and flying an aircraft known to be inferior to its likely opposition. His death attracted much publicity, but he represented only the tip of the RFC's casualty iceberg at the end of 1916. British aircraft losses during the Battle of the Somme, between July 1 and November 17, were 782 from all causes.

ENGINES

French-built engines provided the core of power on which was built Allied air superiority in WWI. One solution to the problem of cooling these early aircraft engines was to keep the crankshaft still and spin the finned cylinders around it. The Le Rhône rotary weighed 308 pounds and produced 110 horsepower. Small fighter aircraft powered by rotary engines, like the Nieuport and Sopwith designs, could turn very quickly, especially to the right, but because they were susceptible to the considerable torque and gyroscopic effect of their engines and propellers, they were tricky to fly. Entering a tight turn to the left, the nose rose sharply; to the right, the nose dropped. Coarse and early application of rudder was necessary to avoid loss of control. OPPOSITE PAGE In the Nieuport 28, the Gnôme Monosoupape 9N rotary was closely and neatly cowled. It delivered 160 horsepower at 1,350 rpm, but was a notoriously thirsty engine and, like all rotaries, it had a very limited operational life.

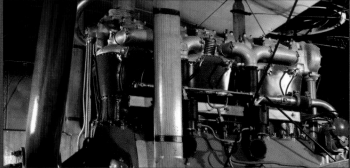

One of the 275-horsepower Isotta-Fraschini engines powering the Caproni Ca.33 at the USAF Museum.

The 200-horsepower Benz IV six-cylinder in-line water-cooled engine mounted in the L.V.G. C.VI flown

Cecil Lewis, author of the airman's classic, *Sagittarius Rising*, wrote: "Pilots in 1916 were lasting, on an average, for three weeks." He described the young RFC pilots who faced this gloomy prospect as "adventurous spirits, the devil-may-care young bloods of England, the fast livers, the furious drivers [who] were not happy unless they were taking risks." Since many of them were flying "pushers" in which they were liable to be out-flown by an Albatros or be crushed by the engine if they crashed, they fought their fears with the bravado of riotous behavior and trivialized the dangers in such songs as "The Dying Airman."

> *The young aviator lay dying*
> *And as in the hangar he lay*
> *To the mechanics who round him were standing*
> *These last parting words he did say*
> *Take the cylinders out of my kidneys*
> *The connecting rod out of my brain*
> *From the small of my back take the camshaft*
> *And assemble the engine again.*

Richthofen *by Jim Dietz*

Slaughter of the Innocents

The Germans began 1917 intent on holding a defensive posture, both on the ground and in the air. They were unable to find sufficient industrial and military capacity to allow a more assertive policy. German fighter pilots rarely ventured across the front lines and almost always fought over their own territory. In Trenchard's view, this defensive stance placed the Germans at a strategic disadvantage, denying their army the benefits of daily reconnaissance. However, it also meant that local air superiority was theirs for the taking. Operating superior fighters in Jastas, the German pilots patrolled at height and waited for Allied aircraft, choosing the time and place for their attacks. Additional squadrons were called forward when necessary by an aircraft warning service, operated by observation officers connected by land-line to the Jasta airfields. The system worked well, and Allied aircrew, maintaining their aggressive operations with inferior aircraft, suffered accordingly. As the casualty list lengthened, Trenchard's demands both for replacements and more squadrons increased the pressure on industry and the training system. New pilots reached squadrons in France with fewer than 20 hours solo flying and often less than 10 hours on the type in which they were to fight. The average time flown by a pilot before becoming a casualty fell from 295 hours in August 1916 to 92 hours in April 1917. Since neophytes were likely to be shot down before they had even mastered their aircraft, let alone accustomed themselves to the challenges of air fighting, their loss perpetuated a vicious cycle — death, replacement demands, inadequate training, early death.

Given the circumstances, it might have been thought that anything that promised to save the life of a trained pilot would have been welcomed, but the official attitude toward parachutes was implacable. The recommendations of the Air Board in London, most of whose members had no experience of flying, are typical of the time: "It is the opinion of the Board that the presence of such an apparatus might impair the fighting spirit of pilots and cause them to abandon machines which might otherwise be capable of returning to base for repair."

In his *Notes of a Lost Pilot*, Jean Villars commented on the fate awaiting the inexperienced airman, but gloomily pointed out that even the aces were likely to share that fate:

The Fokker Dr.I triplane has become associated with the Richthofen Flying Circus, and thereby gained a reputation out of proportion to its numbers and, except in the hands of a few outstanding pilots, its success in combat. Only 320 were built, equipping twenty-four Jastas. (The cockpit at left is at Le Bourget.) Richthofen himself undoubtedly liked the triplanes, saying that they "climb like monkeys and are maneuverable as the devil." However, there were Allied fighters just as nimble, and most were faster. Flying from rough forward airfields, Richthofen achieved nineteen of his last twenty-one victories while flying the Dr.I, and on April 21, 1918, he died in one.

"The veterans want to hunt individually, through over confidence and a desire to work on their own; the novices imitate them through vanity and ignorance. And both finish by being killed, the young by a lack of address and training, the veterans because the pitcher that goes often to the well gets broken at last."

"Bloody April" 1917 marked the nadir of Allied fortunes in the air, with the RFC being especially hard hit. As losses increased, the British determination to persist with an offensive policy seemed driven by the idea that the higher the casualties the greater must be the value of the air service. While the Battle of Arras was being fought, between March 31 and April 27, 1917, the RFC lost 238 aircrew killed or missing, with a further 105 wounded, while the Luftsteitkräfte suffered only 40 casualties. Statistics such as those were alarming, but to the public eye they were buried in the colossal casualty figures of the war as a whole.

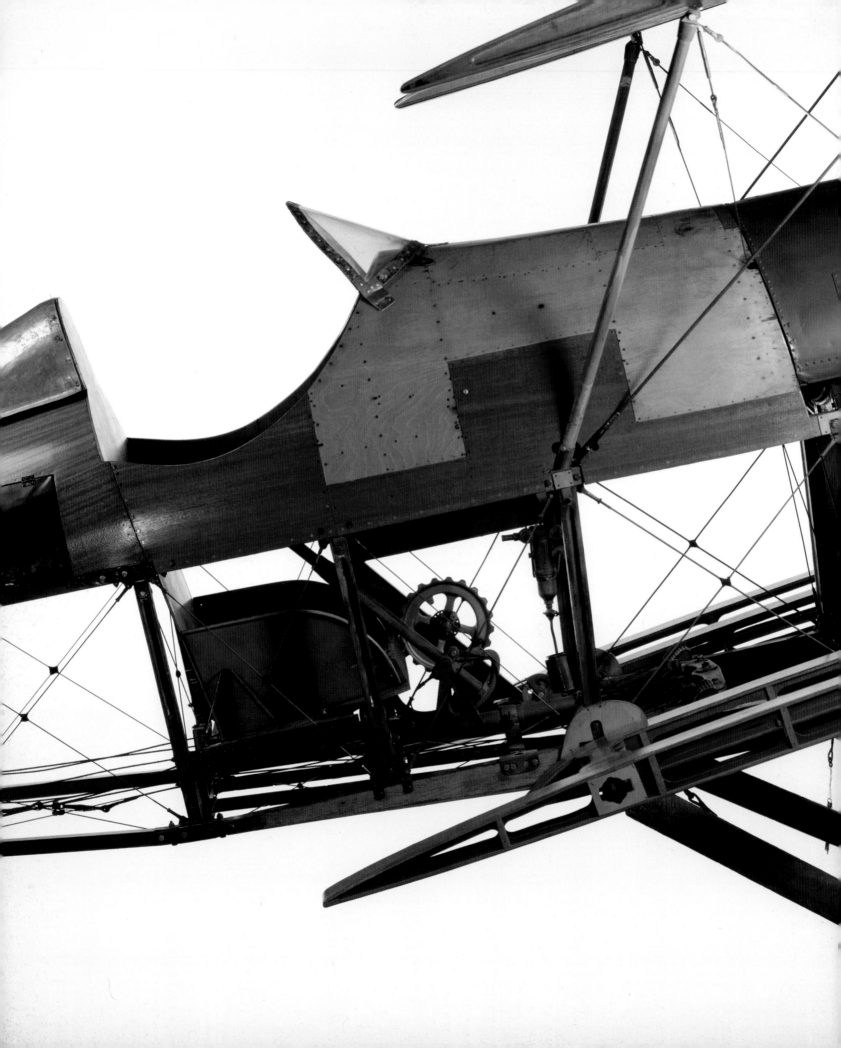

S.E.5

The S.E.5a was a typical fighter of the later stages of WWI. Stripped down to its bare essentials, its simplicity is revealed. The interior of the fuselage is practically empty, in marked contrast to the densely packed fighters of the 1990s. The S.E.5a at left is undergoing restoration at the United States Air Force Museum.

THIS PAGE

RIGHT The RAF's No. 85 Squadron lines up its S.E.5as in the latter stages of the war. The squadron's distinctive hexagon marking can clearly be seen behind the RAF roundel.
BELOW LEFT The specified engine for the S.E.5a was a Hispano-Suiza, but because of production problems most S.E.5as were powered by a "Hisso derivative," the Wolseley Viper. Like its French parent, the Viper was a water-cooled eight-cylinder in-line wide-angle V delivering 200 horsepower. Although it eventually became a reliable engine, the Viper, seen here at the RAF Museum, Hendon, was never as highly regarded as the Hisso. Early-production Vipers suffered frequent failure due to poor-quality components.
BELOW RIGHT The cockpits of 1914 could not compare: the pilot of an S.E.5a, now at Le Bourget, had a cornucopia of instruments and handy devices to aid his flight. Such things as throttle, mixture control, priming pump, oil-pressure gauge, inclinometer, altimeter and airspeed indicator jostled for his attention.

SPAD

In the autumn of 1916, the first examples of a new French fighter arrived in the front line. Less maneuverable than their contemporaries, SPADs were faster and markedly quicker in climbing to height. Pilots used to tightly turning dogfights in Nieuport or Sopwith fighters were sometimes slow to appreciate the qualities of the new aircraft, but in time tactics evolved that made its superiority clear. (A similar situation arose in WWII with the U.S. Navy's Wildcat and Japan's Zero.) Great aces such as Fonck, Guynemer, and Rickenbacker gained their considerable reputations in SPAD fighters.

THIS PAGE
At the Italian Air Force Museum, Vigna di Valle, is a SPAD VII flown by Ernesto Cabruna, an eight-victory ace, while he was with the 77th Squadron in 1918. It is covered in original fabric and bears a heart emblem. A similar aircraft was flown by the premier Italian ace, Francesco Baracca (thirty-four victories), whose aircraft were recognized by the prancing black horse emblem on the fuselage. In 1923, Baracca's mother, Countess Paolina, suggested Enzo Ferrari might use her son's emblem on his now famous line of classic cars.

Suspended in the Musée de l'Air at Le Bourget is a famous aircraft — the SPAD VII Vieux Charles in which Georges Guynemer achieved eighteen of his aerial victories. A look inside the SPAD XIII at the USAF Museum in Dayton reveals that cockpit instrumentation remained relatively simple in 1918 and in this aircraft was neatly arranged on a narrow facia at shoulder level. Windscreens were rudimentary affairs, but in the SPAD, the heavy framing could not have helped the pilot's field of vision.

SOPWITH

The Sopwith Camel shot down more aircraft (1,294) than any other fighter in WWI. There were 5,490 Camels produced and, at the end of the war, the type was flying with thirty-eight RAF squadrons. (Below) The Camel on display at the USAF Museum carries the markings of Lieutenant George A. Vaughn, Jr., 17th Aero Squadron. He was the fourth-ranking U.S. ace of WWI, with thirteen victories.

OPPOSITE PAGE
The most consistently successful British fighter aircraft of WWI were made by Sopwith. The Shuttleworth Collection's Sopwith Triplane is marked as Dixie II, an aircraft of No. 8 Squadron, RNAS, in 1917.

Sopwith Camel

McCudden was one of three brothers to serve with the RFC. He saw combat in France as an observer and gunner before becoming a pilot in 1916. By the beginning of April 1918, twenty-two-year-old James McCudden was the most decorated pilot in the Royal Air Force. The citation to his Victoria Cross concludes with the sentence: "This officer is considered, by the record he has made, by his fearlessness, and by the great service which he has rendered to his country, deserving of the very highest honour." When he was killed in a flying accident on July 9, 1918, his score of aerial victories stood at fifty-seven. As commander of No. 56 Squadron, RFC, he wrote: "I consider it a patrol leader's work to pay more attention to the main points of the fight than to do all the fighting himself. The main points are: (1) arrival of more EA who have tactical advantage, i.e. height; (2) patrol drifting too far east; (3) patrol getting below bulk of enemy formation. As soon as any of these circumstances occur, it is time to take advantage of the SE's superior speed over EA scouts and break off the fight, rally behind leader and climb west of EA until you are above them before attacking them again."

RIGHT *With seventy-five aerial victories, René Paul Fonck was the highest-scoring Allied ace. The citation for his Officier de la Legion d'Honneur citation said that he was a "remarkable officer from every point of view; of admirable fighting ardor." Fonck developed a reputation for studying the tactics of his opponents and conserving ammunition during a dogfight. On two separate occasions, he shot down six enemy aircraft in one day. Unfortunately, as his fame grew, so did his ego and he was not popular. His comments about his own ability included the remarks: "I put my bullets into the target as if I placed them there by hand," and, "I prefer to fly alone…when alone, I perform those little coups of audacity which amuse me."*

my total forty-two. I attacked two Albatros scouts and crashed them, killing the pilots. In the end I was brought down, but am quite OK. Oh! It was a good fight and the Huns were fine sports. One tried to ram me after he was hit and only missed by inches. Am indeed looked after by God, but oh, I do get tired of always living to kill, and am really beginning to feel like a murderer. Shall be so pleased when I am finished."

Ball was not alone in trying to reconcile the prevalent RFC idea that aerial combat was a kind of high stakes game between sportsmen with an enemy's death as the victor's prize. Opponents such as Manfred von Richthofen denigrated the RFC's attitude to combat.

The following month, Captain Albert Ball returned to the front after a much-needed rest from combat. He joined No. 56 Squadron, recently equipped with the new S.E.5, but was not entirely happy with the change from his beloved Nieuport 17, nor was he free of stress. In his letters home during the first week of May he admitted "feeling very old just now," and revealed something of his mental conflict when he told his father: "Have just come off patrol and made

In February 1917, Richthofen wrote: "Englishmen see in flying nothing but a sport … therefore the blood of English pilots will have to flow in streams." His lack of respect for Allied airmen extended to the French, also, whose attacking spirit he said was like "bottled lemonade; it lacks tenacity." Perhaps he had not seen the reckless Guynemer or the icy Fonck in action, and maybe he would have changed his mind if he had heard Albert Duellin, his face and clothing

Richthofen's Flying Circus *by Nicolas Trudgian, courtesy of the Military Gallery, Bath, U.K. In a scene recalling the desolation of the Western Front in 1917, Richthofen watches from his blood red Triplane as a Sopwith Camel struggles to escape, streaming smoke. An Albatros and a Bristol fighter are among the aircraft maneuvering in the background.*

covered in an enemy airman's blood, tell his horrified mechanic: "It is nothing. I shot from very close."

On May 7, 1917, Albert Ball's inner struggle was brought to an end. In the course of a fight with Albatros scouts led by Lothar von Richtofen, Ball's S.E.5 was seen to disappear into cloud. His body, unmarked by any wound, was later recovered by the Germans from the wreckage of his aircraft.

Allied Recovery

Even as the loss of Albert Ball cast an air of gloom over the RFC, the Allied fighter force began to show signs of recovering its superiority. New aircraft and better trained pilots were at last reaching the front-line squadrons. In the months that followed, the British S.E.5s, Bristol Fighters, Sopwith Pups, Triplanes and Camels gained the upper hand, and men such as Edward "Mick" Mannock, James McCudden, South Africa's Andrew Beauchamp-Proctor, and Canada's Billy Bishop and Raymond Collishaw became household names. The outstanding French SPAD became the preferred mount of Georges Guynemer, Charles Nungesser

and the redoubtable René Fonck, who was destined to become the Allied "Ace of Aces" with seventy-five confirmed victories. Belgium's Willy Coppens also operated the SPAD to considerable effect, principally against heavily defended observation balloons.

Effective though the new Allied aircraft were, they were not significantly advanced aerodynamically over their predecessors. To give them the edge in combat, they depended on having more powerful engines, notably the 220-horsepower Hispano-Suiza fitted to the SPAD XIII and the S.E.5a. There were considerable difficulties in developing such engines to an acceptable level of reliability and these delayed the introduction of the new aircraft to squadrons. French industry proved more effective at solving the problems than either the German or British. German engines were dependable, but the standard six-cylinder in-line design had limitations and material shortages denied the possibility of production increases. British engines, such as the Rolls-Royce Eagle or the Bentley rotary, were superb, but their complexity led to reliability problems and made difficult any attempt at mass production. French engines therefore continued to provide the solid core around which Allied air superiority was built in the latter stages of the war.

Having been supremely confident only weeks before, by mid-July 1917, Richthofen, recovering from being shot down and suffering a head wound, was writing: "I can assure you that it is no longer any fun being leader of a fighter unit…for the last three days the English have done as they please. Besides better quality aircraft they have quantity. The D.V [Albatros] is so antiquated and laughably inferior that we can do nothing with it…. You would not believe how low morale is among fighter pilots at the front because of their sorry machines. No one wants to be a fighter pilot any more."

Richthofen's remarks highlighted the astonishingly brief operational life of a fighter aircraft when relatively small improvements could make the difference between success and failure. The Albatros D.V on which he poured such scorn was a development of the D.III, which first appeared with Richthofen's Jasta in December 1916, only eight months before he dismissed its successor as "antiquated."

In an attempt to stem the tide, the German Jastas began operating as fighter wings (Jagdgeschwader). Manfred von Richthofen commanded the first (JG1), comprised of Jastas 4, 6, 10, and 11, each established with two flights of six aircraft. Given ample transport and personnel to allow freedom of movement behind the front, the JGs' mobility enabled them to offset the growing superiority of the Allies by concentrating air power as necessary at critical points. When JG1 appeared, it was instantly recognizable. Richthofen had for some time flown an aircraft painted all red, earning him the nickname of "The Red Baron." The men of his wing followed his flamboyant example, painting their aircraft a variety of bright colors, and were soon known to the RFC as "The Flying Circus."

Ernst Udet's sixty-two victories put him second only to Richthofen on the German list. He was the highest-scoring German ace to survive WWI, largely because he flew with a parachute (not common practice) and used it twice. He was also fortunate to live through a legendary dogfight with Guynemer. Udet's guns jammed and the Frenchman chose to salute and turn away. It was a misplaced act of chivalry — at the time Udet had only six victories.

A Proliferation of Aces

With Immelman and Boelcke gone, and Manfred von Richthofen grounded by his head wound, the Germans were finding, as the Allies had, that other pilots could follow in the footsteps of the established heroes. Apart from Manfred's brother, Lothar, men such as Ernst Udet, Werner Voss and Rudolph Berthold were eager to earn the coveted Blue Max. As the scale of the air war grew, more and more airmen proved capable of surviving long enough to reach the first rung of the status ladder and be called aces. Later studies showed that the achievement often carried the highest possible price. While perhaps 10 percent of all the airmen of either side engaged on the Western Front were killed in action, the figure for "aces" is closer to 25 or 30 percent, a statistic suggesting that the more successful fighter pilots were those who not only survived their first few encounters with the enemy but thereafter actively sought combat, thereby accepting the risk of being shot down more often than others. The great French ace, Georges Guynemer, for example, consistently went looking for trouble, hurling himself into the fray whatever the odds and almost never breaking away with the issue undecided. In gaining his fifty-four victories, Guynemer was shot down eight times and wounded twice before his last flight on September 11, 1917, when he disappeared into cloud during a fight. Neither his aircraft nor his body were ever found, prompting an emotional journalist to write: "He flew so high he could not come down again." In fact, his aircraft fell into an area that was under an intense British artillery bombardment. When the shelling ceased, Guynemer and his aircraft had simply vanished.

(Guynemer is known to have broken off combat once. He fought Ernst Udet for some eight minutes before the German's guns jammed. Offered an easy kill, Guynemer waved at Udet and turned away. Militarily, such gallantry was unwise. At the time, Udet had six victories. He became

Germany's second-most successful ace, with a total of sixty-two.)

Popular culture may have persisted in putting the ace on a pedestal, with pilots such as Richthofen, Mannock and Fonck continuing to personify the fighter pilot as a knightly figure in the public mind, but by mid-1917 German discipline and the British concept of teamwork had transformed most aerial combat into merciless clashes between formations led by a new and implacable breed of national champions. None of the leading three, and very few of their followers, had much time for medieval notions of chivalry. Richthofen was a consummate aerial assassin who savored his victories, and Mannock, perhaps the best all-round fighter leader of the war, repeatedly emphasized his outright hatred of the enemy. A member of his squadron once said of him: "There was absolutely no chivalry in him, and the only good Hun was a dead one." Of the three foremost aces, only Fonck could still be described as a loner. Even though the French had officially formed their escadrilles into groups at Verdun in 1916, they were reluctant to follow the trend, and their leading pilots abhorred the prospect of having the brilliance of their individual prominence dimmed by operations en masse. The effectiveness of the French fighter arm was further affected by the practice of concentrating the most experienced pilots in elite units such as "The Storks," so depriving new pilots in less blessed squadrons of teachers and role models.

The development of formation tactics did not mean that men never had to fight alone. The confused nature of air fighting once opposing formations were engaged was such that pilots often found themselves separated from their comrades, and there were many occasions when a lone Luftstreitkräfte or RFC airman ran into an enemy formation. On September 23, 1917, a single Fokker Dr.I Triplane flown by Werner Voss, who may have been the most talented of German fighter pilots, fought seven S.E.5s of No. 56 Squadron for ten minutes and succeeded in putting holes in all of them. Since his seven opponents, led by James McCudden, claimed well over 100 victories between them, this speaks volumes for the agility of the Dr.I and for its pilot's ability. Still fighting hard, Voss was at last caught by

> "No matter how good the pilot was when it came to maneuvering, the Sopwith Pup would turn twice to an Albatros' once."
>
> JAMES MCCUDDEN, 1917

the guns of Arthur Rhys-Davies and crashed on the British side of the lines, where he was later buried with full military honors. Voss had scored his first victory on March 17 while flying an Albatros D.III and had shot down forty-eight aircraft in just six months. Later in the war, in an even more unequal encounter, Major William Barker, a Canadian, was set upon by elements of four Fokker D.VII Jastas after shooting down a Rumpler two-seater. In the course of the ensuing fight, Barker was wounded in both thighs, had his left elbow shattered, fainted at least twice, and shot down three more of his enemies before surviving a crash-landing near a British balloon unit. Epic though these solo engagements were, they were hardly typical of the air war, which increasingly favored the masses and scorned ideas of individual chivalry.

Climax of the Air War

During the winter of 1917/18, the tempo of the air war slackened, but the lull was merely temporary. Following the entry of the United States into the war on April 6, 1917, Germany faced the prospect of massive American reinforcements arriving on the Western Front in 1918. Desperate to force a confrontation before that occurred, the Germans launched a series of offensives in the spring of 1918, beginning with an assault on the British Army in Picardy.

By careful husbanding of their resources, the Germans succeeded in ensuring superior air strength where it was needed. Although vastly outnumbered elsewhere, they concentrated 730 aircraft in the Picardy area, of which 326 were fighters. The RFC faced them there initially with 579 aircraft, including 261 single-seat fighters. When the German offensive opened on March 21, much of the air effort expended by both sides was devoted to direct support of the armies, but the air-to-air combat was nevertheless fierce, with huge swirling dogfights at heights from ground level to 20,000 feet or more. Pilots spent as many as five or six hours in combat during a day. Two pilots of No. 43 Squadron, RFC, (Captains J. L. Trollope and H. W. Woollett) each destroyed six enemy machines in one day, and René Fonck equaled that feat on the French front. Manfred von Richthofen, his head still bandaged, raised his victory total to seventy-four by shooting down eight aircraft between March 24 and 28.

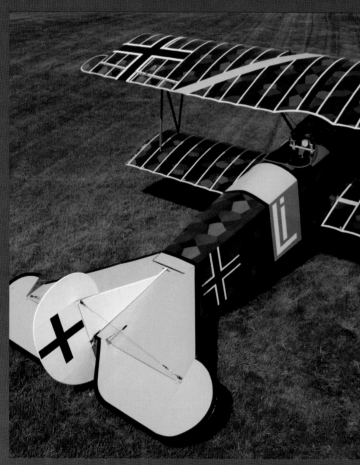

FOKKER D.VII

With his last and most successful fighter design of WWI, Anthony Fokker produced an aircraft that achieved a notoriety unequaled by any other instrument of war. The Fokker D.VII was the only weapon specifically named in the Versailles Treaty: "The German Armies must surrender the following war material: 1700 airplanes —including fighters and bombers, and first — all Fokker D.VIIs...."

The Fokker D.VII was certainly a formidable machine. Although not as fast as the Allied SPADs, it was sensitive yet easy to fly, and had both an impressive rate of climb and excellent maneuverability at all altitudes. Its uncluttered cockpit was dominated by the cocking levers of two Spandau machine guns.

The D.VII exhibited at the Musée de l'Air, Le Bourget, is in the standard German camouflage pattern in use at the end of WWI, while the machine at the USAF Museum is in the exotic lavender color scheme chosen by Lieutenant Rudolph Stark of Jasta 35b.

HENRY BOTTERELL

Henry Botterell was born on November 7, 1896, in Ottawa, Canada. In 1917, he trained as a pilot and joined the Royal Naval Air Service. A crash put him out of action for several months, but he persisted, going through pilot training again and joining No. 208 Squadron, RAF (formerly No. 8 Squadron, RNAS), in France in May 1918. During his service, he flew several fighter types, including the Sopwith Pup, Camel and Snipe, and the S.E.5a. Among his mementoes of the time are diaries, log books, medals, and photographs of a favored nurse and of himself in a Sopwith Camel.

The Balloon Buster, by Robert Taylor, courtesy of the Military Gallery, Bath, U.K. Henry Botterell's Camel has just attacked a German observation balloon north of Arras on August 29, 1918. As the blazing balloon falls, Henry salutes the parachuting observer and heads for base.

In the year 2000, Henry Botterell became one of the few to have lived in three centuries and was probably the last man standing of the aviators who fought in WWI. Dan Patterson caught the determination of his character in a portrait composed soon after Henry Botterell's 104th birthday. Henry Botterell died in January 2003 at the age of 106.

The intensity of the conflict was reflected in the losses. In March and April, the RFC lost 1,032 aircraft, of which 528 were fighters. The Luftstreitkräfte's losses of 629 aircraft and 182 fighters were not nearly so severe, but the dynamics of the struggle were now set firmly against the Germans. These were aircraft that they could not easily replace and a setback from which they would never fully recover. For the aircrew of both sides, this was an especially challenging period. In open cockpits that exposed the crews to biting cold and, at higher altitudes, a debilitating lack of oxygen, they flew knowing that every sortie would involve combat from which some would not return, praying that they would not be among those to die in a "flamer." Strain showed on the faces of the most hardened pilots, and many leaders who had seemed indestructible did not survive the aerial holocaust of 1918. Richthofen himself seemed worn out and depressed, admitting, "I am in wretched sprits after every battle." Mannock, a man who had always had to struggle with his fears, confided to a friend, "There won't be any 'after the war' for me." Within days, Mannock's dismal premonition was realized when he was brought down by ground fire after scoring his seventy-third victory. Richthofen (eighty victories) had died some weeks earlier, on April 21, 1918, shot down during a fight at low level, his destruction claimed by Captain Roy Brown of 209 Squadron, RAF, but almost certainly achieved by gunners of the Australian Field Artillery. Respected leaders Löwenhardt (fifty-three) and McCudden (fifty-seven) were gone, too, both killed in flying accidents.

As the German offensives slowed and they were driven irrevocably onto the defensive, the air battles lost little of their intensity. After starting 1918 with the Albatros D.V and the Fokker Dr.I Triplane, which had difficulty in matching the latest Allied fighters, the Luftstreitkräfte was given new heart by the arrival in April of the Fokker D.VII, an aircraft which, it was claimed, could make good pilots out of mediocre material. The D.VII was not as fast as the SPAD XIII or the S.E.5a, but it was viceless, very maneuverable at all altitudes, a steady gun platform, and had the best rate of climb of any combat aircraft on either side. By the end of the summer, over 800 D.VIIs had been delivered, but it was too late. Although the D.VII Jastas were able, under leaders such as Ernst Udet and Hermann Göring, to score heavily against their enemies, they were overwhelmed by increasingly superior numbers. Richthofen's Flying Circus, now under Göring's command, fought almost to destruction and was withdrawn from the front. The final Allied ground offensives gathered pace and the Luftstreitkräfte units fell back from airfield to airfield, bedeviled by shortages of fuel and lubricants and reduced to salvaging wrecked aircraft for spare parts.

A captured German report, dated June 1, 1918, included the comment: "The supply of material to the front has become essentially dependent on the return of waste material from the front." Well mounted and well led though they were, German fighter pilots were swamped by the rising tide of Allied manpower and industrial strength.

Edward Corringham "Mick" Mannock, VC, DSO, MC, overcame his humble background and virtual blindness in his left eye to become one of the most respected Allied fighter leaders of WWI. His aerial victories have been variously reported from as low as fifty to as high as seventy-three, the latter figure being the official accreditation issued by the Air Ministry after the war. Given his unselfish habit of awarding victories to inexperienced wingmen, it is possible that his score was even higher. The citation to Mannock's Victoria Cross ends with the comment: "This highly distinguished officer during the whole of his career in the Royal Air Force, was an outstanding example of fearless courage, remarkable skill, devotion to duty and self-sacrifice, which has never been surpassed." Mannock's attitude to the enemy was implacable, as is evident from his remark: "I sent one of them down to hell in flames today…I wish Kaiser Bill could have seen him sizzle."

CLOSE AIR SUPPORT

The use of fighter aircraft to attack enemy troops was at first the result of individual initiative rather than any stated policy. It was not until the Battle of the Somme in 1916 that aircraft were given direct orders to engage enemy ground forces. The RFC assigned eighteen aircraft to undertake "close reconnaissance and destructive bombardment." The subsequent attacks, made on an opportunity basis, had a startling effect. A German officer later wrote: "The infantry had no training in defense against low-flying aircraft and had no confidence in their ability to shoot them down ... they were seized with a fear amounting almost to panic..."

The diary of a German soldier confirms this and adds a touch of bitter sarcasm: "During the day one hardly dares to be seen in the trench because of enemy aircraft. They fly so low that it is a wonder they do not pull one out of the trench. Nothing is to be seen of our heroic German airmen. One can hardly calculate how much additional loss of life and strain on the nerves this costs us."

This was a period of Allied air superiority, and the effect of this, combined with Trenchard's incessant offensive policy, was revealed by a letter found on the body of another German soldier, who had spent some time in an area behind the lines: "About our own airmen I am almost ashamed to write. It is scandalous. They fly as far as this village but no further, whereas the English [the RFC] are always over our lines, directing their artillery and getting shells right into our trenches. This moral defeat has a bad effect on us all."

The effectiveness of the RFC's low-level operations on the Somme awakened German interest in the role and encouraged the Allies to continue. However, no significant action was taken until the following year. On May 11, 1917, in an operation designed specifically as ground attack, RFC Nieuports and F.E.2bs struck at German troops with machine-gun fire and 20-pound bombs in support of advancing British infantry.

Until then, low-level sorties over the lines had largely been flown haphazardly, with pilots looking for targets of opportunity. Mannock described the result of such

> *"General Trenchard has not attached very much importance to the delivery of the single engine Caudrons. Of course, the more Caudrons delivered the better. We value the 80 hp Le Rhône engines much more than the machines which contain them."*
>
> ROYAL FLYING CORPS HQ, NOVEMBER 1915

spur-of-the-moment flying in his diary: "Went over the lines from north of Arras to 5 miles behind the German trenches at a height of less than fifteen feet, attacking German balloons. Six of us. All except the new flight commander returned safely but with machines shot to pieces. Hall crashed on our home aerodrome, as did Scudamore. Parry crashed just our side of the lines at Canadian HQ. Redler crashed at Savy but managed to return here later and damaged his machine again on landing. I was the only one to return properly to the aerodrome. We all got our objectives. My fuselage had bullet holes in it, one very near my head, and the wings were more or less riddled. I don't want to go through such an experience again."

The May 11 operation set the pattern for the RFC, which continued to use single-seat fighters for ground attack, modifying them as necessary to carry small bombs and coordinating their operations with infantry assaults. After escorting the troops in the initial phase of an attack, the fighters roamed freely over the battlefield looking for suitable targets. The Germans responded in a similar way, but believed that two-seaters could be more effective, using both the pilot's forward firing guns and the movable gun of the observer in the rear cockpit. By late summer 1917, although soldiers on both sides still feared air attack, they had become accustomed to it and were prepared to fight back. The number of aircraft shot down by ground fire rose, with RFC loss rates often exceeding 30 percent. Understandably, airmen did not like the close-support role; one RFC pilot wrote that trench strafing was "a wasteful employment of highly trained pilots and expensive aeroplanes…rather than face a single trench strafing foray, I would much prefer to go through half a dozen dogfights with Albatroses."

Toward the end of 1917, the Germans introduced new aircraft to the front. Originally designed for "defensive patrol and pursuit" duties, they adapted well to the close-support role. The Hannover and Halberstadt CL series aircraft were formidable two-seaters. Like the RFC's Bristol Fighter, they were maneuverable enough to engage single-seaters in combat with some confidence. They were joined by the

The ungainly Junkers J.1 entered service in the spring of 1917. It was designed to meet a requirement for an armored close-support aircraft and was of all-metal construction. To ensure good downward visibility, the lower wing was only one-third the size of the upper, and to cope with its unusual weight, it was powered by a 200-horsepower Benz engine. Armament consisted of two forward-firing Spandaus for the pilot and a ring-mounted Parabellum machine gun for the observer. Heavy on the controls, its ability to absorb punishment nonetheless made it popular with crews.

Junkers J.1, a large rugged biplane, extensively covered with a steel skin and provided with armor over vulnerable points.

In 1918, the Germans also began to bring a certain amount of order to the chaos of low flying over a battlefield. Special attack units called schlachtstaffen (abbreviated to schlasta) were formed, intended as "a powerful weapon to be employed at the decisive point of attack." They operated in flights of four to six aircraft and, unlike their Allied counterparts, they were not meant to wander freely. Their interventions in the ground battle were controlled and made wherever it was felt they could have the greatest impact. Having seen the effect of low-flying aircraft on their own troops, the German authorities stressed that formations should go over the trenches at minimum altitude to "shatter the enemy's nerve." At the same time, it was recognized that the sight of friendly aircraft in action gave a useful boost to the confidence of hard-pressed soldiers.

In March 1918, the long stalemate of trench warfare was broken by a massive German offensive against the British Third and Fifth Armies. Strengthened by forces freed from the Eastern Front by Russia's collapse and supported by large numbers of aircraft, German troops crashed through the British defensive positions. The seriousness of the situation was reflected in an order from Marshal Foch, the Allied C-in-C, which emphasized that the ground forces could use all the help they could get: "The first duty of fighting aeroplanes is to assist the troops on the ground by incessant attacking with bombs and machine guns on columns, concentrations or bivouacs. Air fighting is not to be sought except as far as is necessary for the fulfilment of this duty."

After many months of stagnation, both sides had to adjust themselves to the very different conditions of mobile warfare. For the airmen, it meant a sudden proliferation of softer targets. Moving armies had to use the roads, often in columns and convoys, giving aircraft the opportunity of catching them in the open. On March 25, 1918, an advancing column of German infantry suffered a single strafing attack of only a few seconds and lost three officers and 135 men. Similar aerial onslaughts slowed the German advance, and it was realized also that attacks on concentrations of troops and supplies behind the battlefront could be effective in destroying the momentum of the enemy's offensive. On June 4, 1918, the French became aware that German infantry were being massed for an assault in a ravine out of reach of artillery fire. In a classic demonstration of what air power could do in such circumstances, 120 Breguet 14s, flying repeated sorties, dropped some 7,000 bombs into the ravine. The planned German advance did not take place.

This was when commanders began to realize just how much massed air power could influence the land battle, and when advocates of using aircraft en masse in critical situations saw their ideas put to the test and largely vindicated, though at considerable cost in men and machines. When the German advances ran out of steam, the Allies responded by initiating their final series of offensives. The

French, British and American squadrons involved devoted over a third of their offensive effort to close support of troops, attacking observation balloons wherever they appeared and strafing anything that moved on the enemy side of the front. Machine-gun posts were silenced, horse-drawn transport stampeded, staff cars shot up and infantry formations scattered. Air attacks on retreating columns hastened the breakup of the enemy armies. Effective though it was, this incessant ground-attack flying was a risky business, as attested to by John Slessor (later Marshal of the Royal Air Force Sir John Slessor), who cited the case of the RFC's No. 80 Squadron, a unit employed almost exclusively in close support: "Their average strength was 22 officers, and in the last ten months of the war no less than 168 officers were struck off the strength from all causes — an average of about 75 percent per month, of whom little less than half were killed."

That the losses were high was undeniable, but so was the evidence that close-support aircraft could exert a powerful influence on the land battle. It was a lesson learned the hard way, and one that would be borne in mind during preparations for another major war, some twenty years later.

BOMBERS AND THEIR "GHASTLY DEW"

When war broke out in 1914, the military establishments had no plans for aircraft to carry bombs, but they had done some trials and the idea that airborne machines could be bombers was already firmly planted in the public mind. Tennyson's poetic "ghastly dew" prediction of 1842 was not alone as a prophecy, and H.G. Wells' 1908 novel, *War in the Air,* was among a number of speculations on the aircraft's potential destructive power. The prewar appearance of German Zeppelin dirigibles only served to heighten public anxieties and, in the absence of empirical evidence, to encourage journalists in their lurid accounts of bombing's anticipated impact on those attacked. Attention was drawn to the vulnerability of such targets as government and communication centers, power stations, ports, bridges and railyards, and it was assumed that shock and panic would be at least as

"For I dipt into the future,
far as human eye could see,
Saw the vision of the world,
and all the wonder there would be;
Saw the heavens fill with commerce,
argosies of magic sails,
Pilots of the purple twilight,
dropping down with costly bales;
Heard the heavens fill with shouting,
and there rain'd a ghastly dew
From the nations' airy navies
grappling in the central blue."

ALFRED, LORD TENNYSON,
"LOCKSLEY HALL," 1842

significant as any physical damage aircraft might inflict. In the event, the Germans were cautious in their use of Zeppelins in the early days of the war, committing the great airships on only a few occasions and then no further than the fighting on the Western Front. They were withdrawn from battlefield operations when three of the seven monsters available were lost to ground fire within a month.

The Zeppelins may have been an awesome sight, but it was the airplane that made bombing a reality, inadequate for the task though it was in 1914. Reconnaissance crews, flying over columns of enemy troops, soon began to carry any weapons that might be suitable for dropping by hand — grenades, 90 mm shells, and fléchettes (steel darts) all served the purpose. It was not long before these opportunistic efforts were officially blessed. In October the RFC issued an instruction requiring all reconnaissance crews to carry bombs, and in November, German units began fitting bomb racks to their aircraft. By early 1915 formal advice was being issued, including recommendations about the targets to be attacked. The targets officially selected as most rewarding for aircraft were generally behind the front lines — artillery positions, massed reserves, road and rail transport, and supply depots. It was realized that bombers could serve best when they struck targets unreachable by artillery. The problem initially was that aircraft were incapable of carrying much of a bomb load. The type most widely used by the Allies for bombing was the Voisin Type III, a version of an ungainly prewar design, with a maximum speed less than 70 mph and a bomb-carrying capacity of only 130 pounds.

Bombing accuracy was not great since it depended on the pilot or observer simply letting go of a bomb when he thought it likely it would hit the target. Even when bomb-racks appeared, bombsights were either absent or very rudimentary, perhaps nothing more than a mark made on a strut outside the cockpit. The racks did at least ease the labor of the "bomber" by providing a mechanical release of a kind.

C.G. Grey described a typical RFC mechanism: "It was a thing exactly like a pipe-rack fixed on the outside of the fuselage, handy for the pilot or passenger. The bombs hung nose downwards and their stems projected up through the holes in the pipe-rack arrangement. There a pin was stuck through each stem and laid across the hole. To the head of the pin a piece of string was tied, and when the 'bomber' wanted to drop the bomb he pulled the string which pulled out the pin which let the stem of the bomb drop out of the rack, and the bomb fell."

Given variables such as height, airspeed and wind, and the distractions of enemy action, it is hardly surprising that getting bombs anywhere near a target was something of a lottery.

(Rudimentary bomb-aiming methods were in use long after WWI. Half a century later, when the development of Soviet missiles forced NATO air forces to adopt low-level tactics, the RAF's force of Vulcan bombers was without a bombsight suitable for the new role. Conventional bombs, dropped from 500 feet or less, were therefore aimed by running the tip of the flight refueling probe through the target and counting to five before releasing the weapons.)

The Strategic Bombing Idea

Air-power visionaries had dreamed of the day when flying machines might leap over intervening armies and navies to strike ruinous blows at the fabric of an enemy nation. Paris was the first capital city to be bombed by an aircraft, although the attack was puny and apparently accomplished at the personal whim of the German pilot. On August 30, 1914, a single Taube monoplane floated unmolested over Paris and scattered some small bombs near the Gare de l'Est. The intrusion caused no more than minor damage, but it did raise the alarm about the lack of defenses against air attack. More disturbing for Parisians was the imperious message dropped with the bombs: "The German Army is at the gates of Paris. There is nothing for you to do but surrender." Aerial threats to Britain were not manifest until December and were even less impressive. Friedrichshafen F.F.29 seaplanes dropped bombs into the sea off Dover harbor and, with the first bomb ever to fall on the British mainland, dug a small hole on open ground near Dover Castle.

More serious German efforts depended on the Zeppelin airships, which had no rivals for lifting power or for range. Of this the Allies were only too well aware, and pre-emptive strikes were launched against Zeppelin bases. Less than two weeks into the war, French Voisins attacked airship sheds near Metz without success, but on October 8, a Sopwith Tabloid of the Royal Naval Air Service carried out an operation that had more than its share of high drama. Flying a final sortie from Antwerp as that city was in the act of surrendering to the advancing Germans, Flight Lieutenant Reggie Marix braved the defenses at only 600 feet to drop two 20-pound bombs on an airship hangar near Dusseldorf. Zeppelin Z IX, full of hydrogen, was inside, and Marix had the satisfaction of seeing flames 500 feet high erupt from the hangar. Seriously damaged by ground fire, the Tabloid came down in open country and Marix pedaled his way to friendly forces on a bicycle donated by a sympathetic Belgian.

The RNAS followed this with a more ambitious and carefully planned strike against the Zeppelins. In November 1914, four Avro 504As were disassembled and shipped to Belfort in France, near the Swiss border. On November 21, three of the aircraft, each armed with four 20-pound bombs, flew more than 120 miles to the airship sheds at Friedrichshafen on Lake Constance. In the attack, damage was done to the sheds and to a Zeppelin. One Avro was shot down and its pilot captured. Possibly the most significant effect of the raid was that it shocked the Germans. They could scarcely believe that enemy aircraft had flown a round trip of over 250 miles and achieved such a deep penetration of their airspace unopposed. They made strenuous efforts to ensure that it could not happen again.

The Zeppelins

The Allies were right to assume that Zeppelins would be used to strike at targets in France and Britain. Operations began in January 1915, when two German naval airships crossed the coast of East Anglia at night, scattering bombs over the ports of Great Yarmouth and King's Lynn. Four people were killed and sixteen injured, the first British civilians to be harmed in the application of a "total war policy." Ineffective though it was, the attack was applauded by the German press, which described the Zeppelin in glowing terms while denying the navy its laurels: "The most modern

Bill Marsalko's painting of Capronis over the Alps captures the essence of these challenging long-range Italian operations against the Austrians. Navigating through mountainous territory in all weather, often with their heavily loaded bombers at heights close to their ceilings, the crews were exposed to the rush of below-zero air for hours in open cockpits. They conducted their strategic campaign with resolution and showed that long-range bombing could be a practical proposition.

air weapon, a triumph of German inventiveness and the sole possession of the German Army, has shown itself capable of carrying the war to the soil of old England! ... This is the best way to shorten the war and thereby in the end the most humane." Such moralizing enthusiasm was premature, as the airship campaign later revealed.

The limitations of the early Zeppelins were considerable. They had a maximum speed of less than 50 mph, operated below 10,000 feet, and carried a typical load of just five 110-pound bombs and twenty 6-pound incendiaries. They were filled with inflammable hydrogen, and were susceptible to bad weather. Initially, they were inhibited in their attacks by the Kaiser's concern for his relatives in the British royal family and his fear of the effect bombing

London would have on world opinion. By mid-1915, however, London was a target, and it was not long before better airships were available. Those of 1916, 650 feet long and powered by six 240-horsepower engines, could fly at over 60 mph above 13,000 feet, and could lift a useful load of more than 70,000 pounds, including four to five tons of bombs. Unfortunately for them, the British defenses had made an even more dramatic improvement, with fighters, anti-aircraft guns and searchlights all ready to make life uncomfortable for the Zeppelin crews.

Zeppelin vulnerability to airplane attack was demonstrated on June 7, 1915, when two were destroyed, one bombed inside its hangar by Farmans of the RNAS, and the other as it returned from an abortive raid on England.

Flight Sub-Lieutenant Reginald Warneford, flying a Morane Parasol, caught the LZ 37 near Bruges and did a bombing run at 150 feet above it, releasing six 20-pound bombs in sequence. As the last bomb left its rack, the huge airship erupted in flame, throwing the little Morane upward, turning it upside down and stopping the engine. As the Zeppelin crashed, Warneford recovered control of his aircraft and completed a forced landing in the dark behind enemy lines. After being on the ground for 35 minutes and repairing a broken fuel line with a piece of cigarette holder, he got airborne again and made his way back to base. Warneford earned the Victoria Cross for his exploit, but did not live long to enjoy his celebrity. He was killed in a flying accident only ten days later.

A second VC for destroying a Zeppelin was awarded in September 1916, the night of the largest ever airship raid on London. Sixteen Zeppelins (twelve naval and four army) set out, but were badly affected by weather. Only the SL 11 reached London. Searchlights exposed the airship to a pilot of the RFC's No. 39 Squadron, Lieutenant William Leefe Robinson, flying a B.E.2c. Closing to within 500 feet of his prey from below, Robinson fired almost three full drums of ammunition into the airship's hull before it began to glow. "In a few seconds," he wrote, "the whole rear part was blazing. I quickly got out of the way of the falling, blazing Zeppelin and being very excited fired off a few red Very lights and dropped a parachute flare." Robinson returned to base to find that his gun mounting had worked loose during the attack and he had inadvertently shot away part of his own wing and badly holed the main spar. The whole incident was witnessed by thousands of Londoners, whose fear and hatred of the Zeppelins found release in an orgy of celebration at the sight of one of them reduced to incandescent wreckage. Robinson was an instant national hero. Few who watched spared a thought for the crew, trapped in the inferno. Pilots' reports, like Robinson's, often carried a euphoric note. Lieutenant W.J. Tempest recorded his destruction of the L31 in October 1916 by saying that the airship "went red like an enormous Chinese lantern and

ABOVE *Crammed together in the boat-shaped nose of the Caproni Ca.36, seen here at the USAFM, two pilots and a gunner braved the elements in open cockpits. The gunner fired a single 7.7 mm Revelli machine gun that traversed on an elevated frame.* LEFT *In Caproni bombers, the rear gunner occupied a precarious and especially exposed railed platform mounted over the central engine and just clear of its whirling propeller. Normal armament for this position was two Revelli machine guns.*

On display in the Grande Galerie of the Musée de l'Air at Le Bourget is a Breguet 14-A2, fully restored by the museum's staff in 1977. Breguet 14s were the outstanding French light bombers of the war, and proved so versatile that they were produced in seventeen variants, filling roles as day and night bombers, reconnaissance machines, air ambulances and floatplanes. By the time production ceased in 1926, over 8,000 Breguet 14s had been built. Advanced they may have been for their time, but in WWI they were still supported in the front line by rudimentary servicing facilities.

then a flame shot out of the front part of her. She then shot up about 200 ft, paused and came roaring down straight on to me. I just managed to corkscrew out of the way as she shot past me, roaring like a furnace." On this occasion, the L31's commander chose to jump rather than be roasted, and his body was found separate from the wreckage, half buried in the ground.

Fifty-one airship raids were made on Britain. Over 5,800 high explosive and incendiary bombs were dropped, killing 557 people and injuring 1,358. Only two raids inflicted substantial damage, one on an engine works and a chemical plant, and the other when it started a fire in a London textile warehouse district. These meager results hardly justified the cost. Almost 100 airships were used on combat operations by the Germans during the war; nearly eighty were lost, over half of them destroyed by Allied action and the rest by accidents or bad weather. Only one crewman survived the inferno of being shot down. Alfred Mühler, the coxswain of Warneford's victim, fell in his detached gondola through the roof of a convent near Ghent and was deposited, unharmed, onto an unoccupied bed.

Winged Destroyers

As experience with tactical bombing was gained by the Allies, and attacks were made on more distant targets, it was a natural progression to think of carrying the war into Germany, using bombing strategically to damage the industrial centers across the Rhine and in the Saar region. In 1916, the RFC was principally concerned with supporting the land battle, and so it was the RNAS that cooperated with the French in drawing up strategic bombing plans. The first daylight raid, launched in October by a combined force,

The A.E.G. G.IV at the National Aviation Museum in Ottawa, Canada, is the only example of a large German bomber to have survived the aftermath of WWI, and the only aircraft left that shows the distinctive German World War I "night lozenge" camouflage pattern. Shipped as a war trophy to Canada in 1919, its original 260-horsepower Mercedes engines were lost in later years and in 1968–69 the aircraft was restored by the RCAF using 160-horsepower Mercedes engines instead. Introduced to service in 1917, the G.IV was used mainly as a tactical bomber, operating close to the front lines in France, Romania, Greece and Italy. Exposed in open cockpits at night in winter, the crew of three (pilot and two gunners) were warmed by electrically heated suits. The G.IV could carry some 800 pounds of bombs and could also be equipped for photographic reconnaissance.

involved fifty-four Sopwith 1½ Strutters, Breguet Michelins, and Capronis (the latter built in France under license) against the Mauser gun factory at Oberndorf. Nine aircraft were lost. More raids followed against other industrial targets, but losses continued to be heavy. Hard lessons were learned about raiding deep into enemy territory in daylight with an unescorted force. However, such lessons were repeatedly forgotten by the airmen of later generations.

Airplanes of all types were modified to carry bombs of various kinds, but the most effective were those designed as bombers from the outset. Neither the Sopwith 1½ Strutter nor the Breguet Michelin was impressive either in its load-carrying ability or general performance, and it was not until the arrival of the D.H.4 and the Breguet 14 B in 1917 that the Allies possessed adequate light bombers. Both types did sterling service until the end of the war, often operating in large numbers and presenting formidable challenges to opposing fighters. By the time they reached the squadrons, much larger aircraft were either flying or on their way and the strategic bombing capabilities were being considerably expanded.

German Giants

Even as the airship assault on Britain was gathering pace, Germany was developing large bombers for a similar role, and by 1917 the Luftstreitkräfte had three main types operational —the A.E.G. G.IV, the Friedrichshafen G.III and the Gotha G.IV, of which the Gotha was the most useful for a strategic campaign. The bomber squadrons, based as close to Britain as Ostend, were at first disguised under the remarkable title of Brieftauben Abteilungen (Carrier Pigeon Units). In daylight on May 25, 1917, twenty-one Gotha "pigeons," foiled by weather in their attempt to reach London, dropped some five tons of bombs on the south coast town of Folkestone, killing ninety-five and injuring almost 200 more. Over seventy British fighters were scrambled but few caught the raiders and only one Gotha was lost. The threatened attack on London, again by day, came nineteen days later. Operating in daylight was a conscious decision, taken in the hope that the bombing would then be accurate enough to ensure hits on such vital points as government buildings, and because it was thought that the British people would be cowed by the sight of enemy bombers flying with impunity over their capital city. Seventeen Gothas reached London on June 13; they dropped over four tons of bombs, killing 162 and injuring more than 400. Other raids followed in July and August, both by day and by night.

The Gothas showed that, even in relatively small numbers, they were a greater threat to life and property than the Zeppelins had ever been. Compared to the air offensives of WWII, the Gotha raids were mere flea bites, but they were inflicted on people generally unfamiliar with aircraft and deeply shocked to find themselves so suddenly in the war's front line. In the strong public reaction to this airborne peril, elements of alarm, indignation and panic were mingled, and there was some decline in factory production because workers were either distracted by day or kept awake at night by the German bombers. An impassioned public outcry left the government in no doubt that something had to be done to curb the raids.

The British Army's most senior soldier, commenting on a War Cabinet meeting held in July 1917 to discuss the bombing, said that among government ministers, "much excitement was shown. One would have thought the world was coming to an end." In a sense, it was. The world in which civilian populations were largely uninvolved in war's bloodshed had indeed come to an end, and in bringing about that revolutionary change, an air offensive succeeded for the first time in directly influencing a government's war

ABOVE *Initially, the U.S.-built Liberty-engined DH-4 was not popular with many American crews, being described in some units as "two wings on a hearse." In time, its superior speed and power earned the DH-4 the respect of friend and foe alike.*
LEFT *An AEG bomber in flight over its parent factory near Berlin.*

strategy. Fighter squadrons were recalled from France for air defense duties, thus affecting the ability of the Allies to achieve air superiority over the front. Major General Trenchard was not amused and, in resisting the recall of further RFC units, was heard to remark that he had "no intention of withdrawing any squadrons from France because in my opinion it does politicians good to be bombed occasionally."

In another move typical of a government under stress, a committee was formed to study the threat and recommend countermeasures. It was given the bureaucratic title of the Committee on Air Organization and Home Defence against Air Raids and was chaired by a distinguished South African, Lieutenant General Jan Smuts. Under his dynamic leadership, the committee's deliberations were swift and its findings comprehensive. The resulting Smuts Report attacked the "competition, friction and waste" resulting from the division of military aviation between the army and the navy. He recommended a strong, unified air defense command, and, in the longer term, the creation of a separate Air Ministry controlling an independent air force.

By August 24, when the first part of the Smuts Report, dealing with air defense, was adopted by the War Cabinet, the daylight Gotha attacks were already diminishing. The British defenses had stiffened and German losses were becoming unacceptably high. In a move that foreshadowed events twenty-three years later, the bombing offensive sought the shelter of the night. During the winter campaign, the Gothas were joined by the Zeppelin-Staaken R.VI, a leviathan manned by a crew of seven and capable of carrying eighteen 220-pound bombs. Its 138-foot wingspan would not be exceeded until the appearance of the Boeing B-29 in WWII. On the night of February 16, 1918, one of these huge aircraft dropped a single bomb of 2,200 pounds on London. It struck the Royal Hospital in Chelsea, causing dozens of casualties.

By May 1918, even the night offensive was proving too costly, and the German bombing offensive against Britain was called off. In twenty-seven raids between May 1917 and May 1918, the German bombers had killed 836 people and injured another 1,994. Compared to the bloodshed suffered every day on the Western Front, it seemed little enough, but there were other effects out of all proportion to the bald statistics, of which the most significant was

certainly not a part of the original German intention. As the startling idea for the creation of the Royal Air Force began to register on the consciousness of the older services, it could be seen that the "pigeons" of the German strategic bombing offensive were coming home to roost in a most unexpected way. Far from forcing the British government to negotiate terms for peace, the Gothas had unleashed the concept of independent air power.

"Bloody Paralysers"

The Germans were not alone in producing large aircraft. Both Russia and Italy had preceded Germany into the big bomber business, and the British requirement for similar machines was expressed by a naval officer as early as 1914. Galled by the inability of the Allies to stop the German advance on Antwerp in December 1914, Commander Charles Rumney Samson, a formidable figure in naval aviation history, sent an impatient message to the Admiralty in London demanding that he should be sent a "bloody paralyser of an aeroplane" so that he could bomb the Germans to a standstill.

The idea of creating an aerial battleship led to wider discussions in the Admiralty's Air Department, which was much more inclined to think of using air power strategically than was the War Office, and so the aircraft builder Frederick Handley Page was asked to design a bomber capable of carrying six 100-pound bombs at a sea level speed of 65 mph. To complicate matters, it also had to have folding wings to ensure it would fit into existing hangars, and it had to have armored protection for its crew, engines and fuel tanks. In 1914, only six years after Wilbur Wright showed Europeans what real flying meant, it was a challenging requirement. The result, which first flew one year after Samson sent his message, was the Handley Page O/100 (The designation indicated the H.P. Type O, and arbitrarily added its 100-foot wingspan. The later O/400 bomber did not have a 400-foot wingspan!). The production version far exceeded the Admiralty's specifications, proving itself capable of reaching 76 mph while loaded with a crew of four, and sixteen 112-pound bombs. It is pertinent to note that, as the prototype O/100 was completing its first flights and bringing closer the day when the Royal Navy could extend its strategic role into the third dimension, the British War Office was concluding that the Army should not engage in

The Handley Page O/400 was the largest British aircraft used against the Germans in WWI and it set the standard of heavy bomber design for the following decade. A huge aircraft for its day, the O/400 became so famous that for years after, all large airplanes were generally referred to as "Handley Pages." Powered by two 360-horsepower Rolls-Royce Eagle VIIIs, a fully loaded O/400 weighed 13,000 pounds and had a top speed of 97 mph. Its service ceiling was 8,500 feet, and it had an operational range of approximately 650 miles. On bombing raids against German targets, crews often had to spend seven hours in the cramped open cockpits.

strategic bombing, and that a requirement for a twin-engined bomber should be canceled. At that time, the generals felt that the RFC had enough to cope with in supporting the land battle without adding the complications of broader horizons.

Handley Page O/100s became operational in November 1916, when they were received in France by the 5th Wing, RNAS, at Dunkirk, and the 3rd Wing, at Luxeuil, near the Swiss border. The winter weather of 1916/17 was severe, and it was not until March 16, 1917 that a single O/100 of the 3rd Wing carried out the first night raid by a British heavy bomber when it attacked the Moulin-les-Metz railway station. RNAS O/100s were employed in a number of attacks on German industrial centers and airfields, and against naval bases, but policy disagreements between the Admiralty and the War Office eventually led to the RFC taking on responsibility for most of the air operations in France from the RNAS. As well, the strength of British public reaction to the Gotha raids forced the RFC to consider the need to retaliate by taking the war to the German people. In October 1917, the 41st Wing, RFC, was formed to conduct a bombing campaign against targets in Germany. Equipped with D.H.4s, F.E.2bs, and a naval squadron of O/100s, it was intended that the wing would operate independently and so avoid having its strength dissipated by the demands of local military commanders. Between its formation and May 1918, the 41st Wing was used in 142 raids, 57 of them over Germany.

Air Power Independent

On April 1, 1918, the second part of the Smuts Report bore fruit. The Royal Flying Corps and the Royal Naval Air Service were combined and the Royal Air Force came into being, setting an example for independently minded airmen the world over. The RAF was to continue supporting the army and the navy, but the new service was also meant to undertake independent strategic operations. This intention was given solid form in June 1918 with the creation of the Independent Bombing Force in France under the command of Major General Sir Hugh Trenchard. He was charged with implementing a strategic bombing offensive against Germany, and by August his command had nine squadrons, five of them equipped with the Handley Page O/400, an improved version of the O/100. (The choice of All Fool's Day as the RAF's birthday was thought appropriate by the other services, who bitterly opposed their loss of control over military air power.)

The bomber crews were well aware that their operations were reprisals. In a letter to his family in Colorado, an American RAF pilot, Lieutenant J.H.L. Gower, wrote: "For every town the Huns burn in France, we have got to demolish one in Germany. And believe me we have a bomb which can lay everything flat within a mile radius." Gower's hyperbole is understandable, given the size of bombs dropped before the HP O/400s arrived. Using a cradle between the undercarriage legs, the big biplanes could lift individual bombs weighing as much as 1,600 pounds. One pilot of No. 207 Squadron, RAF, facing anti-aircraft fire on the approach to a target, was shocked by the lumbering bomber's violent reaction to the release of such a big bomb: "Suddenly we shot up like a lift: we must have been hit underneath!"

In the last five months of the war, the IBF dropped 550 tons of bombs on industrial targets deep inside Germany, including major cities such as Cologne, Frankfurt and Stuttgart. As with the Gotha raids on Britain, the public reaction was strident, and the Luftstreitkräfte was forced to strengthen Germany's fighter defenses. The campaign was not without cost; 109 RAF aircraft were lost, of which sixty-nine were the big Handley Pages. This did not discourage the offensively minded Trenchard. If the war had gone on longer than it did, there is no doubt that the assault on German targets would have been intensified. By November, deliveries of a new, much larger bomber had begun. The Handley Page V/1500 was an aircraft with genuine strategic capabilities. Intended to reach Berlin from bases in England, it could carry thirty 250-pound bombs or two huge bombs of 3,300 pounds each. Three of these giant bombers were bombed up and ready to go when the armistice was signed.

AMERICAN INTERVENTION

When the United States declared war on the Central Powers on April 6, 1917, the American services were far from ready. Only the U.S. Navy was able to make an immediate contribution, joining the struggle against the U-boats in the Atlantic. The U.S. Army, with just 130,000 regular soldiers, was described by one of its senior generals as having "no practical military value as far as the fighting in France was concerned." This harsh judgment certainly applied to the Air Service, which had no aircraft fit for combat and no airmen with any experience of aerial warfare. The limited capabilities of U.S. military aviation had been brutally exposed during the Mexican Punitive Expedition in 1916, and the ensuing year had seen little improvement. In April 1917, the total strength of the U.S. Army Air Service was 131 officers, 1,087 men, and less than 250 aircraft, only half of which were serviceable. None of the machines could be classified as other than a trainer, and many were obsolete even in that role. No bombers or fighters were in service or being procured. Worse still, the American aircraft industry was then incapable of supplying the equipment needed to support an operational air force. In the eight short years since the purchase of the first Wright Military Flyer, the United States had fallen to fourteenth in the world's ranking of aviation powers. Nothing daunted, great plans were made. It was proposed that, by the spring of 1918, the U.S. would produce 22,625 aircraft (12,000 of them for combat) supported by 80 percent spare parts, plus 45,000 engines. The thousands of aircrew to man this armada were to be graduated from flying schools that did not then exist. Given that the U.S. had produced a total of fewer than 1,000 aircraft of all

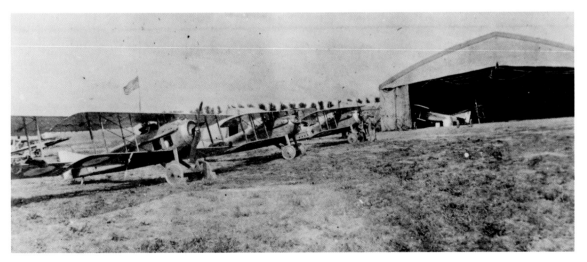

The SPAD XIII was one of the finest fighter aircraft produced in WWI. It was the principal fighter used by the U.S. Army Air Service, which took delivery of 893 during 1918. It was described by Eddie Rickenbacker as "the ultimate aircraft in the war in which aviation developed."

Nieuports in various stages of repair and maintenance in a hangar at Issoudun, home of a U.S. flying school in France in 1918.

types in the fourteen years since Kittyhawk, these were startling figures, and it soon became obvious that the plans could specify what they liked, but good intentions, even when backed by unlimited money, could not make up for years of neglect. (As early as 1911, the Englishman Claude Grahame-White pointed out the growing transatlantic disparity in aviation. His published scorecard of the world's trained pilots that year gave France 387, Britain 128, Germany 46, Italy 38, Russia 37, and the U.S. 31.)

To solve the most pressing problem, it was decided to make use of European designs — in particular, the SPAD single-seat fighter, the Bristol two-seat fighter, the DH-4 reconnaissance/light bomber, and the Caproni triplane heavy bomber. The Handley Page O/400 heavy bomber was later added to the list. Contracts were placed with a number of companies to build these aircraft in the thousands necessary to meet the commitments so freely given for the U.S. to have an air force in the front line by the summer of 1918. The American aircraft industry expanded dramatically in trying to reach the planning objectives, but the task was too great. Herculean efforts were made, but the goals were too ambitious. When the war ended in November 1918, of the forty-five U.S. Air Service squadrons assigned for combat, just twelve were operating DH-4s manufactured in the U.S. The DH-4 was the only combat aircraft made in any numbers in American factories; 3,431 of them were delivered. Of these, some 1,200 arrived in France, but only 417 reached the front.

The failure to live up to the promises made was bitterly resented by American airmen, but it should not be forgotten that in 1917 the United States was trying to accelerate from a standing start to the hectic pace of an air war that had been in progress for three years. Looked at from that point of view, what was accomplished is more creditable. The U.S. aviation industry in 1917 was negligible, but by November 11, 1918 it had grown to a size that had produced over 11,000 aircraft of all types, including nearly 8,000 trainers, and the production rate had risen to no less than 21,000 aircraft per year. In addition, there was one conspicuous success story in the 400-horsepower Liberty engine; over 13,000 of them had been produced by the war's end.

To overcome the U.S. difficulties, arrangements were made for the U.S. Air Service to fly European-built aircraft and use Allied training facilities. Eventually, American flying schools operated in France, and they were not always remembered with affection by the trainees. One of them described the experience of the flying school at Issoudun as: "A sea of frozen mud. Waiting in shivering line before dawn for the spoonsful of gluey porridge slapped into outstretched mess kits, cold as ice. Wretched flying equipment. Broken necks. The flu. A hell of a place, Issoudun."

American Squadrons in Action

U.S. Air Service pilots saw their first combat on April 14, 1918. On that day, Lieutenants Winslow and Campbell of the 94th Squadron ("Hat in the Ring") were on alert duty at Gengault aerodrome. At 8:45 on a dull morning with low cloud, the alarm was given and the Nieuports of Winslow and Campbell roared into the air. As they cleared the airfield, they almost ran into two German single-seaters emerging from the mist, a Pfalz D.III and an Albatros D.V. Taken by surprise, both German aircraft were shot down in rapid succession within sight of the cheering men of the 94th. It was a sensational start to the American air campaign and a wonderful boost for the morale of the newcomers to the front line.

In the weeks that followed, the American buildup gathered pace. As more squadrons became available they were formed into pursuit groups until, by November 1918, there were four groups controlling twelve pursuit squadrons. Observation squadrons received French Salmson 2A.2s, fast and rugged two-seaters powered by a reliable 260-horsepower radial engine. The Salmson was well armed with two Lewis guns for the observer and a forward-firing Vickers, and was maneuverable enough to give a crew a chance against German fighters. As was later recorded, "At the altitudes at which the 91st Squadron worked [5,000 meters], the Salmson had a decided advantage over [Pfalz and Albatros scouts] both in climbing and in horizontal speeds." At the end of the war, there were sixteen observation squadrons in eight groups and over 700 Salmson 2A.2s had been delivered to the U.S. Air Service.

American bombardment squadrons were slower to build up. The 96th was the first into the fray, on June 12, 1918. That they were able to get into action by then was a tribute to the ingenuity of the squadron's mechanics. Their aircraft were Breguet 14 B2s that had been in use at a training school since 1917 and were worn out. Spare parts were impossible to obtain. Master Sergeant James Sawyer and his men scavenged the local area for pieces of discarded farm machinery and used their imagination: "Part of a weather-beaten harvester was used for a tailpost for one of the planes; wagon tires were cut up and used for tail skids, and pieces of an ox-cart tongue were employed to reinforce wing spars. One of the planes carried brace wires which had once served on the telephone line…."

The determination of the 96th to join the battle and their valiant efforts to fight on with dilapidated equipment were brought to a temporary halt by one of the most embarrassing episodes of the American campaign. On July 10, 1918, the squadron's spirit was much in evidence as the commander led his six available Breguets on a late-evening raid against German railway yards. Flying conditions were poor, with heavy cloud, and an unexpectedly strong wind blew the aircraft deep into Germany. After a fruitless search for a break in the weather, the squadron commander turned for home and eventually let down through cloud. With their fuel almost exhausted, the six Breguets landed successfully, only to find themselves in Germany. All the American airmen were captured, and their aircraft taken intact. At one stroke,

the only operational U.S. bombardment force of the time had been lost. The Germans were quick to send Air Service HQ a message: "We thank you for the fine airplanes and equipment you sent us, but what will we do with the Major?"

September saw the arrival of more bombardment squadrons equipped at last with Liberty-engined DH-4s. The Breguet was almost universally popular with American aircrews, but the Liberty DH-4 got mixed reviews. Criticisms were aimed at the length of fuselage separating the pilot and observer, which made communication difficult, and at the unprotected fuel tanks between the cockpits. Some aircrew referred to the DH-4 as "two wings on a hearse" or "the flaming coffin" because it was thought to be more susceptible than other aircraft to bursting into flames when hit by enemy fire. In time, the DH-4's virtues began to be appreciated, and at least one squadron commander concluded that "the Liberty plane was considered the best on the front, and its excellent speed and combat power were well demonstrated in actual combat with enemy planes. The Liberty, at low altitude, could outdistance and outclimb any plane the Germans had."

Enter Billy Mitchell

Major William Mitchell arrived in Paris only a few days after the U.S. declaration of war. He immediately set off to visit French combat units, headquarters, airfields and supply depots. He borrowed French aircraft and flew reconnaissance flights over the battle area. The result was a series of reports to Washington commenting on everything he saw, and offering copious personal observations and recommendations. One of Mitchell's visits was to the British front, where he met the commander of the RFC in France, Major General Sir Hugh Trenchard. Mitchell was profoundly influenced by Trenchard's offensive policies and by his views that air power should be exercised under unified command. These ideas took root in Mitchell's fertile mind and grew into the concepts with which he later so forcefully sought to shape the development of American air power.

A year after his arrival in Paris, Mitchell was a brigadier general and Chief of the U.S. Air Service in France. With the blunting of the final German offensives in 1918, the initiative passed to the Allies and preparations began for a major counter-offensive involving American forces, beginning with an assault on the St. Mihiel salient. Mitchell successfully argued for concentrating Allied air power. General "Hap" Arnold later said that "The air offensive which Mitchell laid on in September 1918 was the greatest thing of its kind seen in the war…the first massed air striking power ever seen." Units of the American, French, British and Italian air forces were gathered on fourteen airfields, bringing together a total of 1,481 aircraft — 701 fighters, 366 observation aircraft, 323 day bombers, and 91 night bombers. Facing them on the other side of the line, the Germans had somewhere between 200 and 300 aircraft of all types. Local air superiority was assured.

Mitchell planned to use his massive air force to overwhelm the opposition. One-third of the force was dedicated to ground support, and the remaining two-thirds was split to attack installations, communications and troop columns behind the lines, as well as the flanks of the St. Mihiel salient.

Besides seeking to defeat the German air force, Mitchell was intent on using his fighters for "attacking his troops on the ground, and protecting our own air and ground troops." Fighters had been used before in attacking ground targets, but mostly in random fashion and not in large numbers. This time the air force was to intervene in the ground war in a big way.

The attack was launched on September 12, 1918, in foul weather, with low cloud and driving rain. Major Hartney, commander of the 1st Pursuit Group, noted the conditions and drew attention to the change in policy: "The weather was atrocious — pouring rain, with low-hanging clouds. This, however, was perfect for part of our plan — low flying. The pilots certainly flew low that day — they could not do otherwise — and the success of this new system [low-altitude strafing and bombing attacks on troop convoys

General Billy Mitchell with his staff officers in 1918. Mitchell believed that military aircraft should be used in overwhelming strength at selected points rather than spread out thinly along the front. In September 1918, as Chief of the U.S. Army Air Service in France, he commanded the first serious attempt to concentrate air power in support of an offensive. The massed air forces, bringing together almost 1,500 aircraft, made a decisive contribution to the success of the Allied armies at St. Mihiel.

and trenches] pointed the way we followed until the end of hostilities. And by low I mean low. The clouds at times formed a solid mist at 100ft and everything had to be done below that. This low flying by an entire group was a revolution in war-time flying."

In spite of the poor conditions, the air forces under Mitchell's command contributed significantly to a successful operation at St. Mihiel. In the subsequent Allied offensive at Meuse-Argonne, Mitchell continued to trust the same tactical principles. This time, however, his relative superiority in numbers was not so great. On September 26, he had some 800 aircraft at his disposal, about three-quarters of them available for operations. The Germans began the battle with about 300 aircraft but, as the offensive progressed, these were reinforced, and by early November the ratio had closed to 700 against 500. Throughout, Mitchell steadfastly refused to spread his forces in an attempt to cover the whole area, but wherever possible operated strong formations and maintained attacks on the German rear areas. Protection was given to forward American troops by patrols of five aircraft assigned to 6-mile fronts. These patrols were flown at low level by the 1st Pursuit Group and had the responsibility of breaking up any German formations attacking American soldiers, at the same time taking every opportunity to strafe German troops and shoot down observation balloons.

Edward Vernon Rickenbacker, former racing driver, soon made his mark as a fighter pilot in France. He achieved six aerial victories in the spring of 1918 while flying Nieuports, but was then grounded by illness throughout the summer. He returned to action in mid-September flying the aircraft he most admired, the SPAD XIII, and was appointed commander of the 94th ("Hat in the Ring") Squadron. By the end of the war in November, he was the leading American ace with twenty-six kills (twenty-two aircraft and four balloons).

Aces Extraordinary

Attacking balloons was a dangerous business. They were heavily guarded by anti-aircraft guns and fighters, and there was also a gauntlet of infantry fire to run. The most celebrated of those who were successful in this hazardous art

was Frank Luke. Between September 12 and 29, Luke, flying a SPAD XIII of the 27th Squadron, shot down the incredible total of fourteen balloons and four aircraft. His meteoric and often undisciplined career ended on the evening of September 29 when he subjected the Germans on the front near Verdun to a lone assault worthy of a Wagnerian epic. As the sun was setting, he flew over the American 7th Balloon Company and dropped a note that warned them to "Watch for burning balloons." The first German balloon fell in flames at 7.05 P.M., and was rapidly followed by another. Luke was momentarily diverted by harassing Fokkers and disposed of two of them before claiming his third balloon. At some point he was hit by ground fire and seriously wounded, but he turned to strafe German troops before crash-landing his SPAD. Once on the ground, he dragged himself from the cockpit and died nearby, pistol in hand.

Another prominent figure in the war's closing battles was Eddie Rickenbacker. He had six victories before a severe ear infection grounded him for much of June, July and August. He returned to action with the 94th Squadron in mid-September and became its commander a few days later. The squadron was equipped with the SPAD XIII, a fighter that suited Rickenbacker's style of aerial combat perfectly. He described it as "more impressive than any other airplane, any automobile, any other piece of equipment I had ever seen…the ultimate aircraft in the war in which aviation developed." At the opening of the Meuse-Argonne offensive, Rickenbacker's personal score had risen to ten enemy aircraft, and on his first day as squadron commander he gave a demonstration of his skill. He set off on a hunting expedition over the front and was rewarded by sighting two L.V.G. observation aircraft escorted by five

Fokkers. Placing himself above them and into sun, he dived onto the last Fokker and destroyed it with one burst. The rest of the escorts broke up in confusion, and Rickenbacker kept his dive going for the L.V.G.s. After exchanging spirited fire with the rear gunners and avoiding the attempt of one L.V.G. to get behind him, he slipped out to one side of the pair and ruddered his SPAD so that the nearer L.V.G. flew through his line of fire. As Rickenbacker himself so colorfully described it, "It burst into flames and tumbled like a great blazing torch to earth, leaving a streamer of black smoke against the blue sky." He went on to take his score of kills to a total of twenty-six (twenty-two aircraft and four balloons) to become America's leading ace of WWI.

The courageous spirit of men such as Luke and Rickenbacker was recognized by the award of America's highest decoration, the Medal of Honor, but not only fighter pilots performed with such valor. On October 2, men of the 308th Infantry Regiment broke through the German line only to be surrounded and pinned down by heavy fire in a deep ravine. Their exact position was unknown, and the 50th Aero Squadron was asked to find what the press was calling the "Lost Battalion." In atrocious weather, several crews took their DH-4s through the area at low level without success, and by October 6 the soldiers' plight was desperate. That morning, Lieutenants Harold Goettler and Erwin Bleckley flew through a number of ravines so low that German gunners were firing down on them. There were more than forty holes in their DH-4 when they landed. Later in the day, they volunteered to try again. They repeatedly flew at tree-top level through the most likely ravine and were raked with gunfire again and again. Already dying, Goettler lifted the shattered DH-4 out of the ravine and crash-landed in front of some French positions. He was dead when the French reached them and Bleckley was dying. Bleckley's mission notes were intact and the search for the "Lost Battalion" was narrowed to a small area. A rescuing U.S. force reached them the next day. Of the 554 men who had entered the ravine, 194 were able to walk out. Lieutenants Harold Goettler and Erwin Bleckley were both awarded the Medal of Honor.

Whenever they were given the chance, American airmen fought well in WWI. Their frustration was that they were never able to fulfill the promises made in the euphoric days following the U.S. declaration of war in 1917. As 1918 drew to its close and German resistance collapsed, American manpower was flooding forward and the great wheels of U.S. industry were shifting into top gear. The blessed relief of the Armistice stopped the massive buildup in its tracks, leaving the promises unfulfilled and many air power questions unanswered.

THE ITALIAN FRONT

War on the southwestern front of the Central Powers broke out in May 1915, with Italy's declaration of war against Austria-Hungary. The Italian Aeronautica del Regio Esercito (Royal Army Air Service) was not well prepared for the conflict, equipped as it mostly was with obsolescent aircraft, mainly Nieuports, Maurice Farmans and Blériots. On the positive side, the Italians were the only country to have an aircraft designed from the outset as a big bomber. The pioneer Italian aircraft constructor, Gianni Caproni, had flown his first trimotor biplane, the Ca.30, in 1913. This led to a production bomber, the Ca.32, early examples of which reached front-line squadrons in mid-1915 and began operations on August 20, when they raided the Austro-Hungarian airfield at Aisovizza.

A curious bureaucratic drama lay behind the acquisition of the Capronis. Giulio Douhet, one of air power's prophets, was commander of the Italian aviation battalion in 1914. Convinced of the potential benefits of the aircraft as a strategic weapon, he used his initiative and personally authorized Caproni to build his bomber. Admirable though

The Ansaldo S.V.A.5 was an exceptional aircraft for its time — robust, fast and long-ranged. It was involved in many operations over Austria, but is best remembered for the Vienna raid of August 9, 1918, when the poet d'Annunzio, in a two-seat S.V.A.9, led a flight of S.V.A.5s over the Austrian capital. In a flamboyant gesture bordering on the theatrical, he bombed the Viennese with leaflets bearing a grandiose message rather than with explosives. The S.V.A.5 at the Caproni Museum is a survivor of d'Annunzio's raid. The pilot was Gino Allegri .

the Ca.32 proved to be, Douhet's superiors removed him from his post to discipline him for exceeding his authority. Refusing to fade away, Douhet continued to promote his doctrine, sowing the seeds of strategic air power where he could. In 1916, he was jailed for a while after he left a paper critical of Italian war policies on a train. Undeterred, he wrote and published essays from his prison cell agitating for an Allied fleet of strategic bombers. In *The Great Aerial Offensive*, he urged Italy to build 1,000 bombers, France 3,000, Britain 4,000 and the United States 12,000. Released from prison in October 1917, he returned to military aviation, but it was not until after the war that Douhet's contributions to air power were reexamined and his intellectual respectability reinstated.

Detail of S.V.A.5 exhibited at the Italian Air Force Museum piloted by Giordano Bruno Granzarolo in D'Annunzio's raid.

Austro-Hungarian airmen had been fighting against Russia and in the Balkans since they entered the war, but by the time Italy became an opponent, their army air service was still a relatively ineffective force. The aircraft were a mixture of outdated German and Austrian designs, provided mainly by the Aviatik and DFW companies, and later by Hansa-Brandenburg, few of which proved to be stellar performers. In 1916, matters were improved by the arrival of such aircraft as the Fokker D.III and the Brandenburg D.I, a fighter with a wing-bracing arrangement that led to it being known as the Starstrutter. Rumpler C.Is and Albatros C.IIIs added an improved reconnaissance capability. Nevertheless, the Austrians were bedeviled to the end of the war by inadequate training and aircraft supply systems. Even after the collapse of Russia and Serbia allowed them to concentrate their efforts against the Italian front, they were never able to gain air superiority. In 1918, the poorly organized Austrian aviation industry produced fewer than 2,000 aircraft and engines, which was barely enough to keep pace with attrition. Courageously as they fought, most Austrian units faced the air war well short of their established strength, both in machines and aircrew.

On the other hand, the Italians, starting from a poor position in 1915, made rapid progress. The aircraft industry, in particular, was organized into an efficient industrial machine, producing airframes, engines and accessories standardized as far as possible and combined into large numbers of effective aircraft. The front-line strength of the Army Air Service grew tenfold during its three and a half years of fighting, and in 1918, Italian industry produced nearly 6,500 aircraft and 15,000 engines. Squadrons were operating aircraft such as the Ansaldo S.V.A.5, one of the best reconnaissance machines of the war, and the great Caproni bombers, both biplane and triplane.

Although the scale of the air war was small compared to that on the Western Front, the struggle was fiercely fought, and both Italy and Austria had their share of aerial heroes. On the Austrian side, the leading aces included Polish-born Godwin Bromowski, who claimed forty victories, mostly in the Albatros D.III, and a half Polish, half English pilot named Frank Linke-Crawford, whose score had reached thirty when he was shot down in his Phönix D.I scout during a confused dogfight with RFC Sopwith Camels and Italian Hanriots. The highest scorer among Italy's forty-three aces was Francesco Baracca, many of whose thirty-four successes came in the SPAD VII. Like so many pilots who were supreme against opponents in the air, such as Richthofen and Mannock, Baracca was killed by intense ground-fire, as he was attacking Austrian troops crossing the Piave River bridges on June 19, 1918.

Another larger-than-life figure in Italian aviation was the poet Gabriele D'Annunzio. Fascinated by aviation and a prolific writer on the subject, he had first flown in 1909 in a biplane piloted by Glenn Curtiss. The experience marked him for life, and he wrote: "Until now I have never really lived. Life on Earth is a creeping, crawling business. It is in the air that one feels the glory of being a man and of conquering the elements." Although fifty-two years old when the war began, D'Annunzio joined the Army Air Service to conduct a personal crusade from the air. He advocated and took part in massed bomber attacks on enemy forces and on distant targets such as the naval base of Pola on the Adriatic. The climax of his campaign came in August 1918, when he flew in an Ansaldo S.V.A.9 to Vienna and bombarded the Austrian capital with leaflets bearing a grandiloquent message: "On the wind of victory that is rising from the rivers of liberty, we only came for the joy of the exploit and in order to demonstrate what we can dare and do when we want, at the time that we choose. Viva l'Italia! In the sky of Vienna, 9 August 1918, Gabriele D'Annunzio."

The Caproni Legacy

After the first long-distance raid in August 1915, the Italians used their big Capronis to good effect, blunting Austrian ground offensives and attacking more distant targets. The strategic bombing missions were extremely challenging, especially those that crossed the Alps in midwinter to strike targets in Austria. Besides facing the threat of enemy fighters, the crews navigated through mountainous territory in all weathers, often operating their heavily loaded bombers at heights close to their ceilings to avoid Alpine peaks. They were exposed to the chilling below-zero slipstream for hours in open cockpits, the rear gunner especially unprotected on his railed platform above the central engine. In pursuing their campaign with such resolution, they showed that long-range bombing was a practical proposition and bolstered the theories of strategists such as Douhet, whose persistent presentation of the case for strategic air power helped to shape the postwar development of military aviation.

Caproni bombers introduced Americans to strategic bombing. An agreement was reached between the United

A pioneer of the strategic bombing concept, Gianni Caproni designed and flew a large multi-engined aircraft less than ten years after the Wright brothers' first flight. He is seen here with an Italian officer, Giulio Laureati, standing in the nose of the second production Ca.300 (later designated Ca.32). This aircraft (serial 479) was delivered to the 1st Caproni squadriglia at La Comina on August 8, 1915, and remained in service until December 1916.

States and Italy for American airmen to be trained to fly the Capronis at Foggia. Managing the program was a U.S. congressman who had volunteered for the Air Service — Fiorello LaGuardia, later mayor of New York. As an Italian-speaking politician whose family roots were in Foggia, he was a natural choice for the job.

Over 400 Americans graduated from the Italian school by the end of the war. The big Caproni was an effective first step on the road to strategic bombing. It could carry almost 2,000 pounds of bombs and had a range of nearly 400 miles. Its American crews, however, acknowledged that it was slow and not very sophisticated. It was flat out at 85 mph and the absence of trimming controls made it an exhausting aircraft to fly. All the big Capronis were tail-heavy, and it was reported that "you had literally to jam your elbow into your stomach and hold the stick forward with one hand while you operated the ailerons with the other." The instruments were pretty basic, too.

One pilot remembered that "The air speed indicator was a rough and ready affair consisting of what we called a 'penny on a string,' a little round disc on a spring on one of the struts outside the cockpit. When the wind was blowing on it, it was blown backwards, and when the wind wasn't so strong, it came forwards. Behind it was a plate on which were the two words 'Minima' and 'Maxima.' If you let it get below 'Minima' you stalled, and if you got above 'Maxima' the wings fell off."

From June 1918, American pilots were assigned to Italian squadrons where they were integrated with Italian crews to fly bombing missions against Austrian targets. Almost one hundred Americans served in the battle area and took part in sixty-five raids, mostly at night. Relatively small and brief though the Italian program was, it was invaluable in providing the U.S. Air Service with its first combat experience in the strategic bombing role.

The definitive variant of the Ca.4 series of Caproni triplanes was the Ca.42, a huge twin-boom machine of almost 100-foot wingspan. Powered by either 275-horsepower Isotta-Fraschini or 400-horsepower Liberty engines, the Ca.42 could carry almost two tons of bombs in the container mounted below the crew nacelle. Thus encumbered, the monster could maintain a speed of about 80 mph and stay airborne for seven hours. The crew shown with Ca.42 14667 give some idea of the bomber's great size.

THE RUSSIAN FRONT

In August 1914, Russian military aviation had over 240 aircraft, which compared favorably, on paper at least, with any other power. However, the machines were almost wholly obsolete, and there were no reserves. Nor were Russian pilots well trained. As a result, losses in the first few months were alarmingly high, an average of 37 percent monthly. By October, volunteer civilian pilots were being officially accepted into operational units "provided that they come with their personal machines."

Russia did possess one aircraft with remarkable potential. Igor Sikorsky's *Russkyi Vitiaz* (Russian Knight), a development of his *Bolshoi Baltiskiy*, flew in July 1913 and was the world's first practical four-engined aircraft. Its success led to an even larger machine named *Il'ya Mourometz* (*I.M.*) after a

The world's first practical four-engined aircraft was flown in Russia in 1913 by Igor Sikorsky. A variant of that aircraft was the Il'ya Mourometz, which had obvious military potential and was developed for use as a bomber. The Czar admired the concept and formed a "Squadron of Flying Ships," which operated with considerable success throughout the war on the Russian front, conducting some four hundred raids while having only two bombers shot down. The basic design of the Il'ya Mourometz was modified into a number of different forms, and a total of seventy-three of the bombers saw operational service from 1915 to 1917.

10th-century hero. On February 12, 1914, an I.M., a monster of over 100-foot wingspan, set up an astonishing record for its time, climbing to 6,560 feet above Moscow while carrying sixteen passengers and a dog! Although designed as a civil aircraft, the military potential was obvious, and a second I.M. was built, suitably modified into the world's first four-engined bomber. In this aircraft, Sikorsky demonstrated his brainchild's capabilities even more impressively. In July 1914, he flew from St. Petersburg to Kiev and back, a roundtrip of some 1,400 miles, completing the return journey in less than thirteen hours with only one stop on the way.

Initially, there was some resistance from field commanders to having the I.M. Complaints about how difficult they were to maintain were followed by requests for it to be replaced by larger numbers of smaller aircraft, but an intervention by the Czar led to the formation of a special "Squadron of Flying Ships." In due course, seventy-three of the huge bombers saw operational service. By any standards, they deserve to be considered among the most impressive military aircraft of the war. Between February 1915 and the chaotic departure of Russia from the conflict after the revolution of 1917, I.M. bombers carried out over four hundred raids on enemy territory and lost only two of their number shot down in the process. Their legendary toughness was well demonstrated in July 1915, when an I.M. was attacked and hit hard by three German fighters. Copiously holed and with two engines dead on the same side, the crippled bomber was still brought back to base by its wounded pilot.

The Il'ya Murometz was one bright spot in a generally somber story for Russian aviators. Troubled throughout the war by a shortage of aircraft, and of adequately trained pilots and technicians, the Russian Army Air Service was never able to match its German opponents, who came to regard a tour of duty on the Eastern Front as something of a respite from the rigors of combat in the west. For much of their equipment the Russians had to rely on importing machines from the Western Allies, especially France, but there were many complaints from commanders that even these were inadequate, since they were mainly aircraft that had already seen better days on the Western Front.

However, there was no doubting the courage and determination of Russian aircrew, and several fighter pilots became aces, including Captain Alexander Kazakov, an ex-cavalry officer. For his first attempt at bringing down an aircraft, he fitted a Morane monoplane with a winch and anchor, intending to drag off his enemy's top wing from above. When the winch jammed, he dived on his opponent and did the job with the Morane's wheels. Kazakov went on to become a regular scourge of enemy airmen, destroying a total of seventeen German aircraft, the last sixteen by the more conventional method of using guns. Possibly even more celebrated, if for different reasons, was the world's first female military pilot, the Princess Eugenie Shakhovskaya, who flew as a reconnaissance pilot on the Riga front.

Russia's failing war effort collapsed entirely with the Bolshevik seizure of power in November 1917. The Russian military disintegrated and factory production ground to a halt. In the chaos that ensued, the German Army invaded huge tracts of territory, and many Russian aircraft, including thirty I.M.s, were destroyed to prevent them falling into enemy hands. By March 1918, Russia had left the war more formally in the Treaty of Brest Litovsk and efforts were being made to reorganize what was now called the Workers' and Peasants' Red Air Fleet. This small force was desperately needed for the further struggles that were to come in the fight to defend the revolution. (In a postscript to Russia's agonies, Igor Sikorsky fled to Paris, and then moved on to the United States. In later years, he added still further to his considerable stature as an aviation pioneer.)

FLYING AND FIGHTING ON THE FRINGES

Military aircraft found parts to play in many of World War I's side shows — in Macedonia, Egypt, Persia, Mesopotamia, the Sudan, East and South West Africa, and on the northwest frontier of India. If the scale of the fighting in those far-flung places was not to be compared with the carnage of the Western Front, the servicemen engaged there soon found that there were challenges enough in dealing with excessive heat and monsoon rains, or blowing dust and sand, while wrestling with machinery and living in tents, eating unfamiliar foods and struggling with debilitating diseases.

In none of these theaters was the military aviation presence large, but the value of aircraft was shown repeatedly in their primary role of reconnaissance, and air-power lessons were learned that were not always so obvious elsewhere. For instance, the potential of air-dropping supplies to sustain troops cut off by the enemy was demonstrated at the Turkish siege of Kut in Mesopotamia. The British garrison was eventually forced to surrender, but air supply enabled them to hold out for 147 days before they did so.

Although it could not be claimed anywhere that aircraft were decisive weapons, in one campaign at least they had a significant effect on the outcome, pointing the way for conflicts yet to come. The ghosts of a battle fought in Palestine by airmen with their wood-and-fabric biplanes would haunt other wars, and never more powerfully than in Iraq, on the road to Basra, more than sixty years later.

Massacre at Megiddo

Turkey's entry into the war on the side of the Central Powers posed an immediate threat to the Suez Canal. In a long, drawn-out struggle, British troops eventually forced the Turkish forces back through the Sinai and into Palestine. By the end of 1917, General Allenby, aided by Arab allies and the guerilla warfare of T.E. Lawrence, had taken Jerusalem and the port of Jaffa. There, not far south of a place called Megiddo, the campaign stagnated until September 1918, by which time Allenby was ready to return to the offensive. He determined to end Turkish resistance with one bold stroke, but the success of his plan depended to a great extent on his use of aircraft. To begin with, the German squadrons supporting the Turks had to be kept on the ground, to prevent both their reconnaissance of forces gathering for the assault, and their interference with the subsequent advance. This was done so well that German aircraft were driven from the skies and RAF Bristol Fighters and S.E.5as kept standing patrols over the enemy airfield at Jenin to ensure that they could no longer even take off.

With air supremacy assured, the RAF was then instructed to render the enemy deaf and dumb by destroying their communications. On September 19, the only Handley Page O/400 in the Middle East dropped sixteen 112-pound bombs on the central telephone exchange used by the Turkish Army headquarters, effectively cutting off the German commander-in-chief, General Liman von Sanders, from the Turkish 7th and 8th Armies in Palestine, and from the 4th Army to the east of the River Jordan. (The pilot on this

The remains of a Turkish Army column devastated by aircraft of General Allenby's Palestine Brigade after being trapped at Wadi el Far on September 21, 1918. Compare similar chaotic scenes on the road to Basra in February 1991.

and Bristol Fighters of No. 1 Australian Squadron circled above the chosen choke points, ready to call in other aircraft once targets appeared. What followed was an awesome demonstration of the destructive power of even small numbers of armed aircraft. Many of the pilots involved were themselves horrified by what happened. Once the Turkish troops recoiled from Allenby's attack and tried to escape, they were caught in defiles that became blocked by abandoned equipment and strewn with the dead and dying. As aircraft refueled and rearmed to return again and again to the killing grounds, the Turks found there was no escape from the endless bombing and machine-gun fire.

mission was Captain Ross Smith, later world famous for his trail-blazing flight from England to Australia.) Even if the O/400 had not brought about such a stunning stroke, its mere presence in the theater would still have had a noticeably positive effect on morale.

In his book *The Seven Pillars of Wisdom*, Lawrence described the impact of the bomber's appearance on the Arabs of Sherif Feisal: "At Um el Surab, the Handley stood majestic on the grass, with Bristols and 9As like fledglings beneath the spread of its wings. Round it admired the Arabs, saying: 'Indeed and at last they have sent us THE aeroplane, of which these things were foals.' Before night, rumours of Feisal's resource went over Jabal Druse and the hollow of Hauran, telling people that the balance was weighed on our side."

Smaller bombers attacked the headquarters of the 7th and 8th Armies, destroying communications and cutting them off from their divisions in the field. Still other aircraft engaged in propaganda warfare, dropping thousands of leaflets describing how well the poorly clothed and fed Turkish troops would be treated as prisoners of war. Finally, reconnaissance identified the narrow defiles behind the Turkish forces through which they would have to retreat once the assault was underway.

Allenby's British and Indian troops launched the ground offensive early on the morning of September 19,

The account covering the Australian squadron's operations offers a graphic picture of the scene: "The panic and slaughter beggared all description. The long, winding, hopeless column of traffic was so broken and wrecked, so utterly unable to escape from the barriers of hill and precipice, that the bombing machines gave up all attempt to estimate the losses under the attack, and were sickened by the slaughter. In all the history of war there can be few more striking records of wholesale destruction."

In a telling comment on the effect of relentless air attack on troops, General von Sanders later wrote that: "the unceasing attack…exacted the most frightful sacrifice from them, severely damaging their morale. The feeling of helplessness in the face of the enemy flyers instilled a paralysis in both officers and men."

By the time it was over, the Turkish 7th and 8th Armies had effectively ceased to exist, and the way to Damascus was open.

NAVAL AIR OPERATIONS

It is well established that the first real efforts to develop strategic air power were undertaken by navies — the Germans with their naval Zeppelins, and the RNAS with its Handley Page O/100s and a number of smaller bombers, including Short 184s and Sopwith 1½ Strutters. In the British services, responsibility for the air defense of the United Kingdom was initially vested in the RNAS, and the best-known naval airmen of WWI (Raymond Collishaw and Roderic Dallas) are those who flew fighters on the Western Front alongside their RFC counterparts. Among these various operations, strategic bombing seemed to be a natural extension of a navy's traditional strategic role, but none of them was necessarily naval in character, carried out as they were from airfields with what were essentially land-based aircraft.

At the beginning of the war it was the opinion of most sailors that, if money was to be spent (some admirals would have said squandered) on naval aviation, the resulting aircraft should be employed chiefly in support of ships. The primary tasks of a naval air service sprang from this premise, and all of them involved extending the reach of the fleet — seeing beyond the horizon, observing the fall of shot from the ships' guns, seeking out and attacking enemy surface ships and submarines, and denying the enemy similar advantages. To do these things, a navy needed some aircraft that could operate from and with ships, and others with sufficient range to patrol the seas from coastal bases.

All at Sea

By 1914, the feasibility of taking aircraft to sea and operating them with naval ships had been sufficiently validated for practical steps to be taken. The idea of using a floating runway in the form of a flat-topped ship was already being considered, but it was not an easy problem for naval architects to solve and it was not universally applauded. Many sailors thought that the proposal to place a number of aircraft in one ship was too much like putting all the aviation eggs in one basket. A better solution, they said, was to spread the aircraft around, placing them separately on individual ships. Britain's Royal Navy led the way in pursuing these developments, keeping its options open by trying both. (The form and function of the modern aircraft carrier had been foreseen in 1896 by the French aviation pioneer, Clément Ader, who described a flush deck ship with hangars below and an aircraft elevator. He also suggested that the ship would steam into wind for launch and recovery, and that the aircraft would have wheels and folding wings.)

At the outbreak of war, the Royal Navy commandeered three cross-Channel steamers (*Empress, Engadine, Riviera*) and converted them to carry four floatplanes each. The aircraft chosen were Short "Folders," so called because they were fitted with wings that folded back along the fuselage, allowing their 67-foot span to be accommodated within the confines of hangars constructed on deck. Folding wings thereafter became a common feature of shipborne aircraft.

The Folders could not fly from the deck, however, and had to be lowered onto the water by crane and recovered the same way. This limited their usefulness, since their rudimentary floats were fragile and operations could not be undertaken from rough

The Short 184 entered service in 1915. It was a useful and reliable rather than sensational performer. Powered by a 260-horsepower Sunbeam Maori, its maximum speed was 88 mph. Armament consisted of one Lewis gun in the rear cockpit, plus one 14-inch torpedo or up to 520 pounds of bombs. On August 12, 1915, during the Dardanelles campaign, a Short 184 launched by HMS Ben-my-Chree *became the first aircraft to sink a ship with a torpedo.*

The Junkers J.9 (military designation D.I) was a determined effort to break away from the standard biplane form of the WWI fighter. It was a monoplane, and it used the metal alloy duralumin for both its tubular frame and corrugated skin. Although quite fast, it did not sufficiently impress the pilots at the German fighter trials in June 1918, but it was recommended for the balloon-busting role on the assumption that it would be tough enough to withstand considerable punishment from ground fire. The example on display at the Musée de l'Air, Le Bourget, is one of only forty-one produced.

water. A better system was the one used on HMS *Hermes* in 1913, in which a floatplane could be launched from a bow-mounted takeoff deck with the aid of a wheeled trolley that remained behind as the aircraft took off. Recovery, however, was sometimes still a problem. Nevertheless, several ships were modified with bow takeoff decks, including *Ben-my-Chree*, a converted Isle of Man ferry, and *Campania*, an ex-Cunard liner. Other nations, including France, Germany, Italy, Japan and Russia, experimented with converting ships to carry aircraft, but they did not add decks. Nevertheless, the Russians naval airmen with the Black Sea Fleet developed operational doctrines that pioneered the battleship/carrier task force.

Short Brothers floatplanes with folding wings continued to form a large part of the RNAS establishment throughout the war. The Short 184 in particular, although principally a reconnaissance machine, was used in several roles, operating from both land and water. (It was called the 184 because the Admiralty designated a type by the serial number of the first aircraft built.) Over 600 were built, and the Short 184 claims the distinction, gained when flying from *Ben-my-Chree* during the Dardanelles campaign, of having been the first to sink an enemy ship with a torpedo. Among the 184's companion floatplanes at sea was the Sopwith Baby, a tiny biplane descended from the Tabloid that won the 1913 Schneider Trophy. The 184 and the Baby

could be carried both by ships with takeoff decks and by light cruisers fitted with cranes.

The principal airborne irritant bothering Royal Navy ships was the German Zeppelin fleet operating in its reconnaissance role. It was soon discovered that floatplanes did not have the performance to deal with the Zeppelins. In exasperation, Admiral Jellicoe complained that he was "unable to propose any means of meeting this menace unless it be by the use of [land planes] rising from the deck of *Campania*, capable of climbing above the Zeppelins, and able to land on the water and be supported sufficiently long by air bags to allow rescue of the pilots."

No sooner said than done. Wheeled Sopwith Pups went to sea and improved matters considerably, even though the pilots had to accept getting wet as an almost inevitable consequence of flying. Not enough ships were modified to carry aircraft, but the Pup's performance suggested a solution to that problem, too. A wooden platform just 20 feet long was installed over the forecastle gun of the cruiser HMS *Yarmouth*, and in June 1917 a Pup was flown from there while the ship steamed into wind at 20 knots. Less than two months later, the *Yarmouth* trial paid off handsomely. On August 21, Flight Sub-Lieutenant B.A. Smart

Developed for low-level, front-line observation, the Junkers J.1 was the first all-metal aircraft to go into series production anywhere in the world. Although heavy, cumbersome, and slow to take off from rough ground, J.1s were immensely strong and well suited for low-level observation. Chrome-nickel sheet-steel enclosed the engine and crew compartment, providing effective protection against ground-fire. There were 227 Junkers J.1s built, but the only one to survive (needing restoration) is at the Canadian National Aviation Museum in Ottawa.

completed his first ever takeoff from a ship and climbed to intercept Zeppelin L.23. The German observers evidently did not see the Pup leave the ship, because the L.23 made no attempt to climb away. Smart was able to get above the Zeppelin at only 9,000 feet and made short work of shooting it down.

As expected, Smart got back on board his ship via a cold immersion in the North Sea. With wheeled machines there was no avoiding that, and the benefits of having an aircraft instantly available were such that, by the end of the war, most large warships were fitted with the necessary platforms, often capable of being rotated so that the parent ship did not have to steam directly into wind to launch successfully. While that was being done, it was thought it might be feasible to land an aircraft on one of the ships modified with takeoff decks over the bow. By 1917, one of these was HMS *Furious*, a conversion from what had been intended as a battle-cruiser. Capable of over 30 knots, *Furious* steaming into wind could get close to the landing speed of a Pup. On August 2, 1917, Squadron Commander E.H. Dunning flew his Pup past the ship's superstructure and side-slipped

across to touch down on the takeoff deck, so completing the first ever landing on a ship. Two days later he repeated the hazardous experiment, lost control and careered over the ship's side to drown in the wreckage of his aircraft. Following this, *Furious* was modified again with what was intended to be a landing deck over the aft end of the ship. Various arresting schemes were tried, some of them in which skids replaced the aircraft's wheels, but the basic problem was the dangerous turbulence in the wake of the ship's superstructure. It was not a practical solution, and it became obvious that the only answer was to have a single uninterrupted deck stretching from bow to stern. The first genuine flat-top, still working up to the end of the war, was HMS *Argus*.

Good though the Pup was, the ultimate WWI shipboard fighter was the Sopwith Camel 2F.1, a navalized version similar to its land-based cousin but with a fuselage that could be broken in half behind the cockpit for stowage on board. Once the British fleet had the Camel, the concern about the presence of Zeppelins was much diminished. Camels struck some heavy blows at the German airships, two of them in ways unconventional for the little fighter. On July 19, 1918, seven Camels took off from HMS *Furious* near the coast of Schleswig-Holstein and attacked the Zeppelins in their lair at Tondern. Zeppelins L.54 and L.60 were destroyed by 50-pound bombs. Only three of the Camel pilots were recovered by the ship; three were interned in Denmark and one was drowned. All seven Camels were lost, but that was judged a small price to pay for two Zeppelins.

The second operation was the result of a parallel development for taking aircraft to sea. On August 11, 1918, using a lighter originally intended for towing flying boats, a Camel flown by Sub-Lieutenant Stuart Culley was launched from behind a destroyer steaming at 30 knots. It was airborne after rolling just 5 feet. Culley climbed for nearly an hour to reach 18,000 feet, close to his ceiling, only to find that Zeppelin L.53 was still several hundred feet above him. At this point, the German captain altered course and passed over the Camel on a reciprocal heading. Culley dragged the stick fully back and managed to empty a Lewis gun drum into the massive belly of the airship before his aircraft stalled and fell away. Flames erupted from the L.53, reducing it to its skeletal frame in seconds. It was the last airship to be shot down in WWI.

In cloudy weather, it took an increasingly anxious Culley some time to sight his parent destroyer. A signal to the Admiralty recording the L.53's destruction by Culley's Camel said, "Your attention is called to Hymn No. 224, Verse 7." Reference to *Hymns Ancient and Modern* revealed the message as: "O Happy band of pilgrims, Look upward to the skies, Where such a light affliction, Shall win so great a prize."

Once it was found, however, he allowed himself an exuberant roll or two over the ship and ditched the Camel alongside with only a pint of fuel remaining. (The ditching was so smoothly done that the aircraft was recovered intact and is now part of the collection at the Imperial War Museum in London.)

Bigger Fish

The principal threat from the German navy in WWI came from its fleet of U-boats. Their depredations in the waters around the British Isles were the cause of particular anxiety. To counter their menace, great reliance was placed on maintaining aircraft on extended maritime patrol. RNAS non-rigid airships (blimps) were very useful for this duty because they were fairly numerous and were able to remain airborne for long periods. With top speeds of no more than 40 mph, they rarely got close enough to a

Developed from an original Curtiss design, the Felixstowe series of flying boats became the principal aircraft used in WWI by the Royal Naval Air Service for long-range anti-submarine and anti-Zeppelin patrols. The Felixstowe F.2A began equipping squadrons in 1917 and set the pattern of British flying boat design for almost twenty years.

submarine to bomb it, but they were equipped with radio and could summon surface ships to any area where a U-boat was seen. This alone sufficed to reduce the threat. A submarine forced to submerge had to use its batteries, which were then good for only 60 miles or so, after which its options were limited.

More directly effective were large flying boats operating from coastal bases. Thanks to the advocacy of John Porte, a British pilot flying with the Curtiss company in 1914, the RNAS acquired two Curtiss America flying boats, based on a design originally intended to fly across the Atlantic nonstop. Designated Curtiss H-4s and called Small Americas, they proved successful but rather underpowered, and were followed by the Curtiss H-12 Large America. Admirable though these were, John Porte, who had become a squadron commander in the RNAS, thought they could be made more seaworthy. The result was the series of Felixstowe aircraft that established the flying boat as a weapon of maritime strategy. From late 1917 on, they bore the brunt of the long-range anti-submarine and anti-Zeppelin patrols carried out by the RNAS.

Among the regular duties of the Felixstowes and Large Americas was flying the "Spider Web" patrol. The "Web," 60 miles across and divided into eight principal sectors, was devised so that some 4,000 square miles of the North Sea between England and Holland could be covered by four flying boats in less than five hours. It took a U-boat ten hours to cross the area at cruising speed. On May 20, 1917, a Large America on Web patrol sighted and sank the UC-36, the first confirmed sinking of a submarine by an aircraft. This was a most successful hunting spell for the Large

Americas, as they proved their adaptability by intercepting and shooting down Zeppelins on May 14 and June 14. A year later, on June 4, 1918, Felixstowes showed their mettle when three of them stood guard over a fourth forced down on the North Sea by fuel-system failure. Attacked by fourteen of the capable Hansa-Brandenburg floatplane fighters, the Felixstowes shot down six of the enemy without loss to themselves.

Curtiss flying boats featured strongly in the U.S. Navy's development of its air arm. When America entered the war in April 1917, the U.S. Navy had six flying boats in service. By the end of the war, there were 1,172, most of them Curtiss aircraft. They were active in covering the approaches to the Normandy and Biscay ports involved in the flow of men and supplies to the American Expeditionary Force. Among the other nations, France, Italy and Austria all produced excellent flying boats. The first of the French F.B.A. series appeared in 1915, seeing service with the French, Italian and Russian navies. In the Adriatic, conditions were ideal for a flying boat war, and the Austrians were quickly into the fray with the Lohner E, which gave rise not only to a large family of Austrian aircraft, but also, after one was captured by the Italians, to the Macchi L.1 and its capable successors.

THE AFTERMATH OF BATTLE

If wartime advances in outright aircraft performance and basic design were not spectacular, military aviation as a whole nevertheless made considerable progress between 1914 and 1918. Aircraft altered the character of warfare forever and caused unprecedented winds of change to blow through the entrenched positions of conservative military thinking. Most of those who in 1914 viewed flying machines as little more than amusing but dangerous toys were forced by four years of seeing them in action to recognize that armed conflict now had a dynamic third dimension capable of considerable exploitation in the future. Limited in performance though the aircraft of 1918 still were, it was fairly evident to those of open mind that aeronautical progress would continue

In 1914, Jacob Lohner of Austria designed a small flying boat that was to have a profound influence on the development of maritime patrol aircraft in the Adriatic. Several hundred Lohner Es and the improved L variant were built during WWI. They were important not only for the contribution they made to the Austrian cause, but also because a captured Lohner L was copied by Macchi and became the forerunner of a line of outstanding Italian flying boats, including several that competed successfully in the postwar Schneider Trophy contests. The Lohner flying boat at the Italian Air Force Museum on the edge of Lake Bracciano is the only surviving example of the type. Seen here in mid-restoration, it is now part of the museum's unique and priceless collection and is exhibited fully restored.

the standard of pilots qualifying for their wings. Britain finished the war having trained almost 22,000 pilots, while France added another 18,000. Despite savage losses, the number of survivors was still impressive. Italy and Germany added over 5,000 surviving pilots each, and many more nations also contributed their share to the 1918 total. The United States, starting almost from scratch in 1917, had over 9,000, with 23,000 more at an early stage of training. These young men, together with the aircraft surplus existing once the shooting stopped, would have a marked influence on postwar aviation.

For the air forces engaged, WWI was a prolonged learning experience. Starting from a point where they were expected to perform reconnaissance duties and little more, the fledgling air services developed several specializations and defined air power's roles. Reconnaissance aircraft were armed and gave birth to the fighting scout, the bomber and the multi-role aircraft. Bombing, at first employed solely for the immediate support of the front lines, developed to include the interdiction of reinforcements and supplies, and then deeper strikes at strategic targets. Fighters were used for low-level strafing of both specific and opportunity targets, giving rise to the close-support ground-attack mission. Many naval air arms experienced similar diversification of roles and, in Britain in particular, were closely involved in both the early strategic bombing efforts and the creation of a rudimentary air defense system for the homeland. In the closing months of the war, operations emphasizing the principle of force concentration by the use of massed air power in coordinated attacks produced significant results and offered compelling lessons for the future.

and that air power was an instrument of great flexibility and extraordinary potential. The air forces wielding it were still young and finding their way, but there were already airmen who believed that their services should cut the umbilical cords linking them to their parent organizations and form command structures independent of armies and navies, the better to develop air power doctrines.

The scale of the aviation expansion also changed things outside the immediate military sphere. To support the demand for aircraft by the thousands, new industries appeared, leaving fewer opportunities for individual enthusiasts to lead the way in aeronautical developments. Where industrial production was the priority, there was little room for inspired independents such as the Wright brothers, Samuel Cody and Santos-Dumont. The backroom workshop was overtaken by the factory production line, and many of the great names of the aviation industry were established. Caproni, Sikorsky, Breguet, A.V. Roe, de Havilland and Boeing were among those building aircraft in 1918 whose names would be at the forefront of aviation for many years to come.

Whatever else the war brought to aviation, it was memorable for the vast increase in the number of trained pilots between 1914 and 1918. Equally notable was the establishment of training systems, which sharply improved

By 1918, there could no longer be any doubt that aircraft had become weapons both versatile and deadly. Rooted in reconnaissance and cultivated in combat, the tree of air power had grown rapidly to cast a significant shadow in just four years, its various branches thrusting out strongly and still spreading.

CHAPTER 3

Commercial Aviation Develops: 1918 to 1939

*The civil aviation industry "must fly by itself.
The Government cannot possibly hold it up in the air."*

WINSTON CHURCHILL, 1920

IN 1911, HARRY HARPER and Claude Grahame-White published a book called *The Aeroplane*. It contained a sweeping but perceptive prediction: "First Europe, and then the globe, will be linked by flight, and nations so knit together that they will grow to be next door neighbors. The conquest of the air will prove, ultimately, to be man's greatest and most glorious triumph. What railways have done for nations, airways will do for the world."

Seven years and a world war later, there had been little progress toward the fulfillment of the prophecy. Commercial aviation remained a hope for the future. There had been advances in engine power and reliability, in the use of aircraft as military instruments, and in the creation of an industry capable of manufacturing aircraft, small and large, in considerable numbers. However, none of the machines available at the end of World War I were designed to carry either freight or passengers. The best that could be done in the short term was to convert those with large load-carrying capacities into interim machines for commercial use. It also seemed that the aviator's ideal of international aerial freedom was unlikely to materialize. The hope that aircraft would be able to soar above territorial constraints, ignoring national barriers as they forged new worldwide links between peoples, had died as airmen fought fiercely to defend national airspace during the war. The Convention of Paris in 1919 confirmed that each state had "complete and exclusive sovereignty over the airspace above its territory."

As the years went by, the pace of civil aircraft evolution quickened and the second interwar decade brought significant changes. Air-cooled radials were generally preferred to liquid-cooled engines, and this trend, together with a growing preference for multi-engine configurations, made for greater reliability and safety. Wooden structures were replaced by metal stressed-skin construction, and the biplane was deposed by the monoplane. Retractable undercarriages and variable-pitch propellers were introduced, and more thought was given to streamlining, all

OPPOSITE PAGE
The era of the great transoceanic flying boat airliners was dominated by Pan American Airways. Juan Trippe promoted his airline as the "Wings of Democracy" and saw it as a diplomatic instrument and standard bearer for the United States. In the 1930s it became the world's largest airline with a global network of routes. Nostalgic posters, timetables and PAA china recall the heady days when PanAm led the way in intercontinental travel. Artifacts from the Seattle Museum of Flight.

of which helped to improve performance and efficiency. Passenger cabins were made more comfortable, although the space available for seating remained restricted, since wider fuselages demanded more power to maintain performance. By the end of the interwar period, airliners had evolved into large, sleek monoplanes with the capacity to carry thirty or more passengers, plus their baggage and a useful amount of freight, across the world's oceans. It was starting to look like global air travel might become an everyday affair, which was a dramatic advance from the days after WWI when it took a leap of faith for most people to entrust even a postcard to an intrepid airman.

THE MAIL COMES FIRST

Even in the first decade of powered flight, when flying was regarded by most people as little more than an exciting pastime for the adventurous or foolhardy, tentative experiments were made in the use of heavier-than-air machines as a means of transport. A few thrill-seeking passengers were carried, and the rare unofficial letter was stuffed into a pilot's pocket. Occasionally, special arrangements were made at air shows for cards and letters to be franked with a commemorative postmark, but no serious attempt was made to establish regularly scheduled mail services. (There were occasions before the advent of powered heavier-than-air machines when mail was carried aloft, notably by the French balloon and pigeon post from Paris during the 1870 Franco-Prussian War and, both before and after WWI, by the great German airships, but none of these established a scheduled mail service.)

The British were the first to launch a formal air mail trial and they did it in India, employing a French pilot for the job. As part of the United Provinces Industrial and Agricultural Exhibition held at Allahabad in 1911, Captain Walter Windham, RN, was invited to bring airplanes from London and demonstrate their capabilities to the Indian people. He arrived with eight machines — six Blériot-type monoplanes and two Sommer biplanes. Once in Allahabad, Windham was asked if he could help in raising funds for a church hostel, and he suggested flying mail across the Jumna River to Naini Junction, using a special postmark and making a small surcharge for the service. The proposal was approved

> *"The conquest of the air will prove, ultimately, to be man's greatest and most glorious triumph."*
>
> HARRY HARPER, THE AEROPLANE, 1911

and, on February 18, 1911, pilot Henri Pequet carried some 6,500 letters and cards over the 5 miles to the delivery point. A regular service was operated for a while, the letters being franked "First Aerial Post, UP Exhibition, Allahabad, 1911."

Having had some success in India, Windham turned his attention to the prospects for air mail in Britain. The Coronation of King George V was imminent, so Windham approached the Post Master General with a scheme to fly mail as part of the celebrations. Arrangements were made for special cards and envelopes to be franked "1st UK Aerial Post" before being sent to Hendon Aerodrome, northwest of London. The first delivery of a sack containing 23 pounds of mail was made on September 9, 1911, when Gustav Hamel braved threatening weather to fly his Blériot from Hendon to Windsor. Commemorative letters to the German Kaiser and the Emperor of Japan were among the correspondence carried, as was a congratulatory message to the new King from the pilots who would be doing the flying. Their letters included a hopeful prophecy: "We believe this important event will become Historical, and its development will lead to a revolution in the present modes of conveying communications between the peoples of the world." Strong tailwinds helped Hamel to rush his first cargo over the 19 miles to Windsor in not much more than ten minutes, at the remarkable average speed of 105 mph. The service was continued until September 26, by which time over 113,000 pieces of mail had been delivered and one aircraft had crashed, pilot Charles Hubert suffering two broken legs in trying to ensure that the mail would get through. On the whole, the exercise was deemed a success, drawing crowds of spectators at both Hendon and Windsor and a generally favorable reaction from the public, although at least one newspaper was inclined to be cynical, commenting that the venture "demonstrated nothing except the ardour with which grown-up people will throw themselves into a game of make-believe." (Almost unnoticed elsewhere, an air mail experiment had been carried out in Denmark a week before Hamel's first flight to Windsor. Robert Svendsen took over 150 postcards about 10 miles across an arm of the Baltic from Middlefart on the island of Fyn to Fredericia in Jutland.)

With remarkable unanimity of purpose, three more nations took wing with the mail within two weeks of the first airborne delivery in Britain. Like the British, the French began overseas, but were more ambitious, sending their first aerial post across the 270 miles between Casablanca and Fez in Morocco. In Italy, pilot Achille Dal Mistro linked Bologna and Venice, completing the 170-mile journey in just under an hour and a half, a dazzling performance only slightly marred by his crash-landing on arrival at the Venice Lido. In the United States, an aviation meet was the excuse to try air mail delivery. A temporary post office was set up during the nine days of an event at Garden City, Long Island, and, starting on September 23, 1911, Earle Ovington flew a Blériot named *Dragonfly* carrying cards and letters from there to the postmaster at Mineola. Compared with the French and Italian efforts, it was not a very challenging performance. Since the flights were mere 6-mile round trips, Ovington could see his destination almost as soon as he took off and he did not even need to land when he got there. He just dropped a mail pouch in a field for a postal worker to collect.

Japan, Germany and Switzerland were among the nations to experiment briefly with air mail in 1912 and 1913, but nowhere did an aerial postal service take root before WWI because the equipment was not yet up to the task. The rudimentary aircraft of the day could not be expected to fly regularly in bad weather or at night, nor were they either mechanically reliable or capable of lifting much of a load. A train service could be counted on, could cope with vast amounts of mail, and often delivered it more quickly.

Even in remote, rugged areas, the supposed advantage of being able to fly in straight lines over obstacles such as mountains and deserts was often illusory, given the performance limitations typical of the available machines.

During the war years, as aircraft performance improved, some effort was made to use them for speeding up postal communications. The British flew official mail over the Channel from 1915 onward, and the Germans and Italians both established internal air mail routes in the latter part of the war, but it was not until March 1918 that a regular international air mail courier service began operating, principally to carry official correspondence between Austria and the Ukraine. Hansa-Brandenburg C.Is were flown from Vienna to Kiev, a route measuring almost 700 miles. Surface communications had been greatly disrupted by the war, and aircraft provided a necessary link between Austrians suffering desperate shortages and their Ukrainian suppliers. The service was maintained until the defeat of the Central Powers and the dissolution of the Austro-Hungarian Empire. (The Italians issued the world's first adhesive air mail postage stamp in May 1917. It was the regular express delivery stamp overprinted "Esperimento Posta Aerea.")

Uncle Sam's Air Mail

Until 1918, air mail in the United States retained little more than the sideshow status it had attracted on Long Island in 1911. Temporary post offices were often set up at air shows to draw customers interested in special delivery postmarks. However, there were those who could see the advantages of a regular aerial postal service, particularly in the United States, where the principal commercial centers were so far apart. As American entry into WWI became more and more probable, it was claimed that flying cross-country

Over 6,400 Curtiss JN-4 Jennies were built and served principally as training aircraft during WWI. After the war, many were sold off as surplus and were used to establish the first air mail services in the U.S. and, in the hands of barnstormers, to introduce aviation to the American people.

mail routes would be good training for pilots who might soon be at war. The argument gained Congressional support and Otto Praeger, the Administration's Second Assistant Postmaster General, joined forces with the National Advisory Committee for Aeronautics (NACA) to draw up a plan for an air mail system. In February 1918, an agreement was reached between the Post Office and the War Department in which the U.S. Army would provide the aircraft, pilots and mechanics for a trial, while the Post Office paid for the fuel and contributed the necessary postal services. Initially, it was planned to link Washington and New York. Curtiss JN-4 Jennies would take off from the Polo Grounds in Potomac Park, land in Philadelphia to change pilots, and then go on to Long Island's Belmont Park. It was expected that the whole trip would take about three hours. May 15, 1918, was the starting date chosen and, to make the most of the occasion, it was arranged that the first takeoff would be witnessed by a crowd of dignitaries led by President Woodrow Wilson and including such luminaries as Alexander Graham Bell and Admiral Peary, the Arctic explorer. As things turned out, it might have been better if the whole affair had been kept quiet until some experience had been gained.

The pilot entrusted with the first flight was 2nd Lieutenant George Boyle. He had gained his wings only a short time before and had been selected more for his political connections than for his known ability. (Boyle's fiancée was the daughter of an Interstate Commerce Commissioner who had helped the Post Office by opposing a takeover of the parcel post by private companies.) His commander, Major Reuben Fleet, was seen briefing him with the aid of a motorist's road map not long before he climbed into the cockpit. A sack containing 140 pounds of mail was loaded aboard the Jenny, and Boyle tried to start the engine. Despite Herculean efforts from the prop-swinging mechanics, the engine remained stubbornly unaroused. As the assembled dignitaries began to fidget at the delay, it was discovered that the fuel tanks were almost dry. Nobody had remembered to refuel the Jenny after it arrived at the Polo Grounds. Nor had anyone thought to make a supply of fuel available, so the ground crew had to drain fuel from other aircraft to get some. All this took time, but eventually, to everyone's relief, the engine burst into life and Boyle got airborne. If any anxiety lingered, it was because the Jenny appeared to leave Washington on a heading diametrically opposed to Philadelphia. Unfortunately, the visual evidence proved to be correct. Some time later, Boyle telephoned to say that he was in a plowed field near Waldorf, in southern Maryland, and that the propeller of the Jenny was damaged. He had, he said, got a little mixed up. A truck was sent off to recover the mailbag.

It was fortunate for the reputations of the Post Office and the Army Air Service that the other three legs of the opening day's operations were flown successfully, although the pilot responsible for the Philadelphia to Long Island leg was late because he delayed his takeoff for an hour waiting

The OX-5 represented a benchmark in the evolution of Curtiss V-8 engines and had the distinction of becoming the first engine to be mass-produced in the U.S. First built in 1913, it had an installed weight of some 400 pounds and delivered 90 horsepower at 1,400 rpm. Produced in thousands during WWI, it powered the Curtiss Jenny and is often known as the engine that made barnstorming possible. Many examples continued to fly in restored antiques beyond the end of the 20th century.

for Boyle. In general, the reports in the following morning's papers were full of praise for the brave airmen who would daily face countless hazards to see that the mail was delivered. Boyle's escapade was hardly mentioned. It was decided to give the young man another chance. To add some insurance, Major Fleet, flying another Jenny, escorted Boyle as far as Baltimore to point him in the right direction. He was shown that, in going north from Washington, the broad expanse of the Chesapeake Bay should be kept off the right wing. That basic truth was burned into Boyle's mind, and when the Major left him near Baltimore, he went on keeping the Bay just where he had been told it should be. As a result, he flew right round its coastline, running down as far south as Cape Charles, opposite Norfolk, Virginia, before landing to find both fuel and his whereabouts. Eventually, several hours after he had set off, he made his way to the vicinity of Philadelphia, where he ran out of fuel and landed in a field, breaking a wing in the process. With that, George Boyle's adventures as an aerial postman came to an end, and Major Fleet sent him back to flying school.

Boyle's escapades apart, the early days of U.S. air mail generally passed without serious incident. Deliveries were made in all weather, and a risky attitude developed with the expectation that the mail would get through no matter what happened. However, the demands of the war in Europe soon led the Army to dissolve its partnership with the Post Office, which, in August 1918, assumed sole responsibility for the air mail service. It did so with the help of six new machines from the Standard Aircraft Corporation powered by 150-horsepower Hispano-Suiza engines. They were faster and had longer range than the Jennies, and proved cheaper to operate. The pilots, all of whom had to have at least 1,000 hours flying, were all ex-Army instructors. After taking over, the Post Office announced its intention of expanding the mail service, including a westward extension over the Allegheny Mountains from New York to Chicago via Cleveland. Trial flights were made and the regular service was planned to start in December 1918, with daily departures from each end at 6 A.M. Before that could happen, WWI came to an end and suddenly there were hundreds of trained pilots and Liberty-engined DH-4s not needed by the Army. All sorts of new routes seemed possible.

In the years that followed, the Air Mail Service, with the ambitious Otto Praeger as its first director, suffered the effects of growing pains. Too much was attempted too quickly. The DH-4s, welcomed as an unexpected bonus, proved at first to be less than ideal for the job of carrying mail. Modifications resulting from hard lessons learned turned the two-seat bomber into a single-seater, with the pilot sitting to the rear in the former gunner's position and the pilot's cockpit converted to a compartment for 400 pounds of mail. Engines were reconditioned and airframes strengthened, with most of the original fabric covering being replaced by plywood. Even so, there were still accidents, as a terse telegram from Dean Smith reported: "On Trip 4 westbound. Flying low. Engine quit. Only place to land on cow. Killed cow. Wrecked plane. Scared me. Smith." In the end, the DH-4 grew into a reliable air mail workhorse, respected by the pilots who flew it. It was some time, however, before the general public warmed to the idea of sending mail by air. There were too many accidents, some of them fatal, and a pilots' strike in 1919 challenged the Post Office policy of ordering aircraft into the air no matter what the conditions. A compromise was reached that gave the pilots more say in determining their fate, but questions remained about whether it was all worthwhile. Many times a pilot's life was put at risk while carrying little more than could be stuffed into his jacket pocket.

On display at the U.S. Postal Museum in Washington, D.C., are examples of three aircraft that played significant roles in the development of the U.S. Air Mail service. Of the two shown, the DH-4 was the air mail workhorse for many years, and the Stinson Reliant was fitted with a hook to collect mailbags from smaller communities "on the fly." A 1911 Wiseman-Cooke aircraft (not shown) made the first mail flight officially sanctioned by a U.S. Post Office. The pilot carried letters 18.5 miles between Petaluma and Santa Rosa, California. The trip took two days to complete. Another air mail pioneer, the Curtiss Jenny, had the distinction of being featured on an air mail stamp in 1918. One hundred of these appeared with the aircraft's image upside down and were immediate collectors' items. By the end of the century, each surviving example was worth some $100,000.

Between October 1919 and July 1921, twenty-six members of the Air Mail Service died in aircraft accidents, nineteen of them pilots. Praeger, who was not a flier, viewed this as part of the challenge inherent in delivering the mail. He continued to expand the system, seeking to open an unbroken route between the Atlantic and Pacific coasts of the United States. A trial run, which drew comparisons to the exploits of the Pony Express, began from Long Island on September 8, 1920. Pilot Randolph Page flew his D.H.4 via Cleveland to Chicago, where he handed over to an American ex-RFC pilot, James Murray, who made it to Iowa City for a night stop. The next day, Murray got to Cheyenne, Wyoming, before nightfall, and he reached Salt Lake City, where John Woodward was waiting, by midday on September 10. Fierce headwinds over the high desert held Woodward back and he had to land in gusty conditions on a small strip at Lovelock, Nevada. Woodward was so rattled by a rough landing that he could not continue. Edison Mouton was sent from Reno to take over, and he reached San Francisco on the afternoon of September 11. In spite of everything, the New York mail had been delivered to the west coast in just under seventy-six hours, almost a day faster than the best time available by rail.

Rugged and adaptable though the rebuilt DH-4s were, the expanded service needed better aircraft. Converted Martin bombers were tried and some of the D.H.s were given two six-cylinder engines instead of the twelve-cylinder Liberty, but neither solution was entirely satisfactory. Then, in mid-1920, it seemed that the ideal machine had been found. The Junkers F.13 (redesignated J.L.6 in its U.S. form) was hailed as the answer to a mailman's prayers. An all-metal monoplane, it could carry up to 1,000 pounds of cargo behind an engine of only 185 hp, and cruise for more than six hours on low-grade fuel. These figures made the DH-4 look unacceptably inefficient. Eight J.L.6s were bought and taken into service.

Within days, one pilot experienced an engine failure and fire in the air and was lucky to escape with minor burns after side-slipping into a cornfield. Another J.L.6, piloted by the first civilian Air Mail Service pilot, Max Miller, was seen to be on fire before it struck the ground near Morristown, New Jersey, killing both Miller and his mechanic. Veteran Dean Smith made sixteen dead-stick landings after engine failures in J.L.6s, and only two weeks after Miller's death, another of the Junkers blew up during a forced landing on a farm in Ohio. The rash of serious accidents led to a storm of public criticism and compelled the withdrawal of the type from service. Investigations found that the problem appeared to be a rigid fuel line that was prone to fracturing. The leaking fuel then pooled in the fuselage under the

Air mail pilots flew in all kinds of weather in open cockpits. To face the hazards, they were appropriately clad in heavy flight suits and carried a parachute. The rugged Stearman mailplane was a trusted machine. This one was operated in Texas by the Universal Division of American Airways on the short-lived CAM 15 route between Amarillo and Brownsville.

demonstration was bound to have an effect. On February 22, 1921, two aircraft left each end of the route, beginning a transcontinental relay race in which mailbags were to be passed to a series of waiting couriers, traveling night and day and spending as little time as possible on the ground. Hopes were high as all four aircraft left on time, but they did not have trouble-free runs. The westbound pair were blocked by snowstorms between Chicago and Omaha and canceled their overnight flights. One of the eastbound aircraft crashed near Elko, Nevada, killing the pilot. The mail was salvaged and sent on in another machine. As darkness fell, the eastbound pilots, low on night-flying experience and lacking navigational aids, profited from the enthusiasm of people along the route. Huge bonfires blazed out to mark the track to Omaha, but when they got there it looked as though the great experiment was doomed, defeated by wintry weather over the plains. The pilots for the next leg were still in Chicago.

Harry Smith, the first of the eastbound pair to arrive in Omaha, went to bed, tired out by his efforts thus far. That left Jack Knight, who, delayed by repairs to a tail-skid, did not reach Omaha until 1 A.M. on February 23. During the previous day, he had already flown his regular mail run from Omaha to Cheyenne, Wyoming, before going back to North Platte, Nebraska, for his leg of the transcontinental epic. Confronted with the news that the operation was grinding to a halt, Knight said he would take his aircraft to Chicago. At 2 A.M. he was on the way to his refueling point at Iowa City. Flying through heavy snow and struggling against an almost irresistible need to close his eyes, he got there at 4:45 A.M. He napped briefly while the aircraft was serviced, but was off once more at 6:30 A.M. with clear skies in front of him. At 8:40 A.M.

engine. Flexible hoses and fuel vents were introduced to cure the problem, but a further fatal crash in February 1921 in which the aircraft was seen to explode in the air brought J.L.6 flying to an end. In its eagerness to improve its economics, the Air Mail Service had been dazzled by the prospects of owning a dream machine and had rushed it into operations without thorough testing, only to be reminded that acting in haste can often impede progress. (Elsewhere the Junkers F.13 developed into one of the most successful small airliners ever built. Over 300 were produced and they served between the wars in almost every corner of the world.)

Fly-by-Nights

The J.L.6 fiasco seriously damaged the Air Mail Service in the eyes of the public, and threatened to ruin Otto Praeger's reputation as its director. The door to criticism now open, other charges were heard; the mail planes were missing too many scheduled deliveries and those that were made were nearly always late, offering little advantage over the trains. Praeger was well aware that the image of his Service needed restoring and he believed he knew how it could be done.

The answer was to operate round the clock. Although it was February and the weather was liable to be unfriendly, it was decided to fly a well-publicized trial between New York and San Francisco. Congress was due to vote on air mail appropriations by the end of the month, and so a successful he landed in Chicago, to be met by a crowd of reporters and photographers. Hungry and exhausted, he first had to deal with having become a national celebrity. Answering questions, he seemed modestly unimpressed by his own exploits: "I got tangled up in the fog and snow a little bit. Once or twice I had to go down and mow some trees to find out where I was, but it did not amount to much." For all that, the headlines proclaimed him "Jack Knight, Ace of the Air Mail Service."

Meanwhile, the mailbags were on their way to New York. Ernest Allison got them there at 4:50 P.M. on February 23, 33 hours and 20 minutes after they left San Francisco and more than 60 hours faster than they could have made it by train. An ecstatic Praeger described the achievement as "the most momentous step in civil aviation" and claimed it would revolutionize postal operations around the globe. No matter that three of the original mail cargos had not arrived as planned. The fourth was enough to ensure the funding and the future of the U.S. Air Mail Service.

> *"There is hardly a day passes that some pilot does not have a thrilling experience in getting the mail through to its destination."*
>
> OTTO PRAEGER, U.S. SECOND ASSISTANT POSTMASTER GENERAL, 1921

Safety First

Nine days after Praeger's triumph, he was out of a job. President Warren G. Harding's Republican administration took office and the new Deputy Postmaster, Edward Shaughnessy, became responsible for the air mail. A steadier hand now held the reins. Initially the organization shrank. Feeder routes were abolished and efforts were concentrated on establishing a reliable coast-to-coast service and improving the safety record. Pilots' opinions were given more weight, parachutes were made available (although not all pilots felt the need for them), and maintenance standards were improved. Perhaps the greatest single advance was made in the development of a night-flying system, the main elements of which were radio stations at the principal airfields, emergency fields in between, and chains of lights along the routes. Terminals had revolving 36-inch lights sweeping their horizons three times a minute; on a clear night, these could be seen for 100 miles. The emergency fields, about every 25 miles, had 18-inch lights, and whole segments were marked by smaller beacons at

3-mile intervals flashing 150 times a minute. The aircraft, too, were equipped with landing lights and luminous instrument panels. These improvements did much to turn night into day for the pilots and, in July 1924, made it possible to begin the world's first air services regularly flown during the hours of darkness.

Almost as significant was the attitude of the management. By 1924, Paul Henderson was the man in charge, and he made it clear that pilot safety was more important than getting the mail through at all costs. There were still hazards to face, but the improvement in the accident record during the 1920s was evidence that swashbuckling and amateurism were things of the past. The transcontinental operation became smoothly professional, with mail deliveries averaging 30 to 35 hours from coast to coast. Each crossing was accomplished by seven pilots, who relieved each other at the Cleveland, Chicago, Omaha, Cheyenne, Salt Lake City, and Reno terminals. The refueling stops in between would have done credit to a motor-racing pit crew. A plane landed, taxied into an open-ended hangar and stopped beneath a fuel hose. The tank was filled and the mail was on its way in only a few minutes, without the pilot leaving the cockpit.

By 1925, both the American general public and the commercial world recognized the advantages of having a safe and efficient air mail service. Major banks were regular customers, and a Chicago woman asked whether she could air mail her two children home from Colorado, only to be told by the postal authorities that their aircraft did not transport "perishable matter." Having made the system a success, the Post Office withdrew from the air mail business. The Air Mail Act of 1925 allowed the Postmaster General to invite bids from contractors for elements of the air mail system. In 1926, a number of private contracts were let and, on August 31, 1927, pilots Dean Smith and Earl Ward flew the last Post Office air mail into New York. The pioneering days of government ownership were over. It had been a stirring adventure, and the pilots involved had relished the challenge. Many years later, when jet aircraft had become commonplace, pioneer airman Hamilton Lee found reasons to regret the march of progress and the

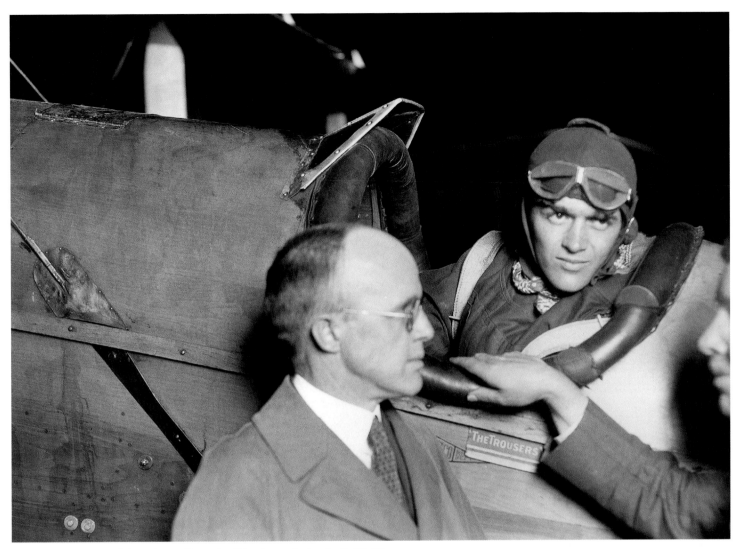

Jack Knight, "Ace of the Air Mail Service," in the cockpit of a D.H.4B.

resulting emphasis on what he regarded as a rather boring professionalism: "Today they sit up there at 35,000 feet. What fun can they have? Oh, those were great days!"

French Flair

During WWI, Pierre Latécoère became a major aircraft manufacturer, turning his Toulouse railway coach factory over to making warplanes. By 1918, he was looking for ways to exploit aviation when the war was over. The fighting on the Western Front was still intense when he startled French officials with an audacious proposal to set up an air mail route nearly 3,000 miles long, running from France through Spain and Morocco to Dakar in Senegal. His ideas did not stop there. Dakar was to be the eastern end of a transatlantic link to Brazil, Uruguay and Argentina. In those days

it took as long as two months to get a reply to a letter sent from Paris to Buenos Aires. Latécoère saw no reason why that could not be cut to one week, revolutionizing business relationships. It was difficult for government officials to imagine any aircraft covering such enormous distances, and Latécoère's ideas were not taken seriously. He was not to be denied, however. Within weeks of the Armistice, he set off in a Salmson 2 to survey the route into Spain. By February 1919, he had the approval of local authorities to operate mailplanes into Spain and Morocco, and a promise from the French government that they would supply him with both a subsidy and surplus military aircraft. Before the end of the year, the Lignes Aériennes Latécoère was operating Breguets on a regular mail service between Toulouse and Casablanca, with stops at Barcelona, Alicante, Malaga and Tangier.

The winter months brought with them blizzards in the Pyrenees, coastal fogs and violent storms. Maintaining a regular flying schedule in such conditions was a challenging business, and sometimes a fatal one. Pilots crashed into mountains and disappeared over the sea. The Breguets, regarded as notably tough warplanes, had unsuspected weaknesses revealed. Latécoère's determined director of operations, Didier Daurat, faced the problems by setting up a rigorous training program in which his aviators became proficient mechanics as well as masters of every aspect of a pilot's art. He also saw to it that the aircraft were strengthened for their peacetime task. By 1923, the results of his efforts were apparent. The line was firmly established and carrying millions of letters annually. The personnel were welded into a disciplined team, a close-knit brotherhood, proud of their accomplishments and dedicated to carrying the mail, which they saw as their sacred duty.

Latécoère believed it was time to extend the route along the African coast, but the problems inherent in doing so were daunting. Up to now, the flying had been done mostly over populated areas. Between Casablanca and Dakar there were vast stretches of desert, with a few isolated settlements around forts and oases. The desert itself was home to nomadic Berber tribes, including bands of armed raiders, to whom a downed airman would be fair game. Nevertheless, arrangements were made for landing rights, airfields, hangars, radio stations and fuel supplies, and a number of sheikhs were promised money in return for their assurances that pilots landing in their territory would be protected. Even as all this was going on, the impatient Latécoère was turning to the next step, contacting governments in South America with proposals for inaugurating air mail services there.

As had been feared, when the route to Dakar opened in 1925, it gave aircrews much unwanted excitement. The sheikhs' assurances notwithstanding, forced landings did lead to confrontations with wandering Berbers, who were just as ready to shoot an aviator as to capture him for ransom. Several airmen were killed, and others escaped by the narrowest of margins. One of those captured was a flamboyant character named Jean Mermoz, an adventurer destined to become one of the aviation world's celebrities. He was bound by his captors and rode in a cage on top of a camel for several days before his ransom of 50,000 francs was paid and he was released. Such hazards were accepted as part of the French air mail pilots' job, and the experience produced a group of unusually

ABOVE *The Latécoère 28.3 was designed as a long-range mailplane. On May 12, 1930, Mermoz, Dabry and Gimie flew one named* Comte de la Vaulx *nonstop from St. Louis, Senegal, to Natal, Brazil. They carried 285 pounds of mail and took a little less than twenty-one hours for the crossing.*
RIGHT *The Latécoère 25 was powered by a 400-horsepower Renault engine that gave it a 110-mph top speed carrying up to 2,420 pounds and four passengers. It was used extensively by Aeropostale on South American routes. A Laté 25 flown by pioneering aviator and author Antoine de Saint-Exupéry is the last surviving example of the type. Carefully restored, it is now on public display in Buenos Aires.*

courageous and talented aviators, including the steadfast Henri Guillaumet and Antoine de Saint-Exupéry, a complex man who later gained international fame and enriched aviation literature as a gifted writer about fliers and flying.

Ambition Denied, Dream Fulfilled

In 1925, aircraft of the Lignes Aériennes Latécoère flew trials that connected Rio de Janeiro with Recife in the north and Buenos Aires in the south. Unfortunately for Latécoère, with the successful conclusion to his campaign for an intercontinental air mail service in sight, he found that he had exhausted his capital. In April 1927, his air mail interests were bought by wealthy French businessman Marcel Bouilloux-Lafont, and Latécoère retreated to his aircraft factory in Toulouse.

The new owner changed the company's name to Aéropostale and began to expand the South American routes. He promoted Jean Mermoz to chief pilot on that side of the Atlantic and bought new equipment. By November 1927, there were regular flights between Buenos Aires and Natal in northern Brazil, with the founding father still very much part of the enterprise. One of his aircraft, the Latécoère 25, was the machine chosen to operate over the long east-coast route. Powered by a 450-horsepower Renault engine, it had a greater range than its predecessors and could accommodate four passengers besides the mail. For the time being, the Atlantic remained a difficult obstacle, so the French government plugged the gap by providing four obsolete destroyers to ferry mail between Africa and South America.

In 1929, Aéropostale added a spur route to Paraguay, and probed the Andes for a passage to Santiago, Chile. The mountains were a formidable obstacle, and most passes at higher altitudes than could be reached by the Latécoère 25. Seeking for a way through on one occasion, Jean Mermoz

Among the most celebrated airline pioneers, Jean Mermoz survived a number of dramatic adventures both in the deserts of North Africa and the mountains of South America.

and his mechanic were caught by downdrafts and forced into a rough landing on a flat-topped ridge at 12,000 feet. With no area big enough to permit a takeoff, the airmen tried for two days to find a way off the ridge but without success. They finally decided that there was only one option. Hauling the aircraft back as far from the precipice as they could, they started the engine. Mermoz opened the throttle and roared off over the edge of the abyss. The plane fell nose down until it gained flying speed and soared out across the plains of Chile.

Repetitions of such alarming adventures were largely, but not completely, avoided when the company acquired some rugged Potez 25 biplanes, capable of climbing to 19,000 feet. On Friday the 13th of June, 1930, Henri Guillaumet's Potez, en route from Santiago to Mendoza, was sucked down through a snowstorm to crash alongside a frozen lake high in the Andes. After two days of huddling in the snow under his aircraft behind an inadequate shield of mailbags, Guillaumet started walking. For another five days, in the worst season of the Andean year, he struggled over ice-covered mountain slopes enduring temperatures that dropped to 20 degrees below zero and facing wind-gusts that sometimes knocked him down. Much as his body demanded rest, he dared not stop moving. On his fifth day of walking, hovering on the edge of delirium, he stumbled up to a woman tending her goats. He had survived another adventure, against all the odds.

Jean Mermoz and Henri Guillaumet began the regular service between Buenos Aires and Santiago in July 1929. Not long after that, with Saint-Exupéry appointed chief of Aéropostale's operations in Argentina, routes were opened as far as Rio Gallegos, near the tip of South America. These continental achievements behind them, the men of Aéropostale set about forging the last link in the chain that

Jean Mermoz, aviation pioneer extraordinary and survivor of so many hazardous incidents over desert, mountain and ocean, was gone. As his friend Saint-Exupéry put it: "Mermoz had done his job and slipped away to rest…"

had begun forming in the mind of Pierre Latécoère in 1917. The long-range Latécoère 28 appeared in 1930, and on May 12 of that year Jean Mermoz flew a floatplane version named *Comte de la Vaulx* with 285 pounds of mail from St. Louis, Senegal, to Natal, Brazil, in a little less than 21 hours. It seemed that French aviators had pursued Latécoère's dream to reality, but when Mermoz tried to fly the return route in July, engine failure forced the aircraft down 350 miles short of the African coast. The crew was rescued but the incident delayed the introduction of a regular transatlantic service for a few more years. By that time Aéropostale had ceased to exist, having merged with other companies such as Air Orient, which flew mail to Saigon, to form a national airline, Air France.

Less than three years after his first crossing, Mermoz followed the same transatlantic route and attracted headlines again. On January 16, 1933, carrying passengers in the three-engined Couzinet 70 named *Arc en Ciel*, he cut the time for the flight to 14 hours and 27 minutes. At a time when crossing the Atlantic by air even once was still a considerable achievement, Mermoz went on to accomplish the feat twenty-three times while carrying the mail. Then, on December 7, 1936, four hours after leaving Dakar in the Latécoère 300 flying boat *Croix du Sud,* he transmitted that he was shutting down an engine. No other message was heard, nor was any trace of the aircraft or its crew ever found.

Air Mail Multi-National

In the years after WWI, as the Americans and the French wrestled with the problems of setting up regular air mail services, other nations were doing much the same thing in their own way. The British, having been among the first to experiment on a small scale, could find no reason to develop an aerial postal service inside their small island, where fast trains could do the job more efficiently over such short distances. Overseas, however, it was a different matter. To politicians brought up in the British imperial tradition, there were very good reasons to strengthen the bonds of Empire with aerial links.

The RAF began to operate a regular mail run in November 1918 when asked to organize a messenger service between London and the British peace delegation in Paris. This was later extended to include other headquarters in Europe. Once this precedent was set, the RAF became involved more widely, carrying both military and civilian mail over the 860 miles between Cairo and Baghdad as early as 1921. In the absence of navigational aids, flying over the featureless desert of the Middle East was not an exercise to be taken lightly. Relief landing grounds were prepared about 20 miles apart along the route, which was marked on the ground by the wheel tracks of vehicles driven across the desert for the purpose. Where the surface was too stony to retain wheel-marks, a furrow was plowed to maintain the line. When night came, it was necessary to bed down until sunrise revealed the route once more.

As described by Wing Commander Hill, RAF, sleeping in the desert was a lively experience: "We sleep outside at the foot of one of the wireless masts, and disengage ourselves as best we can from the attentions of the twin-engined sandfly, who also use Ramadi as an aerodrome. We hope a night breeze will spring up, because the sandfly is very lightly loaded and he cannot land on you in a wind. A hot whisky before turning in is also a help; for during the first half of the night you do not notice the sandfly, and during the second [having drunk your alcohol-laced blood] he becomes laterally unstable and cannot bite you. On leaving Ramadi we climb very slowly, with throttles wide open. As it is summer we probably set out in a shirt, khaki shorts and stockings, with a mackintosh on top just to keep out the morning chill. If we are sensible we are wearing tinted goggles, for the glare of the desert and the perpetual watching of the track tend to fatigue the retina. We now feel that it is time to discard the mackintosh and open the throats of our shirts, as although the top wing is still keeping the cockpit in shadow, the air feels as if it came out of an oven and gently roasts your hand if you put it outside."

To begin with, D.H.9As and D.H.10s were used to cross the desert, but the larger Vickers Vimys and Vernons took over in 1922. The RAF continued to fly mail services over this route until they were absorbed into the more widely based operations of Imperial Airways in 1927.

Looking to the future after WWI, Sir Sefton Brancker, Britain's Director General of Civil Aviation, predicted that "aviation will be the greatest factor in linking up our world-wide Empire." His belief led him to encourage proving flights through Africa, and to India and beyond, notably those flown by Alan Cobham. These were the foundation of the Imperial Airways network, which reached out to carry mail and passengers as far as South Africa, Singapore, Australia and the Americas.

Negotiations to operate services into Australia did not, however, go smoothly. In the 1920s, it had become apparent to most Australians that aircraft were likely to become important to the growth of their enormous country. Indeed, the island continent, with its widely spread centers of population, forbidding interior and meager infrastructure, was seen, like Siberia and northern Canada, as a part of the world where the aircraft would have an unusually significant part to play. A number of small airlines had come into being, such as Qantas (Queensland and Northern Territories Aerial Services), founded in 1920. Many believed that these aerial links binding Australia together, at first principally intended to deliver mail, should be essentially Australian. British proposals, such as the Empire Air Mail Scheme (EAMS) of 1934, therefore generated a great deal of resistance and were kept at arms length under endless discussion for years.

> *"Engine quit. Only place to land on cow. Killed cow. Wrecked plane. Scared me."*
>
> DEAN SMITH, U.S. MAIL PILOT

Air mail was always an essential part of British airline development, but until the second half of the 1930s the volume of mail carried remained low, a victim of high postal rates. The EAMS required the British government to underwrite the aerial shipment of first-class mail between selected points on the Imperial Airways routes, thereby supporting the airline's operations to its far-flung destinations. The subsidy was so successful that some of the Short Empire flying boats introduced shortly before WWII had their passenger-carrying capacity deliberately reduced to allow for an extra half ton of mail on each flight. By 1938 the Empires were operating the most extensive postal service in the world, delivering mail carrying special blue air mail stamps to places as widely separated as South Africa, Australia, New Zealand and Hong Kong.

One remarkable experiment in high-speed air mail delivery was made between Britain and North America in 1938. The Short-Mayo S.20/S.21 Composite consisted of a large four-engined flying boat (*Maia*) and a much smaller four-engined floatplane (*Mercury*). The floatplane, full of fuel and loaded with mail and newspapers, was carried into the air on the back of the flying boat. On July 21, 1938, *Mercury*, flown by Captain D.C.T. Bennett, was released off the Irish coast at Foynes and then flew 2,930 miles to Montreal in 20 hours, 20 minutes. *Mercury* later demonstrated the full extent of its capabilities by flying nonstop to the Orange River in southern Africa after being launched

One solution to the problem of combining a reasonable payload with a transatlantic range was the Short-Mayo Mercury/Maia composite aircraft. The small Mercury mailplane was carried aloft by the Maia flying boat and released over the eastern Atlantic. On July 20, 1938, Captain D.C.T. Bennett in Mercury broke away from Maia over Foynes, Ireland, and reached Montreal 20 hours and 20 minutes later. Overtaken by WWII and more practical aircraft, the Mercury nevertheless made its mark on the record books. On October 6, 1939, the composite pair separated over Dundee, Scotland, and Bennett touched down on the Orange River in South Africa some 42 hours later, having established a floatplane record of 5,997.5 miles that remains unbroken.

over Dundee, Scotland. The distance of 5,997.5 miles set a record for floatplanes that remained unbroken at the end of the 20th century. Interesting though these experiments were, the composite method of traveling long distances with a useful payload was soon overtaken by the development of more capable transport aircraft.

Unlike Britain, Germany had no empire as a framework on which to found an aerial expansion. Stripped of colonial possessions after WWI, the Germans had no readily available markets for their manufactured goods nor easy access to sources of raw materials. Germany needed to rebuild its international trade to begin its recovery as a world power. Transmitting important documents and payments as promptly as possible was a way to help German companies gain an edge in the worldwide marketplace, and the best way to do that in the 1920s was to fly the mail. By 1926, the plethora of small airlines that had formed in Germany after the war had been consolidated into Luft Hansa, and the new national airline began a major expansion of its overseas air mail services. Luft Hansa challenged the British with flights to the Middle East and, through subsidiary companies, offered tough competition for the French in South America. Another subsidiary, Eurasia, began mail operations in China's vast interior with Junkers W.33s and 34s. Extended services from Germany to the Far East, begun in the late 1930s with the trimotor Junkers 52, came to an end with the outbreak of WWII.

On July 22, 1929, the Germans tried something new in the Atlantic when the liner Bremen launched a Heinkel 12 floatplane by catapult to fly ahead over the last 300 miles to New York with the mail. The same thing was done on the return voyage when the ship entered the English Channel, with the Heinkel going on to Southampton, Amsterdam and Bremerhaven. Eventually, the Bremen's sister ship, the Europa, was catapult equipped, too, and the two liners operated the system regularly until 1935, using the larger Heinkel 58 and Junkers 46 floatplanes in the later years.

In the 1930s, the Germans also perfected a system for operating a regular mail service across the South Atlantic. Depot ships, equipped with aircraft servicing facilities and catapults, were stationed several hundred miles off the African and South American coasts. Dornier Wal flying boats alighted alongside the ships, were taken on board for refueling, and then completed their ocean crossing, flying at just 30 feet above the waves to get the benefit of an extra 10 mph or so from "ground effect." Once night flying was introduced for the overland segments of the route in 1935, air mail could reach Rio de Janeiro from Berlin in only three days, and could be in Santiago one day later. Improvements to the North Atlantic service followed in 1936 when Dornier 18 flying boats ran trials from Lisbon to New York via the Azores and Bermuda. In 1937, the Dorniers were replaced by four-engined Blohm & Voss Ha 139 floatplanes. Catapulting these large, elegant aircraft from depot ships allowed their takeoff weight to be increased by more than 3,000 pounds, making it possible for them to carry up to 1,000 pounds of mail as well as sufficient fuel to give them a transoceanic range with adequate reserves. In 1937 and 1938, the Ha 139s *Nordwind*, *Nordmeer* and *Nordstern* between them completed forty one-way flights on the North Atlantic run before being moved to the South Atlantic for the period immediately before WWII.

American Entrepreneurs

In November 1925, five contract air mail (CAM) routes were announced by the U.S. government: CAM 1 (Boston – New York) with Colonial Air Transport, Naugatuck, Connecticut; CAM 2 (Chicago – St. Louis) with Robertson Aircraft Corporation, St. Louis, Missouri; CAM 3 (Chicago – Dallas) with National Air Transport, Chicago, Illinois; CAM 4 (Salt Lake City – Los Angeles) with Western Air Express, Los Angeles, California; and CAM 5 (Elko, Nevada – Pasco, Washington) with Walter Varney, San Francisco, California. As it happened, none of the original five contractors carried the first contract air mail. By early 1926, Ford Air Transport had been awarded CAM routes 6 and 7 (Detroit – Cleveland; Detroit – Chicago), and on February 15, Ford pilot Lawrence Fritz flew the first bag of mail out of Detroit in a Stout 2-AT high-wing monoplane. Over the years that followed, CAMs spread their coverage throughout the United States.

The time had come for the workhorse DH-4s to be replaced. Re-equipment began in May 1926 with the Douglas M series, which could lift 1,000 pounds of mail and fly higher and further than the DH-4. Contractors followed with a variety of aircraft. Western Air Express ordered six Douglas M-2s, National Air Transport had the Curtiss Carrier Pigeon, and Walter

In 1937, four-engined Blohm & Voss Ha 139 floatplanes were used as transatlantic mailplanes. Refueling from depot ships stationed in midocean, they could carry up to 1,000 pounds of mail. In 1937/38, the Ha 139s Nordwind, Nordmeer *and* Nordstern *regularly crossed the North Atlantic, and were also used on the South Atlantic run immediately before WWII.*

Varney used modified Swallows. The Robertsons acquired four military surplus DH-4s for their CAM 2 route, and then hired a young barnstormer named Charles Lindbergh as chief pilot.

One of Lindbergh's defining characteristics was his determination to get the job done. If it held an element of challenge, so much the better. At this stage of his flying career, it may be that he relished the challenge so much that his determination to prevail sometimes overrode his judgment. He later described his feelings for uneventful flying: "The day has been crystal clear and almost cloudless; perfect for flying. It's been almost too perfect for flying the mail, for there's no ability required in holding your course over familiar country with a sharp horizon in every quarter. You simply sit, touching stick and rudder lightly, dreaming of the earth below, of experiences past, of adventures that may come. There's nothing else to do, nothing to match yourself against. It's an evening for beginners, not for pilots of the mail."

Lindbergh's competitive attitude led him into adventures that he (and the Robertsons) could have done without. He flew his first mail on the CAM 2 route out of Chicago on April 15, 1926. Five months later, on September 16, he took off from Peoria after dark, bound for Chicago, and was soon flying over fog. The fog was still there when he got close to his destination, and, try as he might, he could find no way of penetrating the murk. Eventually, after dropping

a flare and searching in vain for a beacon, he climbed to 5,000 feet and bailed out, landing near the wreckage of his DH-4 in a cornfield at Ottawa, Illinois. Seven weeks later, on November 3, he again pressed his luck on a northbound flight, pushing on into heavy rain and snow in a tenacious attempt to get the mail to Chicago. This time he left his cockpit at 14,000 feet and drifted to earth not far from Bloomington, Illinois. The civil aviation authorities were on the verge of grounding Lindbergh for being overly aggressive, but Bill Robertson defended his young chief pilot and made the point that, in both accidents, an inadequate weather reporting system had been a contributing factor. A few months later, all was forgiven as Lindbergh's determination took him all the way to Paris.

The experience Lindbergh gained from flying the mail stood him in good stead and he never lost his affection for the service. On his return from France in 1927, he said: "All Europe looks on our air mail service with reverence. There is nothing like it anywhere abroad." He was quite right. By the end of 1928, twenty-one private companies held contracts for CAM routes and were flying the mail all over the United States. There were FAMs (Foreign Air Mail contracts), too, and Juan Trippe's newly formed Pan American Airways took advantage of the opportunities they offered. Starting with just 90 route miles between Key West and Havana in 1927, by 1931 Pan American was the world's largest airline, flying mail over 15,000 route miles in Central and South America and throughout the Caribbean.

ABOVE AND RIGHT *Walter T. Varney. Of the Contract Air Mail routes created in 1925, none was more challenging than CAM 5 from Pasco, Washington State, through Boise, Idaho, to Elko, Nevada, 460 miles over mountains and high desert. Walter Varney, a flight school and air taxi service operator from San Francisco, concluded that CAM 5 was so uninviting that no one else would want it, and he was right. His bid of eight cents per ounce was the only one submitted. On April 6, 1926, Leon Cuddeback, chief pilot of Varney Air Lines, flying a 90-horsepower Curtiss Swallow mailplane, initiated the service when he left Pasco with ten sacks of mail bound for Elko, the terminus of the first commercial air mail flight in the U.S. Including the stop at Boise, the flight took almost nine hours — an average of slightly less than 54 mph. In 1931, Varney Air Lines became one of four airlines brought together to found United Air Lines.*

Exhortations to use air mail were a feature of early posters and pamphlets. Air mail, the public was assured, "saves days" and is "socially correct." People were told also that "The cheer of your messages and gifts is enhanced by air mail." Colorful postage stamps and decorative imprints added to the novelty and attraction of the new service.

Consolidation and Catastrophe

In 1929, President Herbert Hoover appointed Walter Folger Brown Postmaster General. In so doing, he took the first step toward restructuring the U.S. air transportation system. By the end of his tenure, Brown had seen air mail entrepreneurs such as Varney and Robertson absorbed into larger corporations and had laid the foundations of an airline system that was capable both of steady growth and of encouraging industry to produce modern aircraft, larger and more efficient than their predecessors. Unfortunately, in pursuing this goal and riding roughshod over any opposition, Brown made himself and his measures the targets for a Congressional investigation that began in 1933. The investigating committee charged that the Post Office had favored large airlines unfairly over their smaller competitors and recommended that the government cancel all airline contracts. On February 9, 1934, President Roosevelt did just that. While new contracts were being drawn up, the Air Corps was asked to step into the breach and carry the mail. With only a few days to get organized for what was a very specialized operation, the Chief of the Air Corps was given an almost impossible task, and the disastrous consequences were hardly surprising. By May, when the Air

Corps relinquished its air mail responsibilities, there had been sixty-six crashes and eighteen Army airmen had died.

While the business of carrying the U.S. mail reverted to civilian contract operation in May 1934, it had changed completely in character from its "pony express" days of the 1920s. Mail and passengers now went together and were carried in the aircraft of a few large airlines. The air mail story, once an adventure in its own right, had become part of the all-embracing saga of commercial aviation.

With a Hook and a Prayer

One other enterprising air mail venture by an independent American contractor deserves a mention, if only because it was so different from all others. By the late 1930s, it seemed that air mail was available everywhere in the U.S., but one man believed that the benefits of a direct service were not being felt by small towns, many of which did not even have an airport. Dr. Lytle Adams of Irwin, Pennsylvania, thought it should be possible for aircraft to deliver and pick up mail without ever touching the ground. In 1939, Adams formed All American Aviation to operate modified Stinson Reliants, primarily in Pennsylvania and West Virginia. Pickup sites, consisting of a pair of 30-foot-high steel poles standing

The Douglas M series aircraft began with the M-2, which was originally produced to satisfy an order from Western Air Express for a mailplane capable of carrying 1,000 pounds of freight. They began operations in 1926. Improved variants were later flown by several air mail carriers.

60 feet apart, were set up in open areas near fifty-four small towns. Strung between the poles was a rope secured by spring clips, and attached to the rope was a mailbag. The Stinsons trailed a grappling hook on a cable and flew just above the center of the mailbag's rope. If all went well, the hook snagged the rope and the mail was hauled aboard. The procedure demanded considerable precision from the pilot, and All American's airmen had to have at least ten years experience and a minimum of 4,000 hours in the air before they could be hired.

To the surprise of many officials, the system worked, and after a trial lasting a year, All American was fully certified by the Civil Aeronautics Board. By 1941, the company was serving more than 100 towns and collecting over 400,000 pieces of mail per month. Efforts to extend the service into other parts of the nation, however, were unsuccessful, and the system was gradually overtaken by events as passengers became an increasingly important part of the airline business. By 1949, the pickup sites were gone and All American had adopted more conventional methods. After all, picking up people by grappling hook might not have proved too popular.

ABOVE *All American mail pickup. Stinson Reliants of All American Aviation were modified to carry grappling hooks to snag the mail from outlying areas while still in flight. Only very experienced pilots were hired to perform this challenging aerial feat.* RIGHT *Michael Turner contrasts the old and the new in his painting of a Short Empire flying boat operating on Imperial Airways routes in the Far East.*

The Museum of Flight in Seattle has a splendid collection of commercial aircraft. Seen in the foreground is a Stearman C-3B restored as a Western Air Express air mail carrier used on the CAM 12 route between Cheyenne, Wyoming, and Pueblo, Colorado. Next is a 1928 Swallow Commercial, or "OX-5 Swallow," restored in the colors of Varney Air Lines (CAM 5 — Elko, Nevada, to Pasco, Washington). Beyond that is a replica of Boeing's first aircraft, the B&W 1 floatplane. On the floor beneath is America's first production monoplane, the Ryan M-1. The Museum's M-1 is thought to be the first Ryan airframe built. It was abandoned in 1932 after it overturned during an emergency landing in Paso Robles, California, and was restored in 1980.

LIVE CARGO

Establishing regular and reliable air mail services proved to be a considerable challenge to the airmen of the 1920s. That challenge was compounded by additional problems and responsibilities when passengers were carried. Mail bags did not complain about delays or discomfort, nor were they airsick. Seating had to be provided and serious thought given to improving safety standards. With live cargo aboard, pilots did not have the option, so easily adopted by Lindbergh and others when in difficulty, of abandoning the aircraft.

These things had been considered before, when the German DELAG company was formed to operate scheduled passenger services in Count von Zeppelin's massive creations. The intention was never realized, but DELAG's airships did carry thousands of people safely on unscheduled flights all over Germany before WWI. It was left to a small company in Florida to claim the honor of carrying the first passengers ever to travel by scheduled air service. On January 1, 1914, the St. Petersburg–Tampa Airboat Line began operations when pilot Tony Jannus flew St. Petersburg's Mayor Pheil across the 18 miles of water between St. Petersburg and Tampa. The Benoist XIV flying boat used was not the ideal airliner. Powered by a 75-horsepower engine, it took 23 minutes for the trip and carried only one passenger in its open cockpit. Nevertheless, the service was quite popular and by the end of March,

when the waning of the tourist season brought the Airboat Line's operations to a halt, over 1,200 customers had paid $5 each to fly across Tampa Bay. (Men weighing over 200 pounds were charged extra.) Unfortunately, the venture was not a financial success and the Airboat Line passed into aviation history.

Europeans Take to the Air

It was not until after World War I that further attention was given to developing passenger-carrying airlines, and then some geographical and technological facts of life determined that the Europeans would lead the way. The aircraft available at the end of the war were mostly surplus military

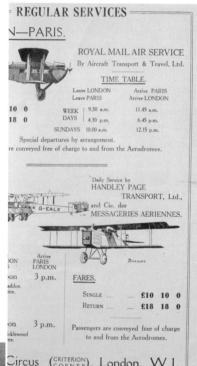
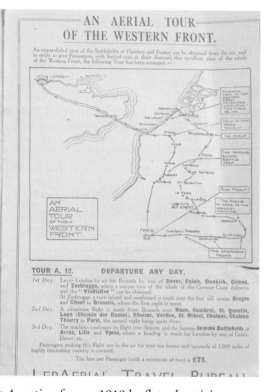

ABOVE *A section from a 1919 leaflet advertizing both regular air services between London and Paris, and a tourist's view of the WWI battlefields.*
LEFT *The Farman Goliath was a twelve-passenger conversion of a WWI bomber. Its obvious limitations notwithstanding, the Goliath was widely used in Europe and some continued in service for more than a decade. Powered by two 260-horsepower Salmson engines, it could cruise at only 75 mph, but in 1919 one example showed unexpected capabilities when it managed to struggle up to over 20,000 feet while carrying fourteen brave and hardy passengers.*

types, not very long-ranged and ill-suited for carrying passengers in either numbers or comfort. In the United States, the railroads offered reliable and comfortable inter-city and transcontinental travel and there was little incentive to develop aerial routes instead. In Europe, much of the rail system had been wrecked during the conflict, and the major centers of population were relatively close together. The aeronautical alternative seemed a logical progression. Aircraft had regularly demonstrated during wartime that they could surmount barriers both natural and manmade, including those notoriously difficult obstacles that continued to defy trains, such as the English Channel. On either side of that unfriendly stretch of water stood two of the world's great cities, only 220 miles apart yet widely separated by the difficulties of a Channel crossing. As the German Gothas had demonstrated, aircraft now had the capacity to reach above and beyond the problem with useful payloads.

In November 1918, the Royal Air Force showed the way when asked to provide air transport from London to Paris for officials attending the Peace Conference. A regular cross-Channel service began on January 10, 1919, and continued until September. Flying converted D.H.4s and Handley Page O/400 bombers, the RAF completed over 700 flights and delivered nearly 1,000 passengers, confirming that such a service was a practical proposition by recording a success rate of 91 percent for the scheduled flights.

Waiting its turn was the Aircraft Transport and Travel Company, formed in 1916 by George Holt-Thomas. On

August 25, 1919, AT&T launched two aircraft from Hounslow (near the future site of Heathrow Airport) to Paris. Pilot Bill Lawford was first away in a D.H.4A, carrying mail and one passenger, but the first scheduled flight was made by Cyril Patteson, who took four passengers across the Channel in a D.H.16. On the same day, a second British airline, Handley Page Transport, sent a proving flight to

Inside, the Goliath had all the trimmings associated with first-class rail travel, including upholstered armchairs and large windows. These could not disguise that it was noisy, smelly and slow. Passengers also had to cope with a stiff breeze swirling down from the crew compartment above. Creature comforts were as sparse as the instruments in the open cockpit. In the winter months, it was necessary for both pilots and passengers to be insulated against the often severe cold.

Paris, taking journalists in one of the company's O/400s converted for seven passengers; regular services followed on September 2. Handley Page added flights to Brussels on September 23, and to Amsterdam in July 1920, introducing O/400s redesigned with a cabin for fourteen passengers and given the civilian designation of O/7s. Apparently the demand for airline seats still exceeded supply, because in February 1920 the Instone shipping company, which had been operating a private service to Paris for its staff, began offering places in their D.H.4As to the general public. Shortly afterward, the Instone Air Line made its mark on aviation history by putting its pilots in uniform, which, as befitted a maritime company, was navy blue. It soon became common practice for airlines all over the world to dress their aircrew in distinctive uniforms, usually in some shade of dark blue.

These British initiatives did not earn the rewards they perhaps deserved. By the end of 1920, all of the British companies were in financial trouble. The British government did not see it as their business to help in establishing private airline companies. Winston Churchill, in many ways an enthusiast for things aeronautical, said that the civil aviation industry "must fly by itself. The Government cannot possibly hold it up in the air." This was in stark contrast to attitudes on the other side of the Channel. The French believed that it was in their national interest to keep themselves at the forefront of the aviation world, and

therefore important to ensure the success of their airlines by granting subsidies. The Farman Company was among those to benefit, beginning operations to London and Brussels in 1919 with twelve-passenger civilian versions of their F.60 Goliath bomber. (The Paris–Brussels route was initiated on March 22, 1919, so opening the world's first regularly scheduled international air service for passengers.)

The Goliath's passenger cabin resembled the interior of a Pullman rail coach, complete with large windows, brass fittings and upholstered armchairs. The aura of comfort was something of an illusion. Sumptuous furniture could not disguise the reality that air travel in the early days of commercial aviation could be less than enjoyable, particularly for those who had not flown before and were likely to be nervous. Noise, vibration, extremes of temperature, and the smells of oil and fuel, together with atmospheric turbulence, combined to give passengers a challenging ride. In aircraft where no bulkhead separated the open cockpit from the cabin, the discomfort level was magnified by the gale swirling round the passengers' seats. Airsickness was frequent and paper bags were a necessity. Then there was the question of aircraft reliability. Most early airliners had their problems, and forced landings in farmer's fields were not uncommon, brought about by either mechanical failures or inclement weather. Even so, pilot George Olley of Handley Page may have been more unfortunate than most in reporting seventeen "involuntary descents" in the course of one epic flight from London to Paris.

The burden of coping with such tribulations while competing with each other and their subsidized French rivals overcame the British airlines. The last straw was added in 1920 when the French cut their air fares. It was too much for AT&T, which was sold off to a new organization, Daimler Airway. Meanwhile other British companies were on an equally slippery slope, and by

The Junkers F.13 carried only four passengers, but established itself as one of the most significant transports of commercial aviation's early days. As the first all-metal monoplane specifically designed as a transport it was at aviation's cutting edge, yet it entered service in July 1919, only a month after its first flight. There were 322 F.13s built and they were flown by air services all over the world.

early 1921 they had all ceased operations. In the face of complete collapse, the government relented and allocated modest subsidies, enough to allow Handley Page, Instone and Daimler to match the fares of their international competitors and take their share of the growing traffic. (In the year ending March 31, 1922, there were 11,042 passengers who crossed the Channel by air. Of those, 5,692 did so by British airlines, while the French carried 4,258.) The struggle for survival remained fierce, and Daimler tried hard to improve efficiency and to operate at high intensity, sometimes managing to have all seven of its aircraft airborne at the same time. Added attractions were the fourteen-year-old cabin boys, who set a precedent that led to the employment of trained stewards and stewardesses by other airlines in later years.

> An instrument panel is "just something to clutter up your cockpit and distract your attention ..."
>
> SLIM LEWIS, AIR MAIL PILOT, 1924

The British government came to realize that airline subsidies were a necessary evil, if only to dissuade the individual companies from cutting each other's throats. Daimler was financially encouraged to develop the route from Manchester to London and Amsterdam, with a connection to Berlin; Instone was allocated London to Brussels and Cologne; while Handley Page concentrated on London to Paris, extending to Basle and Zurich in August 1923. Even these arrangements proved far from satisfactory, and the government finally concluded that a national airline was the only practical answer. This came into being on March 31, 1924, with the formation of Imperial Airways, which inherited the staffs of the independent airlines and a variety of aircraft modified to bewilderingly different standards. Among them were D.H.4As, 16s, 18s, and 34s; Handley Page O/7s, O/10s, and W.8Bs; a Vickers Vimy Commercial; and two Supermarine Sea Eagle amphibians. Re-equipment with more modern aircraft became an early concern of the new national airline. Imperial Airways gathered this motley collection together and began operations on April 26. (At first the national airline was named British Air Transport Service. However, BATS was considered an inappropriate acronym and Imperial Airways was chosen instead.) Having initially been reluctant to become involved in directing the course of civil aviation, the British Government was the first to see to it that most of the national air-transport eggs were put into a single airline's basket.

Germany Rises

Surprisingly, it was neither the enthusiastic French nor the reluctant British but the defeated Germans who were the quickest to develop civil aviation, offering substantial subsidies for the establishment of commercial airlines. The aircraft manufacturing firm AEG (Allgemeine Elektrizitats Gesellschaft), well known for its bombers in WWI, grasped the opportunity, joining forces with the Hamburg-Amerika shipping line to form an airline named Deutsche Luft Reederei. On February 5, 1919, less than three months after the signing of the Armistice, DLR inaugurated its route between Berlin and Weimar. For the first few days newspapers and mail were carried, but on February 10, passengers were added, thus opening the first sustained daily passenger air service in the world. DLR's fleet at first consisted of ex-military aircraft, mostly single-engined L.V.G. C.VIs with room for two seats in the open rear cockpit, but also AEG J.IIs and some of the larger AEG G.Vs and Friedrichshafen G.IIIs.

Before the year was out, a number of other small airlines were launched, spreading out over Germany to build a network of internal routes. New aircraft were needed to meet the demand, so, operating under the restrictions imposed at Versailles barring German industry from building large aircraft, designers such as Junkers and Dornier produced small but efficient aircraft suited to Germany's commercial requirements. Prominent among them was the Junkers F.13, the first all-metal monoplane specifically designed as a transport. First flown on June 25, 1919, the F.13 was in service by July 18. With an enclosed cockpit and a cabin for four passengers, this small airliner became one of the most significant transport aircraft ever produced. There were 322 F.13s built and exported all over the world, establishing air services in East and Central Europe, the U.S.S.R., and South America. Only in the United States, where consistent problems were experienced, was the F.13 less popular. (See "Uncle Sam's Air Mail" earlier in this chapter.) The success was not immediate, however. Not until 1921, when Junkers formed an airline, Junkers-Luftverkehr, and went on to establish routes into Hungary, Switzerland and Austria, did the F.13 became a familiar sight both within Germany and internationally. Junkers also operated a sensible policy of

The largest and most luxuriously appointed airliners of the early 1930s were built by Handley Page. For the first time in a British airliner, all crew members were accommodated inside the aircraft, and up to twenty-four (Empire routes) or thirty-eight (European routes) passengers were seated in unprecedented comfort. Slow and lumbering, the H.P.42s were nevertheless popular, not least because of their unrivaled reputation for safety. Named after legendary heroes such as Hannibal, Heracles, and Horatius, they flew millions of miles in a decade of service without suffering a fatal accident.

encouraging airline development by offering easy terms for purchasing or leasing aircraft.

Anthony Fokker was another who built effective small airliners that were operated by Dutch and Belgian as well as German airlines, notably the Fokker F.III, a five-passenger, high-wing monoplane. It was an F.III that inaugurated a regular service to Moscow. Postwar relations between Germany and the Soviet Union were to be normalized by the Treaty of Rapallo on April 16, 1922, and in preparation for this event, a joint Soviet-German airline was formed in November 1921. It was named Deutsch-Russiche Luftverkehrs GmbH, abbreviated as Deruluft. On May 1, 1922, Deruluft's Fokker F.IIIs began flying mail from Konigsberg, East Prussia, to Moscow via Kaunas and Smolensk, and a passenger service started on August 27. Deruluft added a route to Leningrad in 1928 and continued to operate until March 1937, in its later years using the Tupolev ANT-9 and the Junkers 52/3m.

With new aircraft and support from the Weimar government, German civil aviation seemed full of promise in the early 1920s, but it became clear that a degree of coordination and consolidation was needed if the industry was to prosper. By 1924, the small airlines had been incorporated into two groups — Junkers Luftverkehr and Deutscher Aero-Lloyd. The Lloyd group concentrated its efforts on northwest Europe, while Junkers generally dealt with routes to the north and east. Junkers flew only aircraft manufactured by its own factory, and Lloyd's used those made by anyone else.

Both were still dependent on heavy subsidies, and there remained a need to rationalize the financial situation. On January 6, 1926, the final step was taken when Deutsche Luft Hansa was created to take over all the airlines and affiliates of the Lloyd and Junkers groups. Just six and a half years after the Treaty of Versailles imposed crushing penalties on Germany, the new company controlled assets that accounted for 40 percent of the world's air transport industry.

Imperial Ambitions

It was understandable that European governments, having provided the capital that allowed their airlines to grow, should see them as useful instruments for the furtherance of national interests. It was not by accident that the name of Britain's airline was Imperial Airways. The official charter of the national carrier was explicit in saying that the airline was to be "the chosen instrument of the state for the development of air travel on a commercial basis." British politicians and businessmen, facing Britain's postwar economic decline, saw civil aviation as a lifeline capable of restoring them to their glorious Victorian past. The Secretary of State for Air, Sir Samuel Hoare, wrote: "I saw in the creation of air routes the chance of uniting the scattered countries of the Empire and Commonwealth."

The air mail services of the RAF in the Middle East from 1921 on, and the later trail-blazing flights of Alan Cobham to South Africa, Burma and Australia, laid the foundations of the Imperial Airways route system. (See "Air

Mail Multi-National" earlier in this chapter.) The first leg of the U.K.–Australia route to carry passengers was inaugurated on January 7, 1927, when a D.H.66 Hercules left Basra for Baghdad and Cairo. Three days later, the eastbound service began. The eight-passenger D.H.66 biplane was specially built for the desert route. Its three 420-horsepower Bristol Jupiter engines allowed it to cruise at a modest 110 mph over its range of 400 miles. A complete U.K.–India service did not follow until March 1929, when an Armstrong-Whitworth Argosy took passengers as far as Basle, Switzerland. From there they went by train to Genoa, where a Short Calcutta flying boat waited to take them in easy stages to Cairo via Naples, Corfu, Athens, Suda Bay, Tobruk and Alexandria. In Cairo, they joined the D.H.66 service, which had been extended as far as Karachi. This momentous journey took seven days, weather and aircraft serviceability permitting, and cost £130 one way. None of the Imperial Airways aircraft could be described as speedy, but they had other qualities that appealed to passengers. They were remarkably reliable, and the passenger accommodations were comfortable by the standards of the time, with large square windows offering a panoramic view of the world as it passed by in stately procession.

A more difficult challenge was the route through Africa, the realization by air of Cecil Rhodes' dream of linking the Cape to Cairo. Weather could be unpredictable and severe, and temperatures extremely high at airfields that, south of the Sudan, were over a mile above sea level. Landing grounds had to be established and maintained in areas that were often remote and on ground liable to be washed out by floods or obstructed by termite mounds. Maps covering some sections were sketchy at best, with large areas left blank. Nevertheless, enough was done by February 1931 for a service to be started between London and Khartoum, although the sections from Paris to Athens and from Alexandria to Cairo had to be by train, the former because of the lack of an agreement with the Italian government. Short Calcutta flying boats operated the leg across the Mediterranean, when Armstrong-Whitworth Argosies took over. An Imperial Airways captain recalled that not all of the journey was as luxurious as advertised. Lunch during a refueling stop at Aswan, Egypt, "was served in a tent which in summer was extremely hot. Lunch usually consisted of ham sandwiches, prepared some time earlier, the bread having in the meantime nearly turned to toast and curled up at each corner, while the ham was almost liquid in the heat." When the route was extended beyond Khartoum to Mwanza on Lake Victoria, it was 5,114 miles long and was scheduled to take ten days. The complete service between London and Cape Town began operating in 1932, with aircraft leaving Cape Town and London every Wednesday and reaching their destinations eleven days later.

In 1931, Imperial Airways introduced a fleet of Handley Page H.P.42 biplanes on routes in Europe, Africa and Asia. Even at the time they seemed something of an anachronism. Slow lumbering creatures, they were held aloft by fabric-covered wings spanning 130 feet. With their heavy bracing, fixed undercarriage and ungainly triple-finned tails, they were said to have a built-in headwind. Nevertheless, they were popular with passengers, who enjoyed the opulence of their fittings and the high standard of service provided. They earned a reputation for safety that was unmatched between the wars, and became the first airliner to complete a million commercial air miles without losing a passenger.

Imperial Airways wanted to eliminate the changes passengers endured during long-range flights, shifting between aircraft and using rail services on certain legs. In July 1936, the first Short S.23 "C" class Empire flying boat was launched, and on June 2, 1937, *Canopus* set off from Southampton to inaugurate the through service to Durban. Thereafter, Empire boats were regularly employed over the entire routes between Southampton and both Durban and Sydney. Powered by four 920-horsepower Bristol Pegasus radials, they cruised at about 160 mph and had a range of some 760 miles. The twenty-four passengers were pampered with food produced in a large galley; pâté de foie gras, poached salmon, roast fillet of lamb, peach Melba and crêpes Suzette were among the menu items. Overnight stops were in five-star hotels. Even so, the journey could be something of a

> *"Last year some eighty people in the state of Missouri were kicked to death by mules; over the same period only eight commercial pilots lost their lives. Fine — so long as one remembers that mules probably outnumber airplanes by about 100,000 to one."*
>
> EDITORIAL, WASHINGTON POST, 1927

challenge, since the flying boats were quite noisy and could not fly high enough to avoid rough weather. They were, nevertheless, a considerable improvement on what had been before. Between mid-1938 and the outbreak of war in 1939, the Durban flight schedule was cut to only four and a half days, while Singapore was being reached in five and a half days, and Sydney in another four. For the privilege of beating the time of the fastest ocean liner by three weeks, a return fare from the U.K. to Australia cost £274 (then about $1,100), which in the 1930s would have bought a small house.

Flying High from the Low Countries

One of Imperial Airways' toughest competitors came from small beginnings in the Netherlands. Koninklijke Luchtvaart Maatschappij (KLM) was founded by Albert Plesman in 1919 and made its first flights between Amsterdam and London the following year, using D.H.16s. In a move to support the Dutch aviation industry, Fokkers were added to KLM's inventory and a European route system began to take shape. Plesman's ambition, however, was to link the Netherlands with the East Indian colonies, and he ordered an exploratory flight to Java in 1924. By 1931, KLM was operating a regular service from Amsterdam to Batavia (now Djakarta) in Fokker XIIs. It was the longest route in the world, and the normal fitting of sixteen seats in the Fokkers was reduced to only four, offering more luxurious travel for customers prepared to invest in such a long-range flight.

Plesman's close association with Fokker did not continue long into the 1930s. Good though Fokker's aircraft were, they were overshadowed by more modern designs from the U.S. In 1934, KLM acquired a Douglas DC-2 and, in an inspired piece of public relations, entered it in the MacRobertson England-to-Australia air race of October that year. The DC-2 astonished everyone by finishing second, beaten only by a specialized racing machine and reaching Melbourne less than four days after leaving the United Kingdom.

The twelve-passenger Handley Page W.8F Hamilton was powered by two 230-horsepower Armstrong Siddeley Pumas and a nose-mounted Rolls-Royce Eagle of 360 horsepower. Eight W.8Fs were licence-built in Belgium and flown by Sabena. They had a reputation for reliability, a quality underlined in the 1926 edition of Jane's All the World's Aircraft, *which stated that: "These machines are to be used in the Belgian Congo, and it will readily be understood that absolute freedom from involuntary landings is of the very first importance for service in such a country."*

The most famous of the Junkers corrugated-skin monoplanes made its debut in 1932. Uncompromisingly workmanlike, the Ju 52/3m more than atoned for its angular appearance by proving rugged and dependable. Well over 5,000 were built, seeing service with airlines worldwide and with several air forces. Most often known as "Tante Ju" (Auntie Ju) or "Iron Annie," the Junkers trimotor was a thoroughly practical design that long outlasted many of its rivals. A number were still being operated seventy years after the type's first flight.

The commercial potential was clear, and KLM ordered more Douglas aircraft, self-interest proving more powerful than loyalty to home industry. Fokkers were still used, including the four-engined F.XXII and F.XXXVI, but mostly on shorter European routes. Two years after the MacRobertson race, KLM was the first European airline to fly the revolutionary DC-3, and by 1938, KLM was one of only three airlines (Imperial and Pan American the others) claiming to operate a worldwide network. Using Lockheed landplanes, the Dutch were getting to Sydney a day faster than Imperial's flying boats. With its freedom to buy the best aircraft available, wherever they might be built, KLM moved from strength to strength, a trend of success rudely terminated by the onset of WWII.

In 1920, the Belgian airline SNETA (Syndicat National d'Etudes du Transport Aérien) came into being. Although SNETA joined the rush to establish air services between the western European capitals, flying an assortment of Breguet 14s, D.H.9s, Rumpler C.IVs and Farman Goliaths, a principal Belgian concern was the strengthening of links with the overseas colonies. King Albert was prominent in encouraging the development of air services in Africa. As early as 1922, the Belgian airline LARA (Ligne Aérienne du Roi Albert) was flying Levy-Lepen flying boats between Kinshasa and N'Gombe in the Congo. In May of 1923, SNETA's assets were taken over by the government, which initiated national airline operations with Sabena (a gratifyingly short form of the unwieldy Société Anonyme Belge d'Exploitation de la Navigation Aérienne). Two years later, WWI ace Edmond Thieffry explored a route from Brussels as far as Leopoldville (now Kinshasa). It took him fifty-one days but it laid the groundwork for Belgium's main colonial route. By 1935, Sabena's Savoia Marchetti 73s were carrying passengers and mail to the Congo in five and a half days. The expansion of Sabena's European routes in the 1920s was carried out by Handley Page W.8s, replaced in the 1930s by trimotors, the Fokker F.VIIb and the Junkers Ju52/3m. By 1939, Sabena operated services over most of Europe.

French Fusion

Throughout the late 1920s and early 1930s, the French diligently expanded their network of international air routes, spreading from Europe to destinations in Africa, Asia and South America. The several companies involved built their passenger traffic on the air mail foundations established by

The Bernard 191 Oiseau Canari *(Yellow Bird)* is on display at the Muséé de l'Air et de l'Espace, Le Bourget, near Paris. Originally designed as a transport aircraft for eight passengers, it was modified for transatlantic flight. With Assolant, Lefèvre, Lotti and an American stowaway — Schreiber — on board, the Oiseau Canari completed the first French nonstop crossing of the North Atlantic on June 13 and 14, 1929, flying between Old Orchard (Maine) and Comillas (Spain) in 29 hours, 22 minutes.

The Junkers G.38 was a phenomenon. The gigantic wing was thick enough to allow the engineers access to the four 750-horsepower Junkers engines while airborne and to accommodate a few Lufthansa passengers in the wing roots, from where they could experience the joys (and terrors) of flight through forward-facing windows.

pioneers such as Latécoère, Mermoz, Guillaumet and Saint-Exupéry. By 1933, French air-transport policy needed to change if competitors such as KLM, Lufthansa and Imperial Airways were to be matched. France's civil aviation industry had to be controlled more efficiently, and the French government followed the German and British examples, forming a single national airline out of component parts such as Air Union, Air Orient, the Société Générale de Transport Aérienne (formerly Farman), and the Compagnie Internationale de Navigation Aérienne. On August 30, 1933, Air France was born, inheriting 23,000 miles of routes and a motley collection of 259 aircraft from its predecessors. Thirty-five different types were represented, and not all were in the first flush of youth. The nettle of obsolescence was firmly grasped, however. New aircraft were ordered, the number of types drastically reduced, and the route system rationalized. These measures were successful, and by the eve of WWII, Air France was handling over 100,000 passengers annually. Good though

it was, this figure placed the airline no higher than sixth in the league of passenger/miles flown by the leading European airlines, after Lufthansa, Aeroflot, Imperial Airways, KLM and Ala Littoria.

The designs produced by French aircraft industry during the 1930s to meet the demands of the national airline were often imaginative, with shapes occasionally bordering on the bizarre. Among the more outlandish was the Blériot 125 of 1931, which carried twelve passengers, six in each of two bulbous booms, while the crew of three occupied a separate cockpit capsule sandwiched between two 500-horsepower engines, one pushing and one pulling. Almost equally startling to look at was the massive Latécoère 521 four-engined flying boat of 1936, over 160 feet across the wing and 104 feet long. Its huge hull jutted out below the cockpit area like a prognathous lower jaw, giving the aircraft a belligerent expression. Seventy passengers could be accommodated on the shorter routes of the Mediterranean, and thirty for a transatlantic flight.

The Junkers W 34 continued the line of all-metal Junkers aircraft that began with the Junkers J.1. Considered by many the best bush plane of the 1930s and early 1940s, the Junkers W 34 had excellent flying characteristics and was ruggedly built. Its 600-horsepower Pratt & Whitney R-1340-AN-1 Wasp engine was reliable and easy to service. However, these good qualities were offset by the aircraft's relatively high manufacturing cost. Added to this was a heavy tariff imposed on German aircraft between the wars, and the result was that only nine were imported to Canada. Elsewhere the W 34 was widely used and was the Luftwaffe's standard instrument and navigation trainer until the latter stages of WWII. The Canadian National Aviation Museum's aircraft operated regularly until 1960, and in 1962 was flown from Kamloops, British Columbia, to Ottawa. This was the last flight of any of the Junkers F 13/W 33/W 34 family of aircraft.

Several more conventional aircraft, generally reliable if not outstanding, carried Air France's passengers during the 1930s. The low-wing trimotor Wibault 283.T12 operated services in Europe from the early 1930s, and the high-wing twin-engined Potez 62 flew over routes in South America and the Far East until the outbreak of WWII. The French airliner most closely resembling contemporary U.S. designs was the Bloch 220, an all-metal monoplane powered by two 985-horsepower radials with variable-pitch propellers. State-of-the-art features included retractable undercarriage, split flaps and wing de-icing boots. It carried sixteen passengers in reasonable comfort at a cruising speed of 170 mph. Its larger stable-mate was the trimotor Dewoitine D.338, perhaps the best of the interwar Air France transports. Entering service in 1936, it was used in Europe, the Far East and on the African section of the route to South America. It could accommodate up to twenty-two passengers and cruise at 160 mph over a range of some 1,200 miles. A few of the thirty-one built were still in use in 1946, flying between Paris and Nice.

Lufthansa Leads

From June 30, 1933, Germany's airline made one word out of two and began styling itself Lufthansa. By then it was operating by far the most comprehensive air-route network in Europe. While the British, French and Dutch were primarily concerned with establishing aerial links to their overseas empires, the Germans made the most of their European opportunities. From its birth in 1926, Lufthansa was at the forefront of European airline development, energetically opening up new routes and taking the lead in the newly formed International Air Traffic Association (IATA), an organization set up with the aim of coordinating action on airline timetables, fares and flight safety. In its clandestine but increasingly significant role as the womb nurturing the embryonic Luftwaffe, Lufthansa was helped in its ambitions by generous subsidies and a steady flow of new equipment — modern aircraft, ample aircrew training facilities, effective navigation aids, and new airfields. In Hitler's Third Reich, Lufthansa was fundamental to the resurgence of German air power.

In 1930, Lufthansa led the European airline pack, carrying some 58,000 passengers, mostly over routes within Germany. By 1939, the total had risen to over a quarter of a million, and aircraft bearing the "Flying Crane" symbol were reaching out to destinations all over the world. Crossings of both the North and South Atlantic were regularly accomplished, and Lufthansa was playing a major role in a number of regional airlines serving countries in Latin America and the Far East.

The aircraft flown by Lufthansa during the 1930s included some of the most advanced produced anywhere. As the decade opened, the Lufthansa fleet was composed mostly of useful but aging aircraft, almost all of them relatively small, such as the Junkers F.13 and G.24, and the Rohrbach Roland. At the other end of the scale were two of the largest aircraft in the world, both of them sponsored by the German

> *We shall cast our mantle of safety over the Inland."*
>
> JOHN FLYNN, FOUNDER OF THE AUSTRALIAN FLYING DOCTOR SERVICE

Ministry of Transport and neither of them successful. The Dornier Do X was a gigantic flying boat conceived for the transatlantic routes. It weighed close to 60 tons and, in its final form, was powered by twelve 600-horsepower Curtiss Conquerors mounted in tandem pairs. The intention was to provide for up to 100 passengers, and on one test flight it did carry 169 people — 150 passengers, 10 crew and 9 stowaways. First flown in July 1929, the Do X subsequently undertook a publicity tour lasting ten months around the Atlantic, but it was bedeviled by endless problems and never entered regular service. Two more Do Xs were built for Italy, but were deemed uneconomical and donated to the military.

The landplane stablemate of the Do X was the Junkers G.38, an aircraft of great originality that first flew in November 1929 and was an aerial wonder of its age. Beauty was not an attribute of the G.38, but it was certainly impressive. The wing spanned 144 feet and was nearly 6 feet thick, capacious enough to build small passenger cabins into the wing roots and to allow mechanics access to the four 750-horsepower diesel engines in flight. Thirty-four passengers could be carried, twenty-six in the main cabins, two in a tiny cabin in the extreme nose, and three in each of the wing-roots, from where they enjoyed a superb view through forward-facing windows. Only two G.38s saw service on European routes. The first crashed in 1936, and the second was destroyed in Athens in 1941 by RAF bombing.

The Dornier Do X first flew in 1929 and was the aeronautical giant of its time. It weighed well over 50 tons, its size and shape proving too much even for twelve 600-horsepower Curtiss Conquerors mounted in tandem pairs. Planned for 100 passengers, it once carried 169 people — 150 passengers, 10 crew and 9 stowaways. Endless problems were encountered and the Do X never entered regular service. Apart from the original aircraft, two more Do Xs were built for commercial service in Italy, but their poor performance ensured that they would be donated to the military.

In 1932, Hugo Junkers produced the last and most famous of his corrugated-skin monoplanes, a variant of his single-engined Ju 52. The Ju 52/3m was an angular but workmanlike design initially powered by three 525-horsepower BMW Hornets. Some 5,000 were built in Germany and hundreds more were added in France and Spain after the war. They saw service with numerous airlines in Europe, South America and South Africa, besides being the transport workhorse for the Luftwaffe during WWII. The Ju 52/3m carried some 75 percent of Lufthansa's European traffic in the 1930s. Rugged and reliable, the civil Ju 52/3m carried seventeen passengers, cruised at 150 mph and had a range of some 500 miles. Generally regarded with affection or grudging respect, it attracted nicknames such as "Tante Ju" (Auntie Ju) and "Iron Annie."

Anchored by the dependability of the Ju 52/3m's earlier technology, Lufthansa moved to acquire aircraft of the next generation. In 1932, Swissair's introduction of Lockheed Orions spurred Luft Hansa into seeking competitive German light transports capable of handling four to six passengers. The Heinkel He 70 and Junkers Ju 160 were the results. Besides being an outstanding performer, the He 70 was an aesthetically pleasing aircraft, with a slim streamlined fuselage and elliptical wings and tail surfaces. Against the trend of the times, it was powered by a closely cowled 630-horsepower in-line engine, which blended smoothly into its elegant lines. The He 70 was to exert its influence on high-speed aircraft design for the remainder of the piston-engine era, and its success encouraged Lufthansa to seek a similarly outstanding aircraft of greater capacity. Heinkel's answer was the He 111, a twin-engined aircraft planned for both civil and military roles. The Junkers Ju 86 appeared at the same time and was similarly conceived. Fast, modern aircraft though they both were, neither the He 111 nor the Ju 86 was entirely satisfactory from the airline's point of view, since their cramped bomber fuselages permitted only ten passengers and operations were decidedly uneconomic. Larger four-engined airliners with much greater capacity began to appear in the late 1930s, but these also were built with an eye to future military use. The twenty-six passenger Focke Wulf Fw 200 Condor and the forty-passenger Junkers Ju 90 were the most advanced airliners in service before WWII. The Condor gained world attention in August 1938 when one was flown nonstop from Berlin to New York in 24 hours, 55 minutes, averaging 164 mph. The return journey downwind was completed in 19 hours, 55 minutes, at an average of 205 mph. This was the first time that a four-engined landplane had accomplished nonstop Atlantic crossings. With that achievement, the Condor pointed the way to the future for commercial aviation.

Spreading Soviet Wings

While Lufthansa was building its European dominance, some impressive airline growth was taking place in the Soviet Union. Having gained experience from their collaboration with the Germans in forming Deruluft, the Soviets established a state airline called Dobrolet in 1923. In 1929, Dobrolet merged with another company named Ukrvozdukhput to form Grazdansiy Vozduzhniy Flot, a joint stock company that undertook the expansion of the Soviet airline network called for in the Communist Party's first Five Year Plan. By 1932, the route system measured some 20,000 miles and G.V.F.'s aircraft had carried a total of about 67,000 passengers and over 6,000 tons of mail. In 1932, a new state airline emerged under the name Aeroflot. Over the next three years, the annual figures for the carriage of passengers and freight rose sharply from 27,000 and 900 tons to 111,000 and 11,000 tons. Aeroflot's network reached from Leningrad and Moscow across nine time zones to the shores of the Pacific and the icy Bering Sea, sprouting feeder services along the way. In 1940, Aeroflot carried 350,000 passengers and had overtaken Lufthansa to become the largest of the European-based airlines.

As Aeroflot built the Soviet Union's air transport system, it generally clung to the railways. From Moscow to Vladivostok, for example, it followed the Trans-Siberian Railway's lines closely. The task of reaching the more remote areas of Arctic Siberia, where there were no roads or railways, fell to Aviaarktika, formed in 1930. Using flying boats and floatplanes in the summer months and switching to skis for the long winters, Aviaarktika's pilots followed the Siberian rivers and touched down on the many lakes and coastal inlets of the far north. Some of the pioneering flights undertaken in Siberia during the 1930s were a match for anything accomplished elsewhere. Vasily Molokov's achievements were on an epic scale, culminating in a significant trail-blazing flight in 1936. Using a Dornier Wal, he began in Krasnoyarsk and circumnavigated the Soviet

Fokker F.10 *by Robert Taylor, courtesy of the Military Gallery, Bath, U.K. A Pan American F.10A is seen being loaded at* Vera Cruz, Mexico, in 1931.

Union, flying via Kamchatka, the Arctic Ocean coasts and Archangel to Moscow. Molokov's challenging journey lasted three months and covered over 16,000 miles in some 200 flying hours. Flights like this made it possible to open up the remote areas of the Soviet Union to settlement. With no other means of transport available, aircraft linked settlements with the outside world and brought them the foundations of community life — doctors, teachers, traders and essential supplies.

Airlines, Airlines Everywhere

In the years between the wars, airlines formed all over the world as people accepted the idea that traveling by air was not only for the adventurous few. In many countries, the development was officially encouraged as it was increasingly perceived that aircraft wearing national flags carried prestige on the international stage. Those airlines that appeared in the 1920s included Spain's Iberia, CETA and UAE; Austria's Ölag; Poland's LOT; Switzerland's Ad Astra Aero and Balair; Czechoslovakia's CSA and CLS; and Italy's Transadriatica and Avio Linee Italiane. In Scandinavia, there was Denmark's DDL, Sweden's ABA, Norway's DNL, and Finland's Aero O/Y. On the other side of the Atlantic, some of the world's oldest airlines had their origins in Latin America. Avianca of Colombia has its roots in a company formed in 1919, and Mexicana's ancestor was founded in 1921. In the late 1920s, these were followed by Brazil's Varig, Peru's Faucett, and Chile's Lan-Chile. One of the first in Africa was Wilson Airways of Kenya, which began by operating a single Puss Moth between Nairobi and Lake Victoria in 1929, and later expanded to serve Mombasa, Dar-es-Salaam and Zanzibar.

Back of Beyond

Aircraft had an important role to play in the development of two of the largest countries in the British Commonwealth. Vast areas of Australia and Canada are almost impenetrable on the surface and access to the remoter regions is heavily dependent on air transport.

CURTISS BUSH PLANES

The Curtiss HS-2L was Canada's first bush aircraft and was the predominant Canadian bush plane until 1926.

HS-2Ls flew the first forestry patrols, made the first aerial timber survey in 1919, and in 1924 established the first scheduled air service and the first regular air mail service in Canada. The National Aviation Museum's HS-2L performed the first ever "bush flight" in 1919, but on September 2, 1922, it crashed into Foss Lake, Ontario. The hull and many parts and fittings were retrieved by the museum during a salvage operation in 1968–69. As restored, the aircraft on display incorporates parts from three different aircraft.

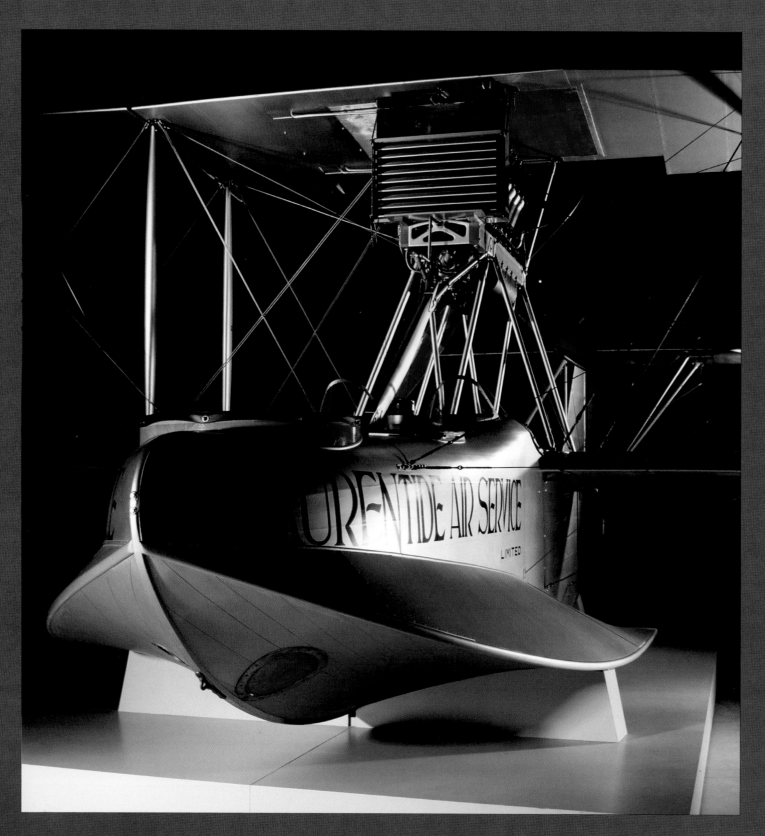

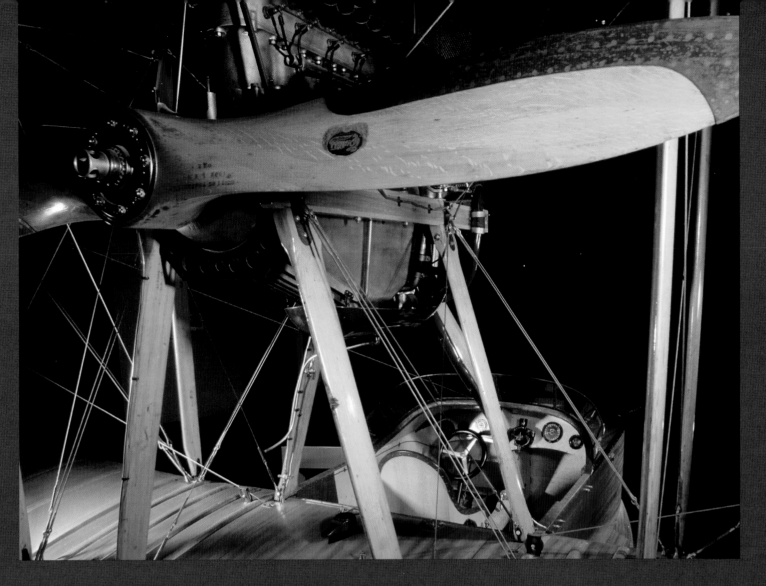

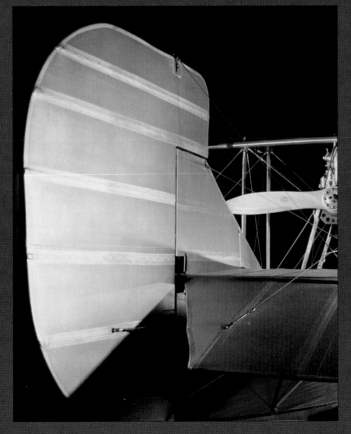

Australia's Qantas began operating a service for Queensland's interior in 1922, and two years later the Laurentide Air Service provided the first regular flights for passengers and freight in Canada, linking Quebec's Rouyn goldfield with the Canadian Pacific Railway. These were the forerunners of services that made it possible for determined pioneers to settle beyond the frontiers of their societies and engage in trapping, fishing, mining, forestry and farming. Similarly adventurous efforts were made in tackling the icy wastes and forests of Siberia and Alaska, and the tropical jungles of New Guinea and the Amazon. For the most part, however, much of the early flying in these areas was unscheduled, with operators reacting as required to the needs of remote communities and individuals.

In the far northern regions, aircraft flew with wheels or floats during the short summers and changed to skis when snow and ice took over the landscape. The tough, independent men who dared to fly over these areas became known as bush pilots. Operating without maps or navigation aids in weather that was often severe, they touched down on uncharted lakes, sandbars in rivers, rocky strips on mountainsides, even on ice floes. They covered in hours territory that would have taken weeks on the ground, carrying supplies both to frontiersmen and to native communities who thereby gained the benefits of the air age before they had seen either rail or road. In the early days, the aircraft invariably had open cockpits and a single engine, circumstances that challenged the fortitude of pilots flying in freezing temperatures behind not always reliable motors. It helped if they were both skilled mechanics and resourceful survivors.

The first bush-flying was undertaken in Canada in 1919, using Curtiss HS-2L flying boats to survey the Quebec wilderness. Capable as they were in the summer, with lakes and rivers everywhere, the HS-2Ls were useless once the deep freeze set in. Year-round operations became possible once rugged aircraft such as the Fairchild FC series appeared, adaptable high-wing landplanes with powerful radial engines and closed, heated cabins. Heating was important on the ground, too, if the aircraft expected to fly again. When the engine was stopped after landing, it was covered by a canvas shroud, within which a burner did its best to keep the temperature above freezing. Engine oil was drained and rushed indoors before it solidified. Immediately before takeoff, the oil was heated on a stove

and poured back into the engine. With luck, these precautions allowed flights to proceed. Even as these techniques of operating in remote areas were devised, and more capable aircraft, such as the Noorduyn Norseman and de Havilland Beaver were introduced, the challenge of flying in the far, frozen north remained ever present.

Flying where none had gone before, some bush pilots carved their names into aviation history. Noel Wien was the first airman to fly north of the Arctic Circle, and the first to cross the Bering Strait from North America to the Soviet Union. Bob Reeve made a business out of landing his Fairchild FC-51 on the glaciers of Alaska's Chugach Range. "Punch" Dickens, flying a Fokker Universal, was the first to cross Canada's Barren Lands to the west of Hudson Bay and later to follow the Mackenzie River from Edmonton, Alberta, to Aklavik on the Arctic Ocean. Renowned for his resourcefulness, Dickens once had to improvise repairs to his aircraft after bending the tips of his propeller and breaking an undercarriage strut on ice-hard snow. Using piping from an abandoned boat to repair the strut, he then sawed 6 inches off each blade of the propeller before taking off to fly back to civilization. Harold Gillam was another with a reputation for surviving accidents. His spirit led a young native American to describe him as "He thrill 'em, chill 'em, spill 'em, but no kill 'em Gillam."

One of the blessings brought to the wilderness by aircraft was the ability to respond quickly to medical emergencies. Nowhere was this more capably demonstrated than in the Australian outback. From the earliest days of outback settlement, the greatest fear of the settlers was their inability to cope with serious injury or illness. To reach medical help, patients often had to endure days of uncomfortable travel by cart. Aircraft offered a solution to the problem, but they were of little use if help could not be summoned. Not until the late 1920s was a pedal-driven generator devised that could provide the power for simple Morse code transmitters. Thanks to the untiring efforts of a remarkable clergyman, the Most Reverend John Flynn, the generators were put in place at the outback stations, and a flying doctor service became a practical proposition. On May 15, 1928, a surgeon named K. St. Vincent Welch began work at Cloncurry, Queensland, as the world's first official flying doctor. For several years he continued as the only one, supported by a single pilot and a D.H.50 biplane.

In time, the idea spread until it became established as an everyday part of Australian life, and the example was copied worldwide.

Monoplanes for Britain

Although Imperial Airways had established its worldwide network with a fleet of large flying boats and biplane anachronisms, new land-based monoplanes were needed for the European and Empire routes by the late 1930s. Since 1933, Imperial had been operating four-engined high-wing monoplanes, Armstrong-Whitworth Atalantas, on its Southern African and Far Eastern routes. They had been both reliable and safe, and at the time they were introduced they were the fastest aircraft in Imperial's sedate fleet, cruising at a modest 118 mph. In 1934, an order was placed with Armstrong-Whitworth for a much larger aircraft, the A.W.27 Ensign. At 123 feet across the wing and 111 feet long, the Ensign was the largest airliner produced in Britain before WWII. It was not, however, a success. Beset by development problems, the prototype did not fly until January 1938, and its four 800-horsepower engines then proved inadequate. For all its great size, it carried only twenty-seven passengers on Empire routes and forty over shorter distances in Europe.

The Ensign's performance was improved by the fitting of Wright Cyclones during the war, and a number of the type flew services to Africa and India until 1946.

One of the most beautiful airliners ever built was produced by de Havilland in 1937. The D.H.91 Albatross was a four-engined cantilever low-wing monoplane with a retractable undercarriage. With its tapered wings and slender streamlined fuselage, the Albatross was a classic. Its four 525-horsepower D.H. Gipsy Twelve engines gave it a top speed of 234 mph, making it the fastest prewar British airliner. However, its modern lines and excellent performance were offset in the eyes of prospective customers by its plywood construction, and only five were built. Meantime, de Havilland continued to specialize in light-weight, high-performance wooden aircraft and went on to design the remarkable Mosquito, one of the best multi-role aircraft of WWII.

The de Havilland factory's ability to produce successful aircraft was consistently demonstrated during the 1930s with a series of wood-and-fabric light biplane transports built for small internal airlines. The twin-engined four-passenger D.H.83 Fox Moth of 1932 (154 built) was followed by the D.H.84 Dragon (202) and the

In 1932, de Havilland produced the D.H.83 Fox Moth, with an open cockpit for the pilot and a cabin below for four passengers. Although larger than the popular Tiger Moth, it used its smaller cousin's wings and borrowed many other parts from earlier de Havilland aircraft. Flown principally as a family transport or air taxi, the Fox Moth later proved useful in a number of roles, including navigation training, surveying, and aerial photography.

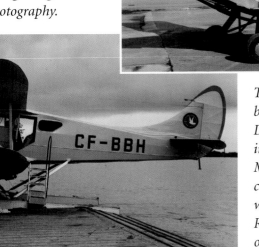

The peak of light transport aircraft development by de Havilland was reached in the D.H.89A Dragon Rapide. First flown in 1934, it remained in production throughout the following decade. More than 700 were built and saw service with civilian and military operators all over the world. Fitted with Fairchild floats, Dragon Rapides were flown on the feeder-line services of Canadian airlines.

four-engined, twelve-passenger D.H.86 (62). The best known of the series came in 1934; the economical and reliable eight-passenger D.H.89 Dragon Rapide. Powered by two D.H. Gipsy Six engines, it cruised at 130 mph and had a range of 580 miles. The D.H.89 and its predecessors saw service in all parts of the world, proving their adaptability to a wide range of local conditions. Jersey Airways, for example, was able to begin services to the Channel Islands in 1933 before airfields were available by operating from island beaches. Over 730 D.H.89s were built, many of which were still flying more than sixty years after the type first flew. Light monoplane transports were produced in Britain by Airspeed; the A.S.5 Courier of 1933 was the first British series production aircraft with a retractable undercarriage, and it was followed by the A.S.6 Envoy, the forerunner of the enormously successful twin-engined military trainer, the A.S.10 Oxford, of which over 8,500 were built.

Among the principal customers for the D.H. biplane airliners were a number of small operators who covered routes not flown by Imperial Airways. Hillman Airways, Spartan Air Lines, United Airways and British Continental Airways, in a move to achieve greater efficiency, joined forces in 1935 to form British Airways. The new company held its own in competition with its European rivals and, as a private company, was not limited to buying British aircraft, unlike the state-sponsored Imperial Airways. The best available aircraft could be acquired, and that often meant choosing airliners such as the Lockheed Electra

from the United States. The commercial success of the new airline and the superiority of its equipment helped to highlight shortcomings in the management of Imperial Airways. A government-appointed committee of inquiry declared that Imperial should undergo drastic reform. In 1938, the British government, with war looming, decided to merge Imperial and British Airways into a nationally owned corporation.

When the British Overseas Airways Corporation finally came into being in 1940, its first duty was to a state already involved in a major war. All thoughts of acquiring new aircraft and consolidating a worldwide network were set aside for the duration. British industry necessarily concentrated on meeting military requirements, and this led to the cancellation of two proposed transport aircraft. The Short S.32 was to have been a pressurized long-haul airliner for the transatlantic route, capable of carrying twenty-four passengers and cruising over its 3,400-mile range at 250 mph. Its companion, the Fairey FC.1, would have taken twenty-six passengers on the shorter overland routes. Both types were under construction but were then abandoned when war broke out. With Germany and Italy similarly affected and France effectively eliminated for the time being, the further development of commercial aircraft was left to the United States.

America's Big Four

With a comprehensive railway system already in place and the national fascination with the automobile well established, the Americans of the 1920s were in no hurry to embrace aerial transport as a way of traveling from place to place within their huge country. Aircraft were still too short-ranged, unreliable and uncomfortable to compete with surface transport, especially since they were not yet fast enough to show significant gains in journey times. The inanimate mails were one thing,

The elegantly streamlined de Havilland 91 Albatross entered service with Imperial Airways in 1938. Twenty-one passengers could be carried at a cruising speed of 210 mph. Only seven were built, and were flown as the "F" series, with names such as Frobisher and Fortuna.

First flown in 1928, Boeing's Model 80 had a fuselage made of welded-steel tubing covered with fabric, and its wooden wingtips were removable so the aircraft could fit into the primitive hangars along its routes. It was the first American airliner designed with passenger comfort and convenience in mind. Initially some pilots were dismayed at being asked to work within an enclosed flight deck, but they, too, soon became accustomed to flying in the absence of an icy blast.

but thinking passengers were another. Intercontinental travel was even less considered. The aircraft that had managed to cross the oceans up to then were obviously unsuitable for passengers (the R 34 airship apart), and those who had flown them were regarded as courageous adventurers, a race apart from ordinary human beings. Paradoxically, it was just such an adventurer, in a single-seat aircraft, who began to change people's minds about the possibilities of air travel. Charles Lindbergh's Atlantic crossing in 1927 fired the imagination of the American public and was instrumental in spurring the development of commercial aviation in the United States.

Although it was air mail that laid the foundations of the airlines in the United States during the 1920s, it would not be true to say that no passengers were being carried. From March 1925, Ryan Airlines operated a passenger service between Los Angeles and San Diego, and Ford carried passengers on its CAM routes out of Detroit from August 1925. Others carrying people as well as mail in the late 1920s included Western Air Express, Colonial Air Transport, Philadelphia Rapid Transit Service, and Boeing, who built a fleet of Model 40A biplanes for the San Francisco-to-Chicago route. However, mail remained the priority; the 40As were designed to carry 1,200 pounds of mail and just two passengers.

With the acquisition of larger aircraft and the rise of flying fever after Lindbergh's achievement, the volume of passenger traffic began to rise. Maddux Air Lines opened a Los Angeles – San Diego service with Ford Trimotors in June 1927, and Standard Airlines began flying Fokker F.VIIs between Los Angeles and Phoenix in November 1927. Boeing

began to catch up in 1928, introducing its own three-engined Model 80s with seats for twelve to eighteen passengers. It was on these aircraft that the first air stewardesses appeared in 1930. In 1928, Transcontinental Air Transport (TAT) was formed and quickly enlarged when it acquired Maddux Air Lines within six months. Ford Trimotors were employed by TAT in an arrangement with the railways that took passengers from New York to Los Angeles in just 48 hours, using overnight rail sleepers from New York to Ohio and from Oklahoma to New Mexico, and day flights, with meals provided, for the remaining legs. Pitcairn Aviation began offering seats in Mailwings between the East Coast cities, and both Pitcairn and TAT introduced the large Curtiss Condor biplanes to their routes in 1930.

All of this fragmented activity did not please Walter Folger Brown, appointed as President Hoover's Postmaster General in 1929. He believed that the nation would be best served by an airline industry that was better organized, with several major competing transcontinental lines and a connecting network of strategically placed feeder lines covering the country. Brown also wanted to see larger, more efficient aircraft in service, offering greater passenger-carrying capacity. As a politician, he was keen to see the government's mail subsidies decline, a possibility if passenger traffic expanded sufficiently. He was aware, too, that an air transport industry that encouraged aircraft manufacturers to build better machines could be important to national defense, helping to create a strong industrial base to support military aviation. Brown used his powers to brush aside the objections of the airline operators, force a series of amalgamations, and establish a number of main transcontinental trunk routes.

FORD TRIMOTOR

Developed from the single-engine Stout Pullman, Ford's ubiquitous Trimotors were produced in various forms, but all were known by the nickname "Tin Goose." The 4-AT version first flew on June 11, 1926, and was later built with wheel, float and ski landing gear. Power was provided by three 300-horsepower Pratt & Whitney Wasp Junior or Wright J-6 engines. Construction was simple and rugged, with most working parts (engines, undercarriage, control cables) clearly visible and easily reached. Ford Trimotors played an important part in developing the U.S. domestic route system and flew with more than 100 airlines in all parts of the world.

Seen beneath the left wing of the EAA's Trimotor at Oshkosh is the oldest surviving example of a Spartan Executive. Built in 1937, the five-seater could cruise at over 200 mph and was unusual for a light transport in having a stick rather than a wheel in the cockpit.

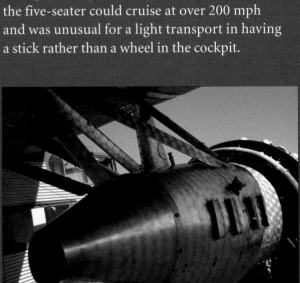

BOEING MODEL 80

The Seattle Museum of Flight's Boeing Model 80A-1 was retired from United Air Lines in 1934. In 1941, it became a cargo aircraft with a construction firm in Alaska. It was recovered from a dump in 1960 and taken to Seattle for restoration. It is the only surviving example of the Boeing Model 80 series. The next generation, in the form of a Douglas DC-3, hovers in the background.

THIS PAGE
TOP The Model 80 brought some comfort to travel — a heated cabin, leather seats, individual reading lights and a lavatory with hot and cold running water. Note the outsize flight instruments mounted at the front of the passenger compartment. The Model 80's biplane configuration was a comforting asset, too, keeping landing speeds low at the high-altitude airports along Boeing Air Transport's San Francisco-to-Chicago route.
BOTTOM In 1930, Miss Ellen Church, a student pilot and registered nurse, convinced Boeing that they should hire female cabin attendants for their Model 80 flights. Until then, it had been the co-pilot's duty to pass out box lunches, serve coffee, and tend to the passengers' needs. She and seven other nurses became America's first stewardesses.

His dictatorial methods gained him many enemies, but Brown ignored criticism. He believed that imposed solutions were best, and he was sure that his choices would serve the national interest. He had no qualms about admitting that: "Competitive bidding in the air mail business is more or less of a myth."

As the dust settled during the months that followed, America's "Big Four" emerged. Transcontinental Air Transport and Western Air Express were pressed together to become Transcontinental and Western Air (TWA), a company that would later keep its initials while changing its name to Trans-World Airlines. American Airways (later American Airlines) had its origins in a dozen smaller companies, and Eastern Air Transport (later Eastern Airlines) was born by joining four, including Pitcairn and the Ludington Line, one of the few early airlines to put passengers ahead of

The Curtiss T-32 Condor was the last biplane airliner built in the U.S. From 1933, forty-five were manufactured, most of which were operated by Eastern Air Transport and American Airlines. As American Airlines took pains to point out, their Condors offered the only transcontinental sleeper service, providing six two-berth compartments from New York to Chicago and Dallas. Safe and comfortable, the Condor was nevertheless soon overtaken by modern monoplanes such as the Boeing 247 and Douglas DC-2.

mail and make a profit. The fourth giant was United Air Lines, founded on such stalwarts as Boeing Air Transport, Varney Air Lines, and Pacific Air Transport. The Brown plan thereby reduced some thirty airlines to four. However, a host of smaller companies remained, over forty of them providing essential feeder services and operating perhaps 500 aircraft between them in the process. With these national building blocks in place, U.S. civil aviation expanded rapidly during the 1930s, establishing itself as the world leader both in terms of traffic volume and in the quality of the transport aircraft flown.

Landplane Leadership

As the number of airline passengers increased in the U.S., so did the demand for more comfortable aircraft and shorter journey times. Reliable though they were, the Ford and Fokker trimotors were noisy and slow, with minimal creature comforts. In 1930, Boeing began to change that with two aircraft called Monomail, sleek single-engined, low-winged cantilever monoplanes of all-metal construction. Markedly advance in design though the Monomail was, however, it was no more than a step toward its remarkable successor, the Boeing 247, an airliner designed to revolutionize air travel. The 247 was a clean, all-metal, stressed-skin, low-wing cantilever monoplane with two neatly cowled engines and a retractable undercarriage. Other sophistications included trim tabs controlled from the cockpit, and, on the 247D, variable-pitch propellers. From the moment of the 247's first flight in February 1933, all other passenger aircraft seemed obsolete. It was small, with seats for only ten passengers, but it was at least 50 mph faster than the existing trimotors and had lower operating costs. United Air Lines, aware of the aircraft's potential from the design stage, ordered sixty, a massive order that monopolized production.

United's monopoly of the 247s had the unforeseen consequence of forcing TWA, now facing the prospect of being unable to compete on an equal footing, to seek new aircraft elsewhere. In August 1932, in a letter to Douglas Aircraft, TWA set out its requirements for a trimotor capable of carrying twelve passengers and cruising at 145 mph over a 1,000-mile range. The safety margin of three engines was still thought to be desirable. Douglas responded with a proposal for a twin-engined aircraft, noting that it would need to survive an engine failure on takeoff with a full load at any airport used by TWA. Acceptance of the proposal led to the DC-1, which first flew on July 1, 1933. It was a revelation, a truly modern airliner that more than matched the 247. In a proving flight across the continent, the DC-1 made it nonstop from Burbank, California, to New York in 11 hours, 5 minutes. With its fuselage stretched by 2 feet and seats for fourteen passengers, it was produced as the DC-2. The DC-2 dramatically confirmed its promise to the world when it won the handicap trophy and came second overall to the specially built D.H. Comet in the 1934 England-to-Australia air race, covering the 11,123 miles in

Steps in the Douglas progression to airliner dominance in the 1930s, from top to bottom: DC-1, DC-2 and DC-3. Originally the Douglas Sleeper Transport, the DC-3 became the most successful piston-engined transport ever built once the sleeping berths were removed. Docile enough in its handling qualities to endear itself to generations of aircrew and simple to maintain, the DC-3 was sufficiently rugged to endure endless punishment from rough fields, severe weather and ham-handed pilots. It was supremely adaptable for all sorts of roles, both civilian and military. By 1939, DC-3s accounted for some 90 percent of the world's airline business. Built primarily in the U.S. but also under licence in the Soviet Union and Japan, over 17,000 DC-3s and derivatives were manufactured and many remained in regular use beyond the end of the 20th century.

The shape of success in commercial aviation in the 1920s and 1930s. Increasingly muscular and reliable radials led the way in the rapid expansion of the world's airline traffic between the world wars. This is a Wright R-1820-G2 Cyclone, the single engine at the business end of the Virginia Aviation Museum's beautifully restored Vultee V-1A, an eight-seat airliner of the early 1930s.

3 days, 18 hours, 17 minutes. Over 200 DC-2s were built and were operated by a variety of airlines, including TWA, American, Eastern and Pan American in the U.S., plus KLM, Iberia, Swissair and a number of others overseas.

Successful though the DC-2 was, it was the harbinger of greater things to come. American Airlines needed to replace the Curtiss Condors of its transcontinental sleeper service. American's president, C.R. Smith, wanted a larger version of the DC-2, with room for fourteen sleeping berths.

Initially reluctant, Donald Douglas was persuaded by Smith's promise to buy twenty aircraft. So was born, almost by accident, the most celebrated transport of the piston-engined era. The DST (Douglas Sleeper Transport) first flew on a day heavy with significance in aviation history. It was December 17, 1935, thirty-two years after Kittyhawk. The DST was noticeably larger than the DC-2, with a fuselage over 2 feet wider and a 95-foot wingspan. It entered transcontinental service as a sleeper in September 1936, but the Douglas assessment that the market for such an aircraft would be limited was correct, and not many were built. However, with the berths removed, the fuselage could accommodate twenty-one seats, and a modified version appeared — the Douglas DC-3.

The DC-3 deserves to be regarded as one of the greatest aircraft ever produced. Initially fitted with 1,000-horsepower Wright Cyclones, it was most often supplied with 1,200-horsepower Pratt & Whitney Twin Wasps. These gave it a cruising speed of 170 mph over an average stage length of 500 miles. Good figures though these were in the mid-1930s, the secrets of the DC-3's success and longevity lie in its sterling qualities as a transport aircraft. Pilots loved it for its forgiving nature, and engineers for the ease with which it was kept flying. Its reliability became legendary, and it was rugged enough to survive the punishment of operating from rough fields and in all kinds of weather. No aircraft, before or since, has matched the DC-3's adaptability — main-route airliner, feederliner, freighter, executive aircraft, and military jack-of-all-trades.

From the beginning, the DC-3's potential was obvious and the Douglas factory was inundated with orders, the U.S. military becoming the largest customer for a version designated C-47. By the time production stopped, a total of 17,299 DC-3s (and derivatives) had been produced; these included 10,654 built in the U.S., 6,157 in the Soviet Union (Li-2s), and 487 in Japan. Their contributions during WWII were so substantial that General Eisenhower rated the C-47 as one of the four most significant items of war-winning equipment. They went on to see

combat again in Korea and in Vietnam, where they were in action as both transports and gunships. After WWII, large numbers of surplus C-47s were converted for civil use and operated into every corner of the globe, from the Arctic's icefields to the dirt strips of the Australian outback. At one time or another, DC-3 types have been flown by almost all of the world's airlines and air forces, and it has proved impossible to replace them with a single type of such wide-ranging capability. Many examples were still flying at the end of the 20th century, more than sixty years after the DST's first flight. Few aircraft can lay claim to such an illustrious history.

The DC-2/3 series was dominant, but Douglas was not the only U.S. aircraft manufacturer to establish a successful line in the 1930s. In 1934, Lockheed introduced the ten-passenger L.10 Electra, a high-speed, twin-engined, all-metal airliner. Smaller than their Boeing and Douglas rivals, they were also faster, and they found immediate favor with airlines in the U.S. and overseas. The much improved L.14 Super Electra followed in 1937. It could cruise at 215 mph with twelve passengers, and its innovations included fixed wingtip slots and Fowler flaps, which increased the wing area for landing. It was the first airliner to enter service with constant-speed, feathering propellers and two-stage superchargers. The eighteen-seat L.18 appeared in 1939 and was the most numerous of the series; 625 were built in the U.S. and another 121 in Japan as the Kawasaki 56.

Fairchild Type 91 *by Robert Taylor, courtesy of the Military Gallery, Bath, U.K. Fairchild 91s were operated by a Pan American subsidiary, Panair do Brasil, and were nicknamed "Jungle Clippers" because of their service in the Amazon region during the 1930s and 1940s. Robert Taylor's sketch shows a 91 leaving its Santos Dumont base at Rio de Janeiro en route to Belem.*

BOEING 247

The Boeing 247 led the way in revolutionizing air travel in the 1930s. It was a low-wing, all-metal, stressed-skin twin-engined monoplane with a retractable undercarriage. Two 550-horsepower Pratt & Whitney Wasp radials provided the power and Hamilton Standard variable-pitch propellers gave the thrust. De-icing boots were fitted on wings and tail. It carried only ten passengers, but the 247 was some 50 mph faster than the airliners of the time and was cheaper to operate. United Air Lines ordered sixty off the drawing board and was the principal operator. The Boeing 247 at Seattle's Museum of Flight is finished in United Airlines colors and maintained in flying condition. The interior is beautifully restored to its original condition, with a soundproofed cabin and seating spaced to offer plenty of leg room. Trim tab and propeller pitch controls were innovations in an airliner cockpit. The trail-blazing design of the 247 won Bill Boeing the 1934 Guggenheim Medal for "successful pioneering and advancement in aircraft manufacturing and support."

Bigger and Better

In 1936, Douglas had discussions with the Big Four plus Pan American, each of which contributed $100,000 toward the cost of developing a four-engined landplane capable of carrying sixty passengers and their baggage over stages of at least 1,000 miles. The new aircraft, initially designated DC-4, first flew on June 7, 1938. It had a triple-finned tail and was the first airliner equipped with a nose-wheel undercarriage. Maintenance problems and disappointing performance led to the aircraft being redesignated DC-4E and used for experimental flying only. The design was shelved and work began on a smaller, simpler DC-4, but it was not ready to fly until 1942.

Meanwhile, in 1935, Boeing had drawn up an ambitious specification for a four-engined airliner, but orders were not forthcoming until 1937, when construction began. Taking the wings, tail and nacelles of the B-17 bomber as the starting point, Boeing added a tubby circular section fuselage capable of carrying thirty-three passengers and five crew to produce the Model 307 Stratoliner. Boeing's concentration on the wartime production of combat aircraft resulted in only ten 307s being built. The prototype was lost during the test program, five went to TWA and three to Pan American. The tenth was sold to Howard Hughes, who had it equipped as a luxurious executive aircraft. Small though the production run was, the Stratoliner was a significant step toward the next generation of airliners and along the road to Boeing's eventual domination of the aircraft industry. It was the first airliner to have a pressurized, air-conditioned fuselage, a feature that made it possible to operate regular passenger services consistently at altitudes well above 10,000 feet.

Plus One

While the Big Four dominated U.S. skies, another airline made its mark internationally. During the 1930s, driven by the determination of Juan Trippe, Pan American Airways grew from its small beginnings as a Caribbean air mail carrier to become the world's largest airline. In the process of shaping Pan American's growth, Trippe often exerted political muscle and rode roughshod over his competition, but the result was an airline that served as a standard bearer for U.S. interests worldwide, and was a testament to his vision of a world made smaller by air travel. Building on the bedrock function of delivering the mail, Pan American first created a network of routes in the Caribbean before expanding to reach the Panama Canal, and then the countries of South America. By the end of 1931, Sikorsky S-40 passenger services extended as far as Santiago, Montevideo and Buenos Aires.

Trippe's airline inevitably had an effect on the affairs of the countries it served. The economic growth, and thereby the social conditions, of the region improved as the various societies, previously relatively remote from one another, were linked by air. Pan American aircraft were seen as symbols of the U.S. administration's "Good Neighbor Policy," and besides their scheduled flights, they undertook humanitarian missions, carrying aid to victims of earthquake, storm and revolution. Some critics, both in the United States and overseas, accused Pan American of becoming too influential in international affairs, but that was probably unjustified; Juan Trippe's aim, as his competitors knew only too well, was to see Pan American make a profit and become an airline of world stature, if necessary by enveloping the competition.

Boeing B307 *by Robert Taylor, courtesy of the Military Gallery, Bath, U.K. Clipper Flying Cloud is seen being loaded at San Juan, Puerto Rico.*

The third and greatest of the Pan American Clippers, and arguably the finest flying boat airliner ever built, was the Boeing 314. First flown in 1938, no civil transport surpassed the 314 in size until the introduction of the Boeing 747 on the transatlantic route in 1970. Boeing's giant Clipper exemplified the gracious days of air travel, offering its passengers comfortable seats, sleeping berths, washrooms, lounge, bar, and a dining room serving meals prepared by celebrated chefs.

In pursuit of his ambitions, Trippe was keen to add the Pacific to his empire. In the summer of 1931, Charles and Anne Lindbergh surveyed a northern route to China via Alaska and Japan, but the U.S. State Department opposed the idea, citing a lack of diplomatic relations with the Soviet Union and deteriorating relations with Japan. The alternative was to use U.S. Pacific islands, but the problems of flying to such tiny destinations over immense stretches of water were formidable. The crossing to Hawaii was the longest over-water flight in the world, and neither Midway nor Wake had the facilities to handle either large aircraft or their passengers. Further on, Guam and the Philippines posed lesser problems. Gambling on the likelihood of an air mail contract, Trippe sent parties to Midway, Wake and Guam in 1935 to build the necessary facilities — air bases, radio stations, hotels — and had survey flights completed by his senior pilot, Captain Eddie Musick, in a Sikorsky S-42. Trials of radio direction finders were carried out and aircrews trained for blind radio-beam approaches. The aircraft with the necessary range and capacity was found in the Martin M-130 flying boat. It was large and graceful, and well equipped from the points of view of safety and comfort. It had dual hydraulic and electrical systems, and its sturdy hull was fitted with multiple bulkheads. Up to thirty-two passengers could be accommodated, with sleeping berths for eighteen, and there was a crew of eight. With fourteen passengers plus a ton of cargo, the M-130 had a range of some 3,200 miles. Its customary cruising speed with a full load was 130 mph. Three M-130s were

built and were named *China, Philippine* and *Hawaii Clippers*. (All three *Clippers* were destroyed in fatal accidents. *Hawaii* disappeared without trace east of Manila in 1938. *Philippine* hit a mountain in cloud near San Francisco in 1943. *China*, the most famous of the three, flew over 3 million miles and survived until 1945, when it crashed during a night landing at Port of Spain, Trinidad.)

To ensure Pacific success, Trippe followed his practice of buying up airlines along the route. He acquired a controlling interest in two Hawaiian airlines — Inter-Island Airways and South Seas Commercial — and in the China National Aviation Corporation. Once an air mail contract was secured, he needed only permission from the British authorities in Hong Kong to carry his route beyond Manila and complete the link with China. British reluctance, inspired by a wish to exclude a competitor to Imperial Airways from the Chinese market, was overcome by initiating negotiations with the Portuguese in nearby Macao. In October 1936, passenger service aboard a Martin *Clipper* was available as far as Manila, and from April 1937, passage was offered all the way to the Chinese mainland. A southern route to New Zealand followed in December 1937, but was suspended after only nine months following two highly publicized fatal accidents to Pan American aircraft that diminished public confidence and reduced transpacific passenger traffic sharply. (These were the *Hawaii Clipper* accident and the loss of a Sikorsky S-42B, together with Captain Eddie Musick and his crew, in a midair explosion near Samoa.)

Stratoliner

Flying Fortress

Clipper

Broader Wings
NOW SPAN THE NATION

THE 1930s: PUBLICITY

Publicity campaigns promoted the aviation companies of the 1930s. Boeing touted aircraft for national defense and for crossing oceans and continents, while TWA spanned the nation and showed cleancut crews in smart uniforms standing in front of shiny new aircraft. Wright engines launched the air age and powered the tonnage of the air.

What cost per ton mile?

Launching THE AIR AGE

Gangplank TO THE AIR AGE

The real payload is the full load

Tons against Time

MODERN ATLAS

In the late 1930s, Zoe Dell Lantis Nutter was employed by the Golden Gate International Exposition as official hostess for the event on Treasure Island in San Francisco. She traveled more than 100,000 miles by air to publicize the fair and promote travel on commercial airlines, later becoming one of the first attendants on passenger airplanes. Also an aviator, Mrs. Nutter has logged more than 2,000 hours as a commercial, multi-engine, instrument pilot, served in the Civil Air Patrol, flown search-and-rescue missions, and having served as president and chair of the board, is a lifetime member of the National Aviation Hall of Fame.

Airline timetables of the 1930s frequently showed good-looking, brightly smiling passengers rushing off cheerfully to exotic destinations. Given the weather through which piston-engined airliners often had to fly, many of the smiles may have been a little forced by the time they arrived.

THE 1930S: CINCINNATI AIRPORT

Completed in 1937, the Lunken Terminal represents the early days of air travel. The airfield had been active since the early 1920s and was formally dedicated by the city of Cincinnati, Ohio, in 1930, becoming the largest municipal airport in the United States.

Embry-Riddle Company, an air mail service company, was founded in 1925 in Cincinnati. In 1927, Embry-Riddle won the contract to deliver mail from Cincinnati to Chicago, and on December 17 of the same year, began flights from Lunken airport using a fleet of ten Waco biplanes. Embry-Riddle was later folded into a larger corporation, AVCO, and in January 1930, reorganized as American Airways, the basis for the future American Airlines.

The murals were painted by William H. Gothard, the painting shown here representing man free of the burdens of surface transportation. Mr. Gothard was the chief conservationist of the Cincinnati Art Museum in 1937.

Prewar propeller-driven airliners such as the Curtiss Condor, Boeing 247, and DC-3s would have taxied onto the ramp just in front of this art deco building. Air travel at that time was a special privilege.

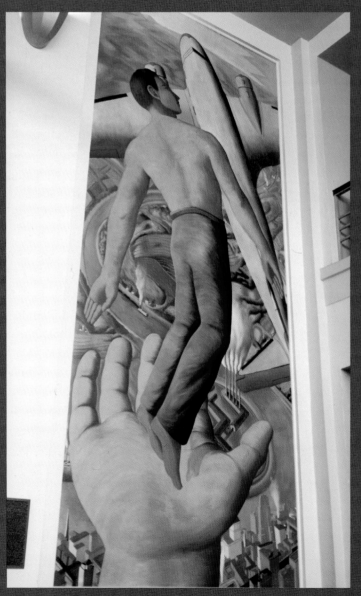

The second four-engined Clipper flying boat to be produced for Pan American Airways was the Martin 130. It was a large, graceful, high-wing aircraft, capable of carrying thirty-two passengers, but limited to fourteen on long-distance transoceanic routes. It was not fast, cruising at 130 mph, but it was as roomy and comfortable as a piston-engined airliner could be made. Just three M-130s were built — named China, Philippine and Hawaii Clippers. They performed magnificently during their relatively brief lives, but all three were eventually lost in fatal accidents.

Refusing to be discouraged, Trippe turned his attention to the Atlantic. Again, there was a problem with the British. It had been agreed that the airlines of the two countries would not initiate a transatlantic service until both were ready, and the British did not yet have a suitable aircraft. Survey flights were carried out by Pan American and Imperial in 1937, using a Sikorsky S-42B and the Short C class *Caledonia,* but neither was then capable of regular passenger services. Now, when Trippe was ready, he was temporarily stymied, since one of the essential Atlantic stepping stones was the British island of Bermuda. Relief for Pan American was at hand, however, in the shape of arguably the greatest civil flying boat ever built, the Boeing 314. It was the largest commercial aircraft to enter service until the appearance of Boeing's 747 thirty years later. Under the wing designed for the huge XB-15 bomber, Boeing hung a capacious double-decked hull capable of holding seventy-four seated passengers or forty in sleeping berths, plus washrooms, a galley, a bar and a dining room. The crew of ten occupied the upper deck, from where the engineers could use walkways inside the wings to reach the engines in flight. Powered by four 1,500-horsepower Wright Double Cyclones, a fully loaded 314 had a range of over 4,000 miles when cruising at 180 mph.

The first of twelve Boeing 314s built, *Yankee Clipper,* was test flown on June 7, 1938. Pan American could now ignore the need for Atlantic stepping stones and bypass Bermuda. In May 1939, *Yankee Clipper* was sent off on an inaugural transatlantic service that avoided Britain, too, flying to Lisbon and Marseilles via the Azores. Accepting the inevitable, and preoccupied with the threat of war, the British gave in and allowed Pan American to operate into the U.K. The scheduled passenger service from New York to Southampton, England, was opened by *Dixie Clipper* on June 28, 1939, and *Yankee Clipper* inaugurated a more northerly route via Botwood, Newfoundland, and Foynes, Ireland, on July 8. The one-way fare was $375. The final link in global circumnavigation was in place, and a determined passenger could fly round the world in ten days or so, but it had all come too late to become common practice. Within a few weeks, Europe was at war, and the Boeing 314s could go no further than the neutral ports of Foynes and Lisbon. By the time the fighting was over, the aviation world had changed. The heyday of the great flying boats was ended, and Juan Trippe's Pan American would never again be the dominant force it had been in the 1930s, when it had pretensions to being a colossus of global proportions, and the world's greatest airline.

CHAPTER 4

Great Names

*"When my brother and I built and flew the first
man-carrying machine, we thought that we were
introducing into the world an invention which
would make further wars practically impossible."*

ORVILLE WRIGHT, 1917

THE MEN WHO FOUNDED the world's aviation industries were as diverse as the aircraft they went on to produce. There were inspirational designers and superb engineers among them, but some just loved the adventure of flying, while others were industrial entrepreneurs with an eye to the future. A few were not only extraordinarily talented but were born into noble families or inherited great wealth, but most were from more humble backgrounds and rose to prominence in aviation because of natural brilliance, determined character or a combination of both. Given that the world of aeronautics was not shocked into real life until the Wright brothers gave their demonstrations to a wider world in 1908, it is perhaps only to be expected that almost two-thirds of them came from the generation born in the 1880s and 1890s. Those featured here, in alphabetical order, are a few of the most significant from France, Italy, Russia, Hungary, Poland, Germany, Holland, Japan, Britain and the United States, but there were many others from elsewhere who had important contributions to make.

OPPOSITE PAGE
Elrey Jeppesen (1907–96) had his pilot's licence signed by Orville Wright. He flew as a barnstormer with Tex Rankin's Flying Circus, and as a commercial pilot with Varney, Boeing and United Airlines. Early in his career he began keeping notes about the routes he flew and airfields he visited, charting radio beacons and let-down procedures. (He claimed that originally his principal intention was to record where to eat and where the restrooms were.) In 1934, Jeppesen published his first Airway Manual, *subsequently developed into a comprehensive system of manuals and charts indispensable to pilots of all kinds. In 1983, Jeppesen was named by the National Aeronautic Association as an Elder Statesman of Aviation for his outstanding contributions to flying. He was later inducted into the National Aviation Hall of Fame. The items of aviation memorabilia shown here were collected by Jeppensen. They are held at the Museum of Flight, Seattle.*

OLEG KONSTANTINOVICH ANTONOV (1906–1984)

Antonov was a Soviet designer from the Moscow region. He graduated from the Leningrad Polytechnic in 1930 and rose through the aircraft industry to become Senior Designer with the Ministry of Aviation after WWII and Designer General in 1962, the year in which he won the Lenin Prize. He was awarded the Order of Lenin twice, and was Deputy to the Supreme Soviet from 1958 to 1966. Anotonov was particularly associated with the large aircraft that formed the backbone of the Soviet transport fleet, both civil and military, notably the AN-22 (world records for payload to height, 1967, and speed with payload, 1972/75), and the AN-124/225 (world's largest aircraft; payload-to-height records, 1985). The rugged and adaptable AN-2 biplane was instrumental in opening up remote areas of the Soviet Union. Over 13,000 were built, operating in various land and floatplane versions specialized for agriculture, freight, firefighting, medical emergency, troop-carrying, photographic survey, television relay, meteorological research, and local passenger transport.

Antonov AN-124.

WALTER H. BEECH (1891–1950)

Walter Herschel Beech began his career in aviation by building a glider of his own design when he was fourteen. A U.S. Army aviator in 1917, he later joined the Swallow Airplane Company, where he rose from test pilot to General Manager. In 1924, Walter Beech co-founded Travel Air Manufacturing Company with Clyde Cessna; the company became the world's largest producer of both monoplane and biplane commercial aircraft. The machines they built received international acclaim by establishing more than 200 performance records. When Travel Air merged with the Curtiss-Wright Airplane Company, Walter Beech became president of the new corporation. However, he desired a more personal participation in aircraft design and manufacture and so co-founded Beech Aircraft Company with his wife, Olive Ann, in 1932. His early Beechcrafts set many distance and speed records and won the prestigious Bendix and McFadden races. Perhaps the most novel among these, with design features years ahead of its time, was the Beech Model 17 Staggerwing biplane. During WWII, Beech turned the entire production of his company over to defense and produced more than 7,400 military aircraft. The C-45 Twin Beech trained over 90 percent of the navigator/bombardiers and 50 percent of the multi-engine pilots for the USAAF. After the war, Walter Beech again applied his genius to producing a new line of light aircraft, the most famous of which was the V-tailed Bonanza.

Beechcraft Bonanza, introduced in 1947.

WILLIAM BOEING (1881–1956)

William Boeing was active in aviation for only eighteen years, but few men can have had such a lasting influence on the aviation industry. A wealthy lumberman in the Pacific Northwest, he had an interest in aviation quickened in 1914 by a flight in a Curtiss pusher float-plane piloted by a barnstormer named Maroney. In 1915, Boeing learned to fly at the Glenn Martin flight school in Los Angeles, and then joined Conrad Westervelt in designing and building an aircraft known as the B&W. Boeing himself carried out the first flight of the B&W (Boeing Model No. 1) on June 29, 1916, and in July he formed the Pacific Aero Products Company to build aircraft that could compete with Curtiss designs. A few months later, with the U.S. drawn into WWI, the first of many government contracts was awarded and the name was changed to the Boeing Airplane Company. By the late 1920s, it had become one of the largest aircraft manufacturers in the United States. The Boeing Company's early success can be largely attributed to the founder's insistence on quality, and to his belief

> *"Our job is to keep everlasting at research and experimentation, to adapt our laboratories to production as soon as possible, and to let no new improvement in flying and flying equipment pass us by."*
>
> WILLIAM E. BOEING, 1929

in the importance of research and development. In 1919, Bill Boeing started a small commercial service, flying mail from Seattle to Victoria, Canada, in his own floatplanes. With this experience gained, in 1926 he made a successful bid to carry mail between San Francisco and Chicago using the Boeing Model 40. To meet the demands of this new venture, he formed the Boeing Air Transport Company, which, in the course of several mergers and acquisitions, became the United Aircraft and Air Transport Corporation, an industrial giant that both built and operated aircraft through its various companies. In 1934, the Air Mail Act decreed that no airline could be directly associated with a company that built aircraft. Bill Boeing was ordered to split his corporation three ways, into the Boeing Airplane Company, the United Aircraft Corporation, and United Air Lines. Bitter at the enforced dismemberment, he resigned and left the aircraft industry, leaving behind him a legacy that helped to shape the future of American commercial and military aviation.

Bill Boeing (center) and Eddie Hubbard (left) prepare to take off in Seattle on the first international air mail delivery from the United States, on March 2, 1919. The next day, the mail was delivered in Vancouver, Canada.

Louis Breguet (1880–1955)

Louis Charles Breguet's family background was in science and engineering, and his interest in aeronautics developed at an early age. In 1905 he built a wind tunnel and began to study the effects of airflow on aerofoils. He was among the few pioneer aircraft designers who grasped the need for thorough preflight testing and the importance of high-quality construction in ensuring that his aircraft were safe to fly. He experimented with rotary-winged flight in 1907 and produced his first fixed-wing aircraft in 1909. His Breguet IV of 1910, nicknamed "the coffee pot," was the first aircraft to lift six people off the ground at once, and on April 22, 1911, *Scientific American* reported that Breguet

himself had flown one of his biplanes for a distance of 5 kilometers with eleven passengers on board. This was believed to be the first time that an aircraft had flown carrying a load equal to its own weight. World War I assured the success of his company, generating orders for some 5,500 of the rugged Breguet 14 reconnaissance aircraft for the Allies. More than 8,000 14s were built by the time production ended in 1926. His more advanced Breguet 19 made history in the postwar years for its ability to fly long distances across oceans and continents, becoming the first aircraft to succeed in nonstop flights across the South Atlantic and from Paris to New York. In 1919, Breguet founded a commercial air transport company, the Compagnie des Messageries Aériennes, which became part of the national airline, Air France, in 1933. Breguet remained an important manufacturer of military aircraft in WWII and afterward produced several large four-engined transports. The Breguet name survived the progressive post-WWII rationalization of the French aircraft industry, eventually merging with Dassault to become Avions Dassault-Breguet.

Breguet 14 A2.

Sydney Camm (1893–1966)

After leaving school at the age of fifteen, Sydney Camm became an apprentice carpenter. He had a consuming interest in making model airplanes and was a founding member of the Windsor Model Aeroplane Club in 1912. He joined the Martin and Handasyde Aircraft Company as a woodworker on the shop floor in 1914, but by the end of WWI had been promoted to the drawing office. In 1923, he was taken on as a senior draftsman at Sopwith's Hawker Engineering Company, and just two years later he was appointed chief designer, a post he held until his death over forty years later. His reputation was that of a hard-driving and intolerant taskmaster, but the results of his efforts speak for themselves. From his earliest years as the Chief, Camm's designs formed a significant part of the Royal Air Force's front line. The Hart and Fury were among the most successful military biplanes of the 1930s,

and the Hurricane bore the brunt of the German assault during the Battle of Britain. Later in the war, the Hawker Typhoon and Tempest proved themselves in the ground-attack role and against the V-1 "flying bombs."

For the jet age, Camm provided the Royal Navy's Sea Hawk and the swept-wing Hunter, which saw service in numerous air forces worldwide. The final masterpiece produced by the Hawker team under his leadership was the world's first successful V/STOL combat aircraft, which entered service with the Royal Air Force in 1969 as the Harrier and was later adopted by the U.S. Marine Corps.

GIANNI CAPRONI, CONTE DE TALIEDO (1886–1957)

Gianni Caproni graduated in civil engineering from the Polytechnic Institute of Munich in 1907. Other degrees followed in electrical engineering from the Montefiore Institute of Leige, and in aeronautical engineering from his studies in Paris. After returning to his native Italy in 1910, he designed and built his first airplane, a single-engine, twin-propeller biplane, the Ca.1. The next year he established the Caproni Company and Flight School, the forerunner of the Caproni organization that was to build 180 different types of aircraft over the next half a century. During World War I, Caproni designed a number of heavy bombers that played a major role in the Allied strategic bombing campaign. The highly successful Ca.33 bomber design was mass produced in England, France and the United States as well as Italy, with an unprecedented total of 745 bombers manufactured by the Milan Caproni works alone. Postwar, Caproni turned his design talents to civil aviation, converting his famous bombers to passenger and cargo aircraft. Among these were the Ca.60 transport, capable of carrying 60 passengers; the six-engined, 6,000-horsepower, Ca.90 biplane, which in 1930 set a world's record for altitude and duration; and the Ca.161, which in 1938 flew to an altitude record for propeller-driven aircraft of 56,000 feet. During WWII he was in charge of all aircraft production in Italy. Between aircraft designs, Gianni Caproni devised and patented many components, including armored and variable-pitch propellers, an anemometer, an engine compressor, steerable undercarriages, and a machine gun driven by centrifugal force. He was awarded the title Count of Taliedo by the King of Italy in 1940 and remained active in his company until his death in 1957.

CLYDE CESSNA (1880–1954)

Clyde Cessna developed his engineering aptitude by working on farm equipment in Kansas, and in time he acquired an automobile dealership. He saw his first airplanes in 1911, the Blériots of John Moisant's aerial exhibition team, and immediately ordered a Blériot fuselage from a catalogue. After designing and building the wings at home, he began teaching himself to fly. More than a dozen crashes later, he abandoned the automobile business and became a barnstormer. For a while during WWI he was involved in manufacturing aircraft in a small way, but it was not until 1924 that he joined Walter Beech in establishing Travel Air. Cessna's wish to build fully cantilevered monoplanes led to design disputes that drove him to separate from Beech in 1927 and form his own company. He produced a series of high-wing cabin monoplanes until the early 1930s, when the onset of the Depression forced a temporary closure of the factory. Production was resumed in 1934 and Cessna aircraft were again successful, being produced in quantity, principally for the private market. Clyde Cessna retired in 1937, handing over the reins to his nephew and one of his sons. As is evident from the number of Cessnas to be found on the flight line of almost any airport, the company Clyde Cessna founded has continued to flourish and has left its mark on aviation the world over, especially at the level of the flying club and the private owner.

Cessna 172.

GLENN CURTISS (1878–1930)

Like his contemporaries, the Wright brothers, Glenn Curtiss was originally a bicycle mechanic. He established a motorcycle factory at Hammondsport, New York, in 1902, and in 1905 set a world speed record of 137 mph riding one of his own machines. Together with Alexander Graham Bell he formed the Aerial Experiment Association in 1907 and, flying the *June Bug*, won the prize for the first public flight in the United States to cover one kilometer. At Reims in 1909 he won the Gordon Bennett cup in his *Golden Arrow* at a speed of 46.5 mph. He had a boundless enthusiasm for flying: "It is hard enough for anyone to map out a course of action and stick to it, particularly in the face of the desires of one's friends; but it is doubly hard for an aviator to stay on the ground waiting for just the right moment to go into the air." His introduction of separate ailerons instead of wing-warping for lateral control involved him in a long, damaging legal battle with the Wright brothers over patents. Curtiss also designed the first practical floatplanes and flying boats. During WWI, his JN series of trainers, known as Jennies, set the standard for American military trainers, and after the war they became a favorite mount of barnstormers. In 1919, a Curtiss flying boat, the NC-4, became the first aircraft to fly across the Atlantic. Just as significant were the in-line V Curtiss engines, especially the OX-5 used in the Jenny, and the D-12, which exerted a notable influence on subsequent in-line large engine design, both in the U.S. and elsewhere. Glenn Curtiss made his last flight as a pilot in May 1930, when he flew a Curtiss Condor from Albany to New York, following the route he took twenty years earlier when he won a $10,000 prize for completing the 135-mile journey in 2 hours, 32 minutes. He died just two months later, still a member of the board of the Curtiss-Wright Corporation.

The U.S. Navy flying boat NC-4, the first airplane to cross the Atlantic Ocean in 1919.

MARCEL DASSAULT (1892–1986)

Dassault was a French aviation pioneer from Paris, born Marcel Bloch. As a schoolboy, he was inspired to a life in aviation when he saw Wilbur Wright fly at Le Mans. He joined Henri Potez to build aircraft during WWI and the interwar years. In WWII he was imprisoned in Buchenwald by the Nazis. Subsequently, he became a Roman Catholic and adopted the name Dassault, which had been his brother's code name in the French Resistance. He founded his own company and began building fighters in the 1950s. In the years that followed, the series continued, bearing names such as Ouragan, Mystère, Mirage and Étendard. The company also produced successful small executive jets such as the Falcon. Dassault had an eye for elegant lines and, for the most part, his aircraft reflected his view that "For a plane to fly well it must be beautiful." Besides his work in the aviation industry, Dassault was a successful politician, serving as a deputy in the French National Assembly.

A Dassault Super Mystère, the first Western European fighter capable of Mach 1 in level flight, shares a hangar with three of its successors — Mach 2 Mirage IIIs.

GEOFFREY DE HAVILLAND (1882–1965)

Geoffrey de Havilland taught himself to fly in 1908, using an aircraft and engine that he had designed and built. In 1912, working at the Royal Aircraft Factory, Farnborough, he produced the B.S.1, aviation's first fast single-seat scout (top speed, 92 mph) and the ancestor of all true fighter aircraft. Among his later designs, the D.H.4 was one of WWI's great combat aircraft, and the only European design to be built in any numbers in the U.S. Geoffrey de Havilland formed his own company north of London in 1920, and in 1925 the first of the D.H. Moths appeared. These remarkable light aircraft changed the character of private flying for people all over the world. During WWII, "D.H." (as he was known) produced one of the most effective combat designs of the war in the Mosquito, a very fast twin-engined multi-role aircraft largely made out of wood. In the 1950s, D.H. pioneered the commercial jet age with the world's first jet airliner (the Comet), built first-generation jet fighters (Vampire, Venom), and expanded the flying performance envelope with experimental aircraft such as the D.H.108 Swallow. The de Havilland Aircraft Company was taken into the Hawker Siddeley organization in 1961, but the name still survives in the Canadian aircraft company.

CLAUDIUS DORNIER (1884–1969)

Claudius Dornier joined the airship research team at the Zeppelin works in 1910, but his original ideas about airplane design led to his moving to a separate establishment at Friedrichshafen in 1914. In the years that followed, Dornier's aircraft introduced many features that were at the cutting edge of aeronautical technology, including the early use of duralumin, metal stressed-skin construction, cantilever torsion-box wings, and jettisonable fuel tanks. Constrained by the terms imposed by the Allies after 1918, he set up foreign subsidiaries to evade the restrictions on the size and performance of aircraft that could be produced in Germany. The remarkable Wal flying boat thereby came into being in Italy and went on to pioneer routes across the Atlantic and the Arctic, gaining a reputation for unrivaled sturdiness and reliability. In 1929, Dornier produced one of the most ambitious aircraft of the interwar years, the Do X flying boat. Powered by twelve engines and weighing well over 100,000 pounds, this phenomenon was intended to carry up to 100 passengers, and was fitted with a lounge, bar and sleeping quarters. For the expansion of the Luftwaffe and during WWII, Dornier concentrated on a series of medium bombers and maritime patrol aircraft, although one remarkable fighter design appeared in the latter stages of the war. The very fast Dornier 335 was unique in being powered by two center-line engines, one conventionally placed in the nose and the other driving an airscrew situated behind the tail.

One that got away. The Do 19 was Dornier's response to a 1935 requirement for a Greman strategic bomber. The "Ural Bomber" program was cancelled in 1937 and only one Do 19 was ever tested.

DONALD DOUGLAS (1892–1981)

An American aircraft designer and manufacturer from Brooklyn, Donald Douglas was educated at the U.S. Naval Academy and MIT. During WWI he became chief engineer to Glenn Martin, and went on to establish the Douglas Aircraft Company in California after the war. The company was responsible for producing the Cloudster, the first aircraft designed to lift its own weight as payload, and the World Cruisers, which completed the first round the world flight in 1924. The Douglas DC-2 attracted international attention in 1934 by carrying fourteen passengers and still managing to finish second in the England–Australia air race. Its famous successor, the DC-3 (C-47, Dakota) appeared in 1936 and has remained in continuous service somewhere in the world ever since. When the economic, social and political effects of aviation are considered, the DC-3 must be seen as an aircraft of particular significance. Other notable aircraft produced by Douglas included the SBD Dauntless, which struck the decisive blows at the Battle of Midway, the A-20 Havoc/Boston, and the A-1 Skyraider, which played such an important close-support role in Vietnam. After WWII, Douglas produced a series of great airliners — the four-engined DC-4 (notable for its performance in the Berlin Airlift) and DC-6, and the jet-liners (DC-8, 9 and 10). Donald Douglas remained as chairman of his company until the merger with McDonnell Aircraft in 1967. (Another merger of note was the marriage of his daughter, Barbara Douglas, to Bruce Arnold, son of General "Hap" Arnold, the "father" of the USAF.) Douglas maintained throughout his jaundiced view of the bureaucracy that often bedevils the aircraft industry, expressed in his remark: "When the weight of paper equals the weight of the airplane, only then can you go flying."

HENRI FARMAN (1874–1958)

Henri Farman was born in Paris of English parents on May 26, 1874. Although educated at the Paris School of Fine Arts as a painter, his first achievements were as a bicycle racer and later an auto-racing champion. With his brother, Maurice, Henri learned to fly in a Voisin and in 1907 he ordered his own aircraft, incorporating his design modifications of wing dihedral and the reduction of the tail to a single plane. These intuitive rather than scientific modifications were the first steps in a long career during which Henri Farman diagnosed and solved a myriad aircraft control and structural problems. In January 1908, Henri Farman won the prestigious Archdeacon prize in his modified machine by demonstrating his ability to fly a circuit of one kilometer, even without adequate lateral control. Soon afterward, he added ailerons to solve this irksome problem. In 1909, Henri Farman began one of the first formal flight-training schools and in 1914 founded the Farman Aviation Works, which produced more than 12,000 military aircraft for France in WWI. After the war, the Farman brothers enjoyed both financial and technical success with a series of advanced designs, including the twin-engined Goliath, which was capable of carrying twelve passengers. With this aircraft, they established their airline, Farman Lines, which was a forerunner of Air France.

Inevitably called "The Flying Dutchman," Anthony Fokker was born in Java, the son of a wealthy coffee planter. He was educated in Holland and was drawn to aviation by Wilbur Wright's exhibition of flying at Reims in 1908. He took an aeronautics course in Germany and, in 1911, made his first "hop" in an airplane that he had helped to design and build. The Fokker Aviatik Company was registered in Berlin in 1912 and became a principal manufacturer of combat aircraft for the Luftstreitkräfte (the German Air Service) in WWI. Fokker's first warplane was basically a copy of the 1914 Morane-Saulnier monoplane, but it was developed into the legendary E series (Eindeckers), the first true fighters to be fitted with machine guns firing forward through the propeller. The interrupter gear that made this possible was developed by Fokker's design staff. Like many of his contemporary pioneers in aircraft manufacturing, Fokker soon became more of a businessman than a designer, but he put together a competent team that, under his leadership and direction, generated a string of outstanding aircraft. In WWI, the Dr.I Triplane and the D.VII were flown with great success by the leading German aces. After the war, Fokker set up a factory in Holland, in the process smuggling over 200 of his aircraft from Germany without the knowledge of the Allies. In 1922, he immigrated to the United States and established the Fokker Aircraft Corporation of America. The company's civil aircraft designs were involved in many notable achievements in the 1920s, including the first non-stop crossing of the U.S. by air, the first aerial crossing of the Pacific, and the first flights over both Poles.

LEFT *Anthony Fokker ready for flight in a KLM F.VII trimotor.*
RIGHT *Germany's best WWI fighter — the Fokker D.VII.*

Ernst Heinkel (1888–1958)

In 1911, Ernst Heinkel joined the Luft Verkehrs Gesellschaft (L.V.G.) factory and designed their first production aircraft, the B.1 tractor biplane. He later worked for Albatros before moving on to join Igor Etrich at the Hansa und Brandenburgische Flugzeugwerke. While at Hansa Brandenburg during WWI, Heinkel gained a reputation for designing effective reconnaissance machines and marine aircraft. In 1922, he founded his own aircraft factory at Warnemünde, Germany, and for the rest of the 1920s relied mainly on foreign contracts for the survival of his company. Japan, Hungary, Denmark, Jugoslavia, Sweden and the Soviet Union all made use of Heinkel designs. By the 1930s, Ernst Heinkel's team was increasingly committed to producing aircraft in secret for the buildup of the Luftwaffe, but there was international acclaim for the aerodynamically advanced He 70, an elegantly streamlined low-wing monoplane with a four-passenger cabin. This was followed by a wolf in sheep's clothing, the He 111, which flew initially as an airliner but became the backbone of the Luftwaffe's medium bomber force. More than 6,000 He 111 were built during WWII. As the war progressed, the Heinkel organization expanded steadily, until by the end of 1944 it employed some 50,000 people in twenty-seven factories, three repair plants and twelve engine and airframe design bureaus. Ernst Heinkel's success was due not only to his talents as a designer, but also to his business acumen and knack for recognizing talent in others. It was under his patronage that the world's first turbojet-powered aircraft, the He 178, was developed and flown.

Heinkel He 70.

Jiro Horikoshi (1905–1982)

Considered one of the world's greatest designers, Jiro Horikoshi became a legendary figure in the Japanese aircraft industry. He joined the Nagoya Works of Mitsubishi Industries in 1927 and quickly revealed his talent. In 1934, he took on the challenge of developing the first naval monoplane fighter and produced the A5M (Claude), which proved markedly superior to its opponents over Shanghai in 1937. Horikoshi then went to work on a successor to the A5M, which had to be equally nimble but with much-improved range. The result was the extraordinary A6M Zero-Sen, a fighter that took the Allies by surprise and swept all before it in the early months of the Pacific war. Horikoshi was instrumental in pioneering such advanced features as flush riveting, lightweight alloys, and the retractable undercarriage. His influence on the Japanese aircraft industry was profound.

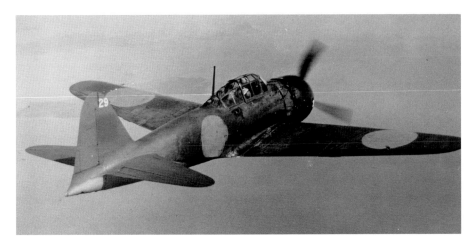

A6M Zero-Sen.

HOWARD HUGHES (1905–1976)

Billionaire oilman, film producer and aviator, Howard Hughes became notorious for his eccentric behavior. He began indulging an obsession with aviation by getting his pilot's licence in 1927. Already heavily involved in the Hollywood film industry, he combined his passions in the classic WWI movie *Hell's Angels,* made in 1930. For a while, in 1932, he worked under an assumed name as an American Airways co-pilot, before turning his attention to designing, building and flying aircraft. Speed captivated him and he did well in the annual All-American air races, but it was in the breaking of records that his wealth made it possible for him to excel. Working with designer Richard Palmer in 1934, he built the H-1, a racer with exceptionally clean lines, designed from the outset to be the fastest landplane in the world. On September 13, 1935, Hughes captured the world landplane speed record, pushing the H-1 to an average speed of 352 mph before running out of fuel and landing in a bean field. Flying a suitably repaired H-1 fitted with higher aspect-ratio wings, Hughes shattered the U.S. transcontinental record on January 19, 1937, crossing from Los Angeles to Newark in just under seven and a half hours, averaging 332 mph for the 2,490 miles. The global record then beckoned, and in July 1938 he and his crew flew a specially equipped Lockheed Super Electra round the Northern Hemisphere in little more than 91 hours, cutting the previous best time, set solo by Wiley Post, in half. Given the opportunity to buy into Trans-Continental and Western Airlines, he did so and soon became the sole proprietor. (Trans-Continental and Western Airlines was the original name behind the TWA logo. It was not changed until 1950, when it became Trans-World Airlines to reflect the company's worldwide interests.) Keen though he was to spend money in making TWA the world's best-equipped airline, Hughes was not an ideal owner. His reclusive character and his continued involvement in other businesses such as moviemaking and building aircraft led to poor corporate decision-making, and TWA suffered accordingly. It was 1960 before TWA's serious financial problems forced Hughes to relinquish his control of the airline. Perhaps his most controversial creation, an achievement and a failure at the same time, was the gigantic wooden flying boat that became known as the "Spruce Goose." Intended to carry up to 700 troops and to operate as an alternative to the troopship of WWII, this vast aircraft was not completed until 1947, by which time it had been overtaken by events. Hughes flew it just once, in a straight line for one mile just above the waters of Los Angeles harbor, after which it was relegated to the role of museum piece. Increasingly remote and unpredictable after sustaining severe injuries in the crash of his XF-11 reconnaissance aircraft in 1946, Hughes became a recluse. He suffered a stroke and died while on board a chartered Learjet flying from Acapulco to Houston.

Hughes' "Spruce Goose."

SERGEI ILYUSHIN (1894–1977)

The early life of Sergei Ilyushin did not suggest his eventual rise to prominence in the Soviet aircraft industry. Born to a peasant family near Vologda, some 300 miles north of Moscow, Ilyushin was serving as a mechanic in the Imperial Russian Air Service when he was first noticed by Igor Sikorsky. By the time of the Russian Revolution, he was the chief mechanic for Sikorsky's Il'ya Mourometz bombers. After winning a scholarship to the Zhukovsky Air Academy, he began designing gliders, and their success eventually led to his being rewarded with his own design bureau. His most famous WWII design was the IL-2 Shturmovik, a heavily armored attack aircraft that Ilyushin himself called "a flying tank." Joseph Stalin wrote: "They [IL-2s] are as essential to the Red Army as air and bread." In the postwar years, the Ilyushin bureau produced a series of successful bombers and transports, including the first Soviet jet bomber, the IL-28

(Beagle), and the wide-bodied, 350-seat IL-86 (Camber). During his long career, Sergei Ilyushin was involved with the design of more than fifty aircraft.

IL-28 "Beagle."

KELLY JOHNSON (1910–1990)

Clarence Leonard "Kelly" Johnson gained his Masters degree in aeronautical engineering from the University of Michigan in 1933. While in college, he had worked as a consultant on the aerodynamic design of automobiles for the annual Indianapolis races. On leaving Michigan, he joined the Lockheed Corporation as a tool designer. After assignments as flight test engineer, stress analyst, aerodynamicist, weight engineer, and wind-tunnel engineer, he became chief research engineer in 1938. He was significantly involved in forty different Lockheed designs, and his creative thinking led to many innovations throughout the aerospace industry. Nineteen Lockheed machines were primarily Johnson products, among them some of the best-known aircraft in the world, including the Hudson bomber, the Constellation and Super-Constellation transports, the P-38 fighter, the F-80 Shooting Star and its derivative T-33 trainer, the F-94 interceptor, and the Jetstar executive jet. Managing Lockheed's Advanced Development Projects Division (colloquially known as the "Skunk Works"), he developed the first American Mach 2 aircraft, the F-104

Starfighter, the high flying U-2 reconnaissance aircraft, and the Mach 3 SR-71 Blackbird. In 1975, he retired as senior vice president of Lockheed. Among his many awards, he received two Collier trophies, two Theodore Von Karman awards, and the National Medal of Science. He was also awarded the Medal of Freedom for his "significant contributions to the quality of American life" in the advancement of aeronautics. His genius in the design and production of state-of-the-art aircraft has never been surpassed.

F-80 Shooting Star.

HUGO JUNKERS (1859–1935)

A generation older than most of the pioneers of powered flight, Hugo Junkers was in his fiftieth year before he took a serious interest in aviation. He was then a professor of mechanical engineering at Aachen University, and the founder of a factory that dealt in sheet metal for boilers and ventilation equipment. He became convinced that sheet metal processing techniques could be applied to the manufacturing of aircraft and in 1915 produced the Junkers J.1, an all-metal cantilever monoplane. The J.1 was too heavy to be practical, but in subsequent designs Junkers used a duralumin frame covered by duralumin corrugated sheet, and these proved more successful. After the war, he turned his attention to commercial aircraft, and by June 1919, the Junkers F.13 (initially J.13), the world's first all-metal airliner, was flying. It was a small machine, with an enclosed cabin for four passengers, but it made a remarkable

contribution to the development of commercial aviation. Over 300 were built and they saw service with airlines all over the world, the last being retired by Varig in Brazil in 1948. Junkers aircraft were used by Amundsen in the Arctic, and in 1928, a W.33 was the first aircraft to cross the North Atlantic nonstop from east to west. In 1921, Junkers formed his own airline to operate the F.13, inaugurating routes between Germany and Hungary, Austria and Switzerland. Small though they were, by 1926, when the Junkers airline was absorbed into the new national airline, Deutsche Luft Hansa, the F.13s had flown almost ten million miles in carrying over a quarter of a million passengers. At the other end of the scale, in 1929 the Junkers factory built the four-engined 144-foot-wingspan G.38 airliner, which could carry thirty-four passengers and was the largest aircraft of its day. This was followed in 1931 by the famous Ju.52/3m, a trimotor transport constructed with the Junkers trademark corrugated skin, which was destined to become a familiar sight for decades in both peace and war. Despite this, because of financial difficulties, the Junkers concern was taken over by the state in 1933, just two years before Hugo Junkers died.

THEODORE VON KARMAN (1881–1963)

Born in Budapest, Hungary, Theodore von Karman received a fellowship to Gottingen University, where he undertook the investigation of aerodynamic drag and the construction of one of Europe's first wind tunnels. He then accepted the Chair of Aeronautics at the Technische Hochschule in Aachen, Germany. His presence made the school an international center for aeronautical research. In reaction to growing Nazi influence in German academic circles, von Karman moved to California in 1930, where he was director of the Guggenheim Aeronautics Laboratory until 1949. He helped to create the Advisory Group on Aeronautical Research and Development for the NATO countries, serving as chairman of that body from 1951 until his death. Theodore Von Karman's contributions to aeronautics included research into rotary flight, composite materials, the longitudinal stability of aircraft, the theory of motion and turbulence in fluids, laminar flow and skin friction, resistance in compressible fluids, and supersonic aerodynamics. His ideas influenced the design of the first aircraft recognized as having exceeded the speed of sound, the Bell X-1. In 1954 he was awarded the Wright Brothers Trophy and was the first U.S. Medal of Science recipient. Although Von Karman's primary interest was aeronautics, he was a mathematical genius, writer and educator, authoring nearly 150 books and articles on engineering, physics and mathematics. His capacity for stimulating research colleagues and students, for building research organizations and for organizing international scientific meetings was renowned. He founded the NASA Jet Propulsion Laboratory and the Aerojet Corporation. His genius touched almost every aspect of contemporary aerospace endeavor.

GLENN MARTIN (1886–1955)

Working as a motor mechanic but inspired by stories of the Wright brothers' achievements, Glenn Martin built his first glider in 1905. By 1909 he had built a primitive biplane in a rented church and flown it in short hops. He then gradually established himself as a regular participant in air shows and competitions. In 1912, the *Los Angeles Times* reported "Pacific Aerial Delivery Route Number 1 Opened by Glenn Martin" after he had flown a sack of mail from Los Angeles to nearby Compton. He developed a parachute and had it successfully demonstrated in 1913, but, although its lifesaving properties were obvious, it failed to interest the authorities. In 1917, after a period as part of the Wright-Martin Corporation, he broke away to found his own company and was invited by the U.S. Army to design a bomber with a performance superior to the Handley Page O/400. The resulting MB-1 and MB-2 became standard equipment in the U.S. Army's bomber squadrons after WWI and featured in Billy Mitchell's 1921 bombing trials against naval vessels. In later years, the Martin factory produced aircraft that filled a wide variety of roles, both civil and military. Among the most famous types were the M-130 Clipper flying boats, the revolutionary B-10 of the early 1930s, and, during WWII, the B-26 Marauder and the large Mariner flying boats. Glenn Martin remained as chairman of his company until he died.

JAMES MCDONNELL (1899–1980)

James Smith McDonnell was born in Denver, Colorado, the son of an Arkansas cotton grower. He earned a masters degree in aeronautical engineering from the Massachusetts Institute of Technology in 1924. He believed that an aeronautical engineer should know how to fly and so joined the Army Air Corps to learn, receiving his wings as a reserve Second Lieutenant in 1924. His subsequent career in the American aircraft industry saw him rise from design engineer to the chairman of the board of one of the world's most respected aerospace giants, the McDonnell Douglas Corporation. Among his notable achievements were the U.S. Navy's first carrier-based jet fighter, the FH-1 Phantom, and the F-4 Phantom II, for which he was awarded the prestigious Collier Trophy in 1966. After merging with Douglas Aircraft, the new corporation produced the DC-10 wide-body airliner, and the superb F-15 Eagle fighter. Although his companies produced a predominance of military aircraft, McDonnell was dedicated to the cause of peace in the world, but a peace founded on strength and firm support for the United Nations and the North Atlantic Treaty Organization. He was also a believer in the human exploration of space, and his company developed the *Mercury 7* spacecraft for America's first manned space program. It was his view that "The creative conquest of space will serve as a wonderful substitute for war."

One of McDonnell's most famous and successful jets, the F-4 Phantom II.

WILLY MESSERSCHMITT (1898–1978)

A graduate of the Munich Institute of Technology, Willy Messerschmitt spent the early 1920s building gliders before turning to powered machines. The history of aerial warfare might have been different if he had not survived an accident in his first light aircraft, the M-17 Ello. Coming in to land from its first flight, the M-17 struck high-tension cables and crashed, injuring both the test pilot and Messerschmitt. Notably ambitious, he joined the Nazi party and became friends with Hermann Göring, a fact that later helped him to overcome the antagonism of Hitler's Secretary of State for Aviation, Erhard Milch. In 1927, when Messerschmitt's company was merged with BFW (Bayerische Flugzeugwerke), he became chief designer of the new organization. In 1934, he produced the excellent Bf108 Taifun, an advanced technology monoplane that featured slotted flaps and ailerons as well as leading-edge slats. The lessons learned during the design phase of the Bf108 were invaluable when Messerschmitt came to design a fighter to meet specifications issued by the Luftwaffe in 1934. The resulting aircraft, the Bf109, first flew in 1935 and subsequently earned a place in aviation history as one of the most outstanding combat aircraft ever produced. In its various forms, more than 33,000 were built, and between them they recorded more aerial victories than any other fighter.

The international acclaim for the Bf108 and Bf109 brought their chief designer such prestige that the BFW management agreed to change the name of the company to Messerschmitt, and named Willy Messerschmitt himself as chairman and managing director. In 1939, a specially prepared Me209 captured the world speed record at 469 mph, a figure that remained unchallenged by piston-engined aircraft for over thirty years. During WWII, the Messerschmitt empire grew to embody establishments all over Germany, the principal factories at Regensburg and Augsburg alone employing 33,000 workers by 1944. They were responsible for well over 40 percent of the combat aircraft produced for the Third Reich, including two notable firsts — the rocket-propelled Me163 Komet and the jet-powered Me262, which was introduced to combat during 1944.

ARTEM MIKOYAN (1905–1970)

Armenian Artem Mikoyan graduated from the Zhukovsky Air Academy in 1936 and began work by designing transport aircraft. His outstanding abilities were rewarded when, in 1938, he set up his own design bureau. In collaboration with Mikhail Gurevich, he produced a series of outstanding fighters bearing the acronym MiG, derived from the initial letters of their surnames. Over 3,000 MiG-3s were built during WWII, and the postwar period saw the introduction of the first Soviet swept-wing jet fighter, the MiG-15 (Fagot), which proved a formidable opponent for the UN forces during the Korean War. Subsequent MiG designs ensured that the Soviet, later, Russian Air Force was always equipped with modern, effective front-line fighters, comparable to their counterparts in the West. The MiG-21 (Fishbed) was capable of Mach 2 and became the most widely used fighter aircraft in the world, with more than 10,000 of all variants being built. The MiG-23 (Flogger) was a variable geometry aircraft, and the remarkable MiG-25 (Foxbat), the prototype of which first flew in 1964, was capable of speeds close to Mach 3. Mikoyan was still the head of his design bureau when he died in 1970.

MiG-21.

REGINALD MITCHELL (1895–1937)

Reginald Joseph Mitchell, born at Stoke-on-Trent, England, showed an early interest in his life's work while still at school, designing and building model airplanes without benefit of plans or instructions. He had artistic flair and a vivid imagination, and these were combined with a talent for mathematics. His power of concentration was intense and Henry Royce described him as being "slow to decide, but quick to act." In 1916, after a five-year apprenticeship with a locomotive works, Mitchell joined Supermarine Aviation in Southampton. He was promoted to chief designer in 1919 at the age of twenty-four and to chief engineer the following year. After WWI, Supermarine manufactured commercial flying boats, but also became known for building the racing aircraft that represented Britain in the international Schneider Trophy competition. A chubby little flying boat, the *Sea Lion*, won the race in 1922, but Mitchell's design team went on to produce the series of elegant floatplanes that won the race three times in succession and, with the beautiful S.6B, gave Britain permanent possession of the trophy in 1931. In spite of the drag of its floats, the S.6B went on to become the first aircraft to exceed 400 mph and set a world speed record of 407.5 mph. Mitchell's flying boat designs served with many maritime squadrons of the RAF between the wars, and his Walrus became the backbone of the RAF's air-sea rescue operations in WWII. Mitchell's crowning achievement was the Spitfire, a fighter he designed while in the grip of a terminal illness. Its beautiful lines and exceptional handling qualities have become legendary, and its remarkable development potential was shown by the fact that it remained in the front rank of combat aircraft from the first day of WWII to the last.

Reginald Mitchell and Henry Royce.

John Knudsen Northrop (1895–1981)

Jack Northrop, although he came from a poor family, was a naturally gifted mathematician and technician who developed into a sophisticated aero-engineer. He began his career as a project engineer with the Loughead Aircraft Company in 1916, and later worked with Donald Douglas before becoming a co-founder of Lockheed in 1927. His genius became evident with the appearance of the Vega, a novel design with a monocoque fuselage and cantilever wing, which produced unusually high performance for the time and was flown by such record-breaking pilots as Wiley Post, Amelia Earhart and Hubert Wilkins. In the 1930s, he was chief engineer of the Northrop Corporation, which was then a subsidiary of Douglas Aircraft. He founded Northrop Aircraft Inc. in 1939, and served as its president and director of engineering. Noted as a gifted designer, he was responsible for many original aircraft, including the P-61 Black Widow night fighter and the F-89 Scorpion all-weather interceptor. He is particularly remembered for his work on a number of "flying wing" designs. Immediately after WWII, the USAF showed some interest in his flying wings, and they flew as the piston-engined XB-35 and the jet-powered XB-49. Although not successful at the time, the basic Northrop idea returned half a century later as the USAF's global strike aircraft — the "stealthy" B-2 Spirit.

Hans von Ohain (1911–1998)

Hans Joachim-Pabst von Ohain conceived his theories of gas-turbine power plants while studying for a doctorate in physics and applied mechanics at the University of Gottingen in 1933. In 1934, he developed these theories, designed and financed the building of a working model, and applied for a patent, which was issued in 1935. Von Ohain recognized that more sophisticated testing and development were essential before practical application was possible and he convinced Ernst Heinkel to allow him to undertake development work at the Heinkel factory as a private venture. While there he designed and built three different engines, the last of which was the HeS 3B. On August 27, 1939, this was the engine that powered the world's first jet aircraft, the Heinkel 178, on its first flight. Two years later he produced the HeS 011 axial-flow engine, which was considered to be the world's most powerful turbo-jet at the end of WWII. In 1947, he emigrated to the U.S. and became a research engineer for the U.S. Air Force at its engine development center. In 1963, von Ohain became chief scientist of the Aerospace Research Laboratories, and, in 1975, chief scientist of the Aero Propulsion Laboratory. After his retirement in 1979, he became professor of mechanical engineering at the University of Dayton and served as a consultant to government and the aviation industry. Throughout his career, he displayed the same analytical insight, initiative and drive he had shown during his early days of turbo-jet development. His work involved such varied fields as the colloid-gas core reactor for propulsion and power generation, electrofluid dynamics, advanced diffusers and ejectors, dynamic energy transfer, and V/STOL aircraft.

FREDERICK HANDLEY PAGE (1885–1962)

The first company in Britain incorporated for the purpose of manufacturing aircraft was set up by Frederick Handley Page in 1909. His first aircraft, small inherently stable crescent-winged monoplanes, were not particularly successful, and it was not until WWI that the name Handley Page became generally well known. During the war, his company produced the first British heavy bombers, the O/100 and O/400, which carried out a strategic bombing campaign against German industrial centers. In 1919, the Handley Page Transport airline was founded, using converted O/400s as interim airliners to open a service between London and Paris. The Handley

Page W.8 that followed was one of the first aircraft specifically designed for commercial aviation. The Handley Page slot, a device that smoothed out turbulent flow over the wing and delayed the onset of a stall, was introduced in 1920. Slotted flaps and ailerons came later, making lower takeoff and landing speeds possible and contributing significantly to flight safety. Just eight Handley Page H.P.42 biplane airliners were built and operated in the 1930s. Slow and stately they certainly were, but they flew over ten million miles without losing a passenger. Handley Page continued to build large military aircraft between the wars, and in WWII his Hampden and Halifax bombers played a large part in the air assault on Germany. As aviation moved into the jet age, Handley Page produced the Victor, a four-engined aircraft that served the RAF first as a nuclear-armed bomber and then as a tanker. On a smaller scale, the H.P.115 research aircraft provided data on the handling characteristics of delta wings, which contributed to the successful development of the Concorde supersonic airliner. Frederick Handley Page continued as chairman and managing director of his company until the end of his life.

H.P. 42 Heracles.

ZYGMUNT PULAWSKI (1901–1930)

The inspired Polish designer Zygmunt Pulawski was only twenty-nine when he was killed piloting one of his own aircraft. The son of a factory worker, he attended Warsaw Technical University and graduated in 1925. He had already shown his talent for aircraft design and was sent to the Breguet works near Paris to gain experience. He later qualified as a Polish Air Force pilot before joining the company that became the Panstwowe Zaklady Lotnicze (PZL) concern in 1928. Given the job of designing a single-seat fighter, Pulawski created an all-metal monoplane with a high wing cranked near the fuselage. This gull-wing shape, sharply tapered in chord and thickness at the root, was introduced to provide the pilot with the best possible all-round view from the cockpit and became known as the Pulawski wing. During the International Fighter Contest at Bucharest in 1930, the Pulawski P-7 proved superior in most respects to contemporary fighters. The originality of the P fighter's design, with its very advanced stressed-skin construction, aroused considerable international interest. Later models

placed Poland in the forefront of the fighter development world and were ordered in quantity by the air forces of Poland, Bulgaria, Greece, Romania and Turkey. Other industrial nations were quick to copy many of the P fighter's design features. Pulawski was able to develop his ideas as an aircraft designer for less than four years, but his pioneering work had a lasting influence on interwar fighter design.

P-11 A.

ALLIOT VERDON ROE (1877–1958)

Before he made his mark in aviation, A.V. Roe had quite a varied career. He began as an apprentice in the Lancashire and Yorkshire Railway Locomotive Works, served as a naval fitter in Portsmouth Dockyard, went to sea as an engineer, and worked in the motor industry. At some point, he won a £75 prize in a model aircraft competition organized by the London *Daily Mail* newspaper and used that money to begin building a full-size airplane based on the design of his model.

He was the first Englishman to design, build and fly his own airplane. Roe himself has described the results: "My first machine was a biplane…. Experiments were made with the machine towed by cars, by means of about a hundred feet of cable. The machine could be steered up and down all right, and the landings were quite good, but if it got sideways beyond a certain angle I could not get it back…if the cable was released I could land. Unfortunately, inexperienced 'towers' would insist on hanging on, with a resulting smash." He moved on from this to a triplane powered by a nine-horsepower twin-cylinder engine. The wings were covered in "a thin yellow butter paper, which was very satisfactory in dry weather, but very apt to stretch and get soppy in the wet."

In all of his early machines, Roe was involved in "a very great number of smashes," but remained undeterred in his determination to build practical aircraft. These were not long in coming. In 1912, the British government ordered three Avro biplanes, and these provided the basis for the design of the 1913 Avro 504, an outstanding biplane that operated in the trainer, bomber and reconnaissance roles throughout WWI. Over 12,000 Avro 504s were built and saw service in several air forces. In the 1920s, Avro produced a number of excellent biplanes, including the Aldershot bomber and the little Avian, which featured in a number of record-breaking solo long-distance flights. A.V. Roe sold his company to Armstrong Siddeley in 1928, but went on to form Saunders-Roe and concentrate on building flying boats, including the postwar development of a jet-powered flying boat fighter, the SR/A1.

A.V. Roe seated precariously in one of his fragile triplanes, 1909.

The Honorable Charles Rolls (1877–1910); Sir Henry Royce (1863–1933)

Aristocratic, rich and well educated, Charles Rolls had an adventurous spirit and a love of speed. He indulged his enthusiasm for racing first as a cyclist and then by driving cars. Ballooning was another of his activities, and in 1901 he was among those who founded the Aero Club. In 1906 he went into partnership with Henry Royce to build quality cars. Royce, by contrast, was an orphan with a background of poverty. After being an apprentice at a locomotive works, he had worked hard to improve himself, holding down jobs while going to night school. He started his own engineering firm in 1884 and built his first car in 1904. His partnership with Charles Rolls produced the 1906 Rolls-Royce Silver Ghost, a car that laid the foundation of the company's reputation for quality. Rolls gained the Royal Aero Club's Aviator's Certificate No. 2 in 1910 and then became the first man to fly across the English Channel from England to France, and the first to complete a nonstop double crossing. Later that year he was killed in the crash of his Wright biplane during an airshow at Bournemouth. Royce retained the name of the partnership and, in WWI, began manufacturing aero-engines. His designs, under the names Eagle, Falcon, and Hawk, were so successful that they comprised some 60 percent of all British engines being built by the end of the war. Royce was actively involved with the design of his company's engines until his death in 1933,

> *"I invent nothing; inventors go broke."*
>
> Sir Henry Royce, after the Schneider Trophy races

and was instrumental in the production of the engines that powered the RAF's winning Schneider Trophy floatplanes in 1929 and 1931. Those same engines were the basis for the Merlin, which proved so effective in aircraft such as the Hurricane, Spitfire, Lancaster, and Mustang in WWII. Sir Henry's guidelines for future generations of company engineers, dictated before his death and known as the "Rolls-Royce Bible," is a document that has remained an industrial secret ever since.

ABOVE *The statue of Charles Rolls stands on the seafront at Dover in England. In 1901 he became an aeronaut and helped to found the Aero Club (later the Royal Aero Club). In 1904 he entered into partnership with Henry Royce, so establishing the world-famous Rolls-Royce company. In 1910 he received Aviator's Certificate No. 2 from the Royal Aero Club, and on June 2 of that year he became the first man to fly nonstop across the English Channel both ways, flying a Wright Type A. In July 1910 he was killed when the Wright biplane broke up in midair. He was Britain's first aircraft fatality.*

LEFT *Charles Rolls with Katharine and Orville Wright at Pau, 1909.*

Elbert L. "Burt" Rutan (1943–)

Elbert L. "Burt" Rutan was born at Dinuba, California, on June 17, 1943. As a schoolboy he designed award-winning model aircraft; he learned to fly at age sixteen. In 1965 he received his aeronautical engineering degree from California Polytechnic University and began a career as a civilian flight-test engineer for the United States Air Force. After leaving the Air Force in 1974, Rutan launched his first private company, the Rutan Aircraft Factory, to market his original light aircraft designs, among them the VariEze, Quickie and Long-EZ. In this period, the concept for the world-flight *Voyager* aircraft was developed. In 1982, Rutan founded Scaled Composites, Inc., and developed prototypes of several aircraft, including the Beech Starship. Burt Rutan's unconventional designs are characterized by the use of lightweight composite materials, a practice that is akin to the earlier transition in aircraft construction from wood and fabric to metal. On December 23, 1986, Rutan's *Voyager* aircraft returned to its starting point at Mojave, California, having completed an around-the-world flight of 25,000 miles in 216 hours, nonstop and unrefueled. Burt Rutan stands out among aircraft designers of the late 20th century because he has imagination to be different, producing aircraft conspicuous for their unusual shape and novel construction.

Horace, Eustace and Oswald Short (1872–1917, 1875–1932, 1883–1969)

The two younger Short brothers, Eustace and Oswald, began their aeronautical careers by buying a balloon in 1897. They started to build their own balloons in 1900, and by 1904 they were supplying balloons both to the British Army and to private citizens. They were joined by their brother Horace in 1908 and established the first airplane manufacturing company in Britain. Their first successful machines were Wright biplanes, one of which was used by Charles Rolls for the first double crossing of the English Channel, but the experience gained from their construction enabled them to go on to design aircraft of their own. In Britain, they pioneered multi-engined aircraft and folding-wing designs for naval operations. In general, Short Brothers did more for naval aviation in its early days than any other British firm. It was a Short 184 floatplane that was the first aircraft to sink a ship at sea.

The Short Sunderland flying boat hunted German U-boats in WWII.

The company's most famous aircraft of the interwar years were the *Empire* flying boats that were used by Imperial Airways on their routes to Africa and Asia. They gave rise to the Sunderland, a maritime patrol aircraft essential to the prosecution of the battle against German U-boats in WWII.

IGOR SIKORSKY (1889–1972)

Igor Ivan Sikorsky was a pioneer of Russian aviation, inspired as a schoolboy by stories of Leonardo da Vinci's ideas and the Wright brothers' achievements. After studying aeronautics in Paris, he returned to Kiev in 1909 and began experimenting with helicopters. Temporarily discouraged by several failures, he turned to fixed-wing aviation with more success. In 1912 he was appointed designer and chief engineer of the aircraft division of the Russo-Baltic Railway Factories, and in 1913 built the world's

> *"Aeronautics was neither an industry nor a science. It was a miracle."*
> IGOR SIKORSKY

first four-engined airplane, the Bolshoi Baltisky Type B (Le Grand). From this was developed the *Il'ya Mourometz*, variations of which were the first four-engined bombers to enter front-line service and were successfully used for bombing operations during WWI. With the coming of the Bolshevik Revolution, Sikorsky left Russia, first for Paris and then for the United States. Overcoming initial hardships, he founded the Sikorsky Aero Engineering Corporation in 1923 with the help of friends, including the composer Rachmaninoff. He began by building his S-29A, an all-metal twin-engined transport. Although it was built of a motley collection of materials and crashed on its first flight, the S-29A was eventually something of a success, performing well for years until being destroyed while mimicking a WWI Gotha bomber for the Howard Hughes film *Hell's Angels*. Sikorsky's most successful aircraft of the interwar years were the S-38 amphibian and the S-42 flying boat, built primarily to meet the requirements of Pan-American Airways. However, his dream of designing a practical helicopter had never died and in 1939 he demonstrated his VS-300. A later model, the R-4, accepted by the U.S. Army at the end of 1942, became the world's first rotary-wing aircraft produced in quantity. Since those early days, Sikorsky helicopters have developed into familiar, capable machines, providing invaluable services in many roles with civilian and military organizations all over the world. Igor Sikorsky did not claim to have invented the helicopter, but it can be said that he played a large part in perfecting it and that he, more than anyone else, was responsible for developing the technology to the point where helicopters could be mass produced. He deservedly received a great many honors in his lifetime, including the National Medal for Science and the Wright Brother's Memorial Trophy.

The Sikorsky H-37 Mojave from the Vietnam era.

Tom Sopwith (1888–1989)

Mechanical aptitude and bounding enthusiasm for the new medium led Thomas Octave Murdoch Sopwith into aviation. In 1910, he bought a monoplane and taught himself to fly by trial and error, being awarded his pilot's certificate on November 22. Less than a month later, he won a prize of £4,000 for the longest flight of the year into continental Europe, covering 177 miles in 3 hours and 40 minutes. In the years before WWI, he founded the Sopwith Aviation Company at Kingston-on-Thames, and later Britain's first major flying school. Hugh Trenchard, destined to become the RAF's first Chief of Staff, was among his pupils. The remarkable little Sopwith Tabloid drew attention to the new company's capabilities by winning the 1914 Schneider Trophy at Monaco. It became the ancestor of a string of outstanding combat aircraft produced by the Sopwith factory, notably the Pup, Triplane, Camel and Snipe. Altogether, more than 18,000 aircraft of sixteen types were built, a remarkable contribution to the Allied war effort. In the postwar collapse of the aviation industry, Sopwith was forced to liquidate his company. However, by November 1920, a new company, Hawker Engineering, was set up with Tom Sopwith and Harry Hawker among its directors. This was the foundation for the formation of Hawker Aircraft in 1933, a company that during WWII continued the Sopwith tradition of building superb combat aircraft, including the Hurricane, Typhoon and Tempest. In the major reorganization of the British aircraft industry undertaken after the war, Sir Thomas Sopwith was the founding president of the Hawker Siddeley Group, and he retained a consulting role in the affairs of his company until well into his nineties.

The Sopwith Camel was the most successful fighter aircraft of WWI, shooting down almost 1,300 enemy machines in one year of operation.

ANDREI TUPOLEV (1888–1972)

Andrei Tupolev entered the Moscow Higher Technical School in 1908 and studied under Nikolai Zhukovsky, a pioneer of Russian aviation. One of the founders of the Central Institute of Aerodynamics and Hydrodynamics, he was its first assistant director from 1918 to 1935. In 1920, he added the post of chief of the Institute's Aircraft Design Bureau and produced a series of original designs for the first Soviet all-metal aircraft. Foremost among them was the ANT-4 (TB-1) of 1925, which became the first all-metal, low-wing, twin-engined bomber in the world to enter quantity production. In 1934, his eight-engined ANT-20, the *Maxim Gorky*, was the largest aircraft in the world, with a 207-foot wingspan. Built for propaganda purposes, it was equipped with a radio station, a printing press, a photographic studio, a film projector and screen, plus, on the outside, an illuminated message system backed up by loudspeakers. Its cabins and sleeping berths could accommodate nearly 100 people. World distance records were set by ANT-25 long-range monoplanes in 1937 when they flew across the Arctic to the U.S., first to Washington State and then to California.

Arrested during the Soviet purges, Tupolev was sent to the Gulag but released during WWII and awarded the Stalin Prize for his design of the Tu-2 medium bomber. After the war, Tupolev's design team were responsible for a string of remarkable jet and turbo-prop aircraft, including the Tu-104 jet and the huge Tu-114 turbo-prop airliners, the Tu-144 supersonic transport, and the Tu-22 Blinder, Tu-26 Backfire and Tu-95 Bear bombers. Andrei Tupolev's remarkable career spanned sixty-four years and resulted in more than one hundred designs. His academic brilliance and innovative powers kept him at the forefront of the aeronautical world throughout his working life.

Tu-114 turbo-prop airliner approaching touchdown.

BARNES WALLIS (1887–1979)

Barnes Neville Wallis was originally trained as a marine engineer, but by 1913 he was designing airships built by the Vickers Company. In 1924, Vickers established the Airship Guarantee Company and appointed Wallis as chief engineer. He designed the R-100, a most successful airship that was completed in 1929 and crossed the Atlantic both ways in 1930. The R-100 featured geodetic construction, a lattice-work structure capable of surviving considerable punishment. Having become chief designer of Vickers Aviation, Wallis designed both the long-range Wellesley and the Wellington, a twin-engined bomber that bore the brunt of RAF Bomber Command's efforts in the early months of WWII. Both aircraft employed geodetic structures, and the Wellington often provided ample evidence of its ability to absorb and survive battle damage.

During WWII, Wallis involved himself in weapon design and was responsible for the bouncing bombs used in the destruction of the Ruhr dams in 1943, and for the massive Tallboy and Grand Slam bombs used against targets such as V-2 sites, viaducts and the battleship *Tirpitz*. After the war, Wallis turned to advanced aeronautical projects and developed the variable-sweep wing, subsequently used successfully in the General Dynamics F-111 and the Panavia Tornado. To the end of his life, Sir Barnes Wallis continued his investigations at the frontiers of aeronautical research, promoting such advanced concepts as a STOL hypersonic airliner capable of linking London to Sydney in three hours. Given his record of original achievement, it is possible to believe his contention that such an aircraft might be more economical than either the Concorde or the 747.

The R-100 made a double crossing of the Atlantic in 1930.

FRANK WHITTLE (1907–1997)

Frank Whittle became a Royal Air Force aircraft apprentice in 1923 at the age of sixteen. He was selected as a cadet for officer and pilot training at the RAF College, Cranwell, in 1926, and was commissioned as a pilot officer in 1928. While still a Cranwell cadet, he wrote a thesis entitled "Future Developments in Aircraft Design" that included his first ideas about rocket propulsion and gas turbines. He continued his studies after graduation from Cranwell and, despite lack of official interest in his work, filed for his first gas turbine patent in 1930. Whittle's brother officers regarded his ideas with some skepticism, calling his proposed engine "Whittle's Flaming Touch-hole." After serving as a pilot with several RAF units, he attended Cambridge University and graduated with First Class Honors in Mechanical Sciences in 1936. By then his designs were reaching the point where prototype production could be considered and a small company called Power Jets was formed to do the necessary work on an engine known as the WU (Whittle Unit). In 1937, the WU achieved a controlled run on a test-bed. Official apathy continued to obstruct development, but Whittle persisted and his W.1 engine eventually flew from Cranwell in the experimental Gloster E28/39 aircraft on May 15, 1941. Developments of Whittle's centrifugal flow engines later powered the Gloster Meteor, the only

> *"Sir Frank is one of the great engineers of the 20th century. He has helped to change both the way we live and the world in which we live and his work has made possible the kinds of journey our ancestors never even imagined. His pioneering work on jet engines, his perseverance over the development of the project and his continuing contribution to science and technology are never to be forgotten."*
>
> MARGARET THATCHER, BRITISH PRIME MINISTER, COMMENTING ON SIR FRANK WHITTLE, 1986

Allied jet aircraft to become operational in WWII. In October 1941, several engineers took an example of the W.1X and the drawings for the W.2B to General Electric in the U.S. This was the starting point for American jet-engine development. By April 1942, GE had a W.2B running on test, and only six months later two of them powered the Bell XP-59A on its first flight. Sir Frank Whittle retired from the RAF with the rank of Air Commodore and later served as technical advisor to British Overseas Airways and as a professor at the U.S. Naval Academy. His work on jet propulsion led directly to the revolutionary advances in aviation experienced during the second half of the 20th century.

Sir Frank Whittle after receiving one of his many awards, this one at the National Air & Space Museum, Washington, D.C., in 1986.

WILBUR AND ORVILLE WRIGHT (1867-1912, 1871-1948)

In 1892, Wilbur and Orville Wright, the sons of a United Brethren Church bishop, opened a shop on the west side of Dayton, Ohio, for selling and repairing bicycles. Their formal education had ended with graduation from high school, but they were blessed with both high intelligence and marked mechanical ability. By 1895 they were manufacturing their own bicycles, but they sought other outlets for their considerable talents. A year earlier they

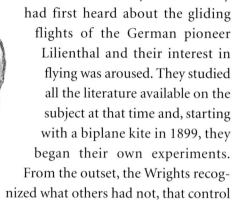

had first heard about the gliding flights of the German pioneer Lilienthal and their interest in flying was aroused. They studied all the literature available on the subject at that time and, starting with a biplane kite in 1899, they began their own experiments. From the outset, the Wrights recognized what others had not, that control was an essential element of successful flight. Their first biplane glider, built in 1900, featured a system, later known as wing-warping, that altered the shape of the wings and made lateral control possible. A "horizontal rudder" was fitted for vertical control. They built other gliders in 1901 and 1902, discovering in the process that Lilienthal's calculations were inaccurate and having to derive their own.

They built a wind tunnel to test wing shapes before trying them out on the dunes of Kill Devil Hill near Kitty Hawk, North Carolina. Vertical rudders were added to provide balanced flight. Once satisfied that the basic control problems had been solved, they developed their own engine and designed propellers from scratch. In the summer of 1903, they began constructing the first Wright Flyer, but it was winter before it was complete. On the morning of December 17, 1903, Orville Wright

became the first man ever to experience sustained, controlled, powered flight, traveling 120 feet across the sands below Kill Devil Hill. The fourth flight of the day, made by Wilbur, covered 852 feet and lasted for fifty-nine seconds. The occasion went largely unnoticed. They returned to Dayton and continued their work, refining their Flyers until they were practical flying machines. It was not until 1908 that the true magnitude of their achievements was widely

ABOVE *Katharine Wright stands behind Hubert Latham to watch the flying at Pau, 1909.*
LEFT *Louis Blériot (on left) listens to a discussion between fellow pioneer aviators.*

Orville, resting on the cane he used after his 1908 accident at Fort Myer, with Wilbur and King Edward VII.

recognized, when Wilbur at Le Mans, France, and Orville at Fort Myer, Washington, D.C., publicly demonstrated their mastery in the air. In 1909, the U.S. Army bought a Wright Flyer; it was the world's first military aircraft. Curiously, the Wrights' inspiration then seemed to fade. The basic design of their aircraft changed very little, and by 1910 leadership in the world of aviation was passing to others. Wilbur died of typhoid in 1912 and thereafter Orville retired into the background, content to concentrate on research rather than the business of flying until his death in 1948.

The Wright brothers were never commanding public figures, nor were they much given to self-promotion, but between them they produced the stroke of genius that solved a mystery of the ages and opened the door to powered flight for the rest of mankind. Their place in history is secure.

> *"In the photographic darkroom at home we pass moments of as thrilling interest as any in the field, when the image begins to appear on the plate and it is yet an open question whether we have a picture of a flying machine, or merely a patch of open sky."*
>
> WILBUR WRIGHT IN A LECTURE TO THE WESTERN SOCIETY OF ENGINEERS, SEPTEMBER 18, 1901

BIBLIOGRAPHY

Abate, Rosario and Gregory Alegi, Giorgio Apostolo. *Aeroplani Caproni.* Trento, Italy: Museo Caproni, 1992

Allen, Oliver E. *The Airline Builders.* Alexandria, Virginia: Time-Life Books, 1981

Almond, Peter. *Aviation: the Early Years.* Köln, Germany: Könemann, 1997

Anderton, David A. *History of the U.S. Air Force.* New York: Military Press, 1981

Angelucci, Enzo. *World Encyclopedia of Civil Aircraft.* New York: Crown Publishers, 1982

Angelucci, Enzo. *Rand McNally Encyclopedia of Military Aircraft.* New York: Military Press, 1983

Baker, David. *Flight and Flying: A Chronology.* New York: Facts On File, 1994

Baldry, Dennis, ed. *The Hamlyn History of Aviation.* London: Hamlyn, 1996

Bauer, E.E. *Boeing in Peace & War.* Enumclaw, Washington: TABA Publishing, 1991

Bickers, Richard Townshend. *A Century of Manned Flight.* Broadstone, U.K.: CLB, 1998

Bickers, Richard Townshend. *The First Great Air War.* London: Hodder & Stoughton, 1988

Biddle, Wayne. *Barons of the Sky.* New York: Simon & Schuster, 1991

Bonds, Ray, ed. *The Story of Aviation.* New York: Barnes & Noble, 1997

Bowen, Ezra. *Knights of the Air.* Alexandria, Virginia: Time-Life Books, 1980

Bowyer, Chaz. *For Valour: The Air VCs.* London: William Kimber, 1978

Bowyer, Chaz. *History of the RAF.* London: Hamlyn, 1982

Boyne, Walter J. *The Leading Edge.* New York: Stewart, Tabori & Chang, 1986

Boyne, Walter J. *The Smithsonian Book of Flight.* Washington, D.C.: Smithsonian Books, 1987

Boyne, Walter J. *Silver Wings.* New York: Simon & Schuster, 1993

Brett, Bernard. *History of World Sea Power.* London: Hamlyn, 1985

Brown, David and Christopher Shores, Kenneth Macksey. *Air Warfare.* Enfield, U.K.: Guinness Superlatives, 1976

Burge, C.G., ed. *Encyclopaedia of Aviation.* London: Pitman, 1935

Chant, Christopher. *Twentieth Century War Machines: Air.* London: Chancellor Press, 1999

Chant, Christopher. *The History of Aviation.* London: Tiger Books International, 1998

Chant, Christopher. *Pioneers of Aviation.* Rochester, U.K.: Grange Books, 2001

Coffman, Edward M. *The War to End All Wars.* Madison, Wisconsin: University of Wisconsin Press, 1986

Cooksley, Peter G. *Air Warfare.* London: Arms & Armour Press, 1997

Corn, Joseph J. *The Winged Gospel.* New York: Oxford University Press, 1983

Coster, Graham, ed. *The Wild Blue Yonder.* London: Picador, 1997

Cross, Robin. *The Bombers.* New York: Bantam Press, 1987

Crouch, Tom D. *Blériot XI.* Washington, D.C.: Smithsonian Institution Press, 1982

Cunningham, Robert E. *Aces High.* St. Louis, Missouri, General Dynamics Corporation, 1977

Davies, R.E.G. *Aeroflot.* Rockville, Maryland: Paladwr Press, 1992

Davies, R.E.G. *Delta.* Miami, Florida: Paladwr Press, 1990

Davies, R.E.G. *Fallacies and Fantasies of Air Transport History.* McLean, Virginia: Paladwr Press, 1994

Davies, R.E.G. *Lufthansa.* New York: Orion Books, 1991

Dick, Ron and Dan Patterson. *American Eagles.* Charlottesville, Virginia: Howell Press, 1997

Donald, David, ed. *The Classic Civil Aircraft Guide.* Edison, New Jersey: Chartwell Books, 1999.

Franks, Norman. *Aircraft versus Aircraft.* New York: Macmillan, 1986

Fritzsche, Peter. *A Nation of Fliers.* Cambridge, Massachusetts: Harvard University Press, 1992

Gibbs-Smith, Charles H. *Aviation: An Historical Survey.* London: Science Museum, 1985

Gildemeister, Jerry. *Avian Dreamers.* Union, Oregon: Bear Wallow, 1991

Glines, Carroll V. and Harry M. Zubkoff and F. Clifton Berry. *Flights.* Montgomery, Alabama: Community Communications, 1994

Green, William and Gordon Swanborough. *The Complete Book of Fighters.* New York: Smithmark, 1994

Greenwood, John T., ed. *Milestones of Aviation.* New York: Hugh Lauter Levin Associates, 1989

Gunston, Bill, ed. *Chronicle of Aviation.* London: Chronicle Communications, 1992

Hallion, Richard P. *Legacy of Flight.* Seattle: University of Washington Press, 1977

Hallion, Richard P. *Strike from the Sky.* Washington, D.C.: Smithsonian Institute Press, 1989

Halpern, John. *Early Birds.* New York: E.P. Dutton, 1981

Harrison, James P. *Mastering the Sky.* New York: Sarpedon, 1996

Hengi, B.I. *Airlines Remembered.* Leicester, U.K.: Midland Publishing, 2000

Heppenheimer, T.A. *Turbulent Skies.* New York: John Wiley & Sons, 1995

Heppenheimer, T.A. *A Brief History of Flight.* New York: John Wiley & Sons, 2001

Holmes, Donald B. *Air Mail.* New York: Clarkson N. Potter, 1981

Howard, Fred. *Wilbur & Orville.* New York: Knopf, 1987

Jackson, Donald Dale. *Flying the Mail.* Alexandria, Virginia: Time-Life Books, 1982

Jackson, Robert. *The Sky Their Frontier.* Shrewsbury, U.K.: Airlife, 1983

Jarrett, Philip, ed. *Biplane to Monoplane.* London: Putnam, 1997

Johnson, J.E. "Johnnie." *The Story of Air Fighting.* London: Hutchinson, 1985

Josephy, Alvin M. *The American Heritage History of Flight.* New York: American Heritage Publishing, 1962

Kasmann, Ferdinand C.W. *World Speed Record Aircraft.* London: Putnam, 1990

Kennett, Lee. *The First Air War.* New York: The Free Press, 1991

Knott, Richard C. *The American Flying Boat.* Annapolis, Maryland: Naval Institute Press, 1979

Layman, R.D. *Naval Aviation in the First World War.* Annapolis, Maryland: Naval Institute Press, 1996

Leary, William M., ed. *From Airships to Airbus (Vol 1).* Washington, D.C.: Smithsonian Institution Press, 1995

Lewis, Cecil. *Sagittarius Rising.* New York: Harcourt, Brace & Co., 1936

Liddle, Peter H. *The Airman's War, 1914–18.* Poole, U.K.: Blandford Press, 1987

Longstreet, Stephen. *The Canvas Falcons.* New York: Barnes & Noble, 1995

Mackworth-Praed, Ben. *Aviation: The Pioneer Years.* London: Studio Editions, 1990

March, Daniel J. and John Heathcott, eds. *The Aerospace Encyclopedia of Air Warfare (Vol 1).* London: Aerospace Publishing, 1997

Marriott, Leo. *80 Years of Civil Aviation.* Edison, New Jersey: Chartwell Books, 1997

Mason, Francis K. *Aces of the Air.* New York: Mayflower Books, 1981

Mason, Francis K. *The British Bomber since 1914.* London: Putnam, 1994

Mason, Francis K. *The British Fighter since 1912.* London: Putnam, 1992

Maurer Maurer, ed. *The U.S. Air Service in World War I* (4 vols). Washington, D.C.: The Office of Air Force History, 1978

Millbrooke, Anne. *Aviation History.* Englewood, Colorado: Jeppesen Sanderson, 1999

Mondey, David, ed. *Aviation.* London: Octopus Books, 1980

Moolman, Valerie. *Women Aloft.* Alexandria, Virginia: Time-Life Books, 1981

Morrow, John H. *The Great War in the Air.* Washington, D.C.: Smithsonian Institution Press, 1993

Musciano, Walter A. *Warbirds of the Sea.* Atglen, Pennsylvania: Schiffer Publishing, 1994

Nicolaou, Stéphane. *Aviateurs dans la Grande Guerre.* Le Bourget, France: Musée de l'Air et de l'Espace, 1998

Nicolaou, Stéphane. *Reims — 1909.* Le Bourget, France: Musée de l'Air et de l'Espace, 1999

Oliver, David. *Wings over Water.* Edison, New Jersey: Chartwell Books, 1999

Oughton, Frederick. *The Personal Diary of 'Mick' Mannock.* London: Neville Spearman, 1966

Prendergast, Curtis. *The First Aviators.* Alexandria, Virginia: Time-Life Books, 1981

Prior, Rupert. *Flying: The Golden Years.* London: Tiger Books, 1994

Rabinowitz, Harold. *Conquer the Sky.* Metro Books, New York, 1996

Rawlings, John D.R. *The History of the Royal Air Force.* Feltham, U.K.: Temple Press, 1984

Redding, Robert and Bill Yenne. *Boeing, Planemaker to the World.* Greenwich, Connecticut: Bison Books, 1983

Regan, Geoffrey. *Air Force Blunders.* Enfield, U.K.: Guinness Publishing, 1996

Rickenbacker, Edward V. *Fighting the Flying Circus.* New York: Avon Books, 1967

Rickenbacker, Edward V. *Rickenbacker: An Autobiography.*

Sampson, Anthony. *Empires of the Sky.* Random House, New York, 1984

Simkins, Peter. *Air Fighting 1914–18.* London: Imperial War Museum, 1978

Smith, Herschel. *A History of Aircraft Piston Engines.* Manhattan, Kansas: Sunflower University Press, 1986

Szurovy, Geza. *Classic American Airlines.* Osceola, Wisconsin: MBI Publishing, 2000

Taylor, John W.R. *Jane's Fighting Aircraft of World War I.* New York: Military Press, 1990

Taylor, John W.R. *Combat Aircraft of the World.* New York: Putnam, 1969

Taylor, John W.R. and Michael Taylor and David Mondey. *Air Facts & Feats.* Enfield, UK: Guinness Superlatives, 1977

Taylor John W.R. and Kenneth Munson. *History of Aviation.* New York: Crown Publishers, 1972

Taylor, John W.R. *Passenger Aircraft and Airlines.* London: Marshall Cavendish, 1975

Taylor, Michael J.H. *Great Moments in Aviation.* London: Prion, 1989

Taylor, Michael J.H. *The World's Commercial Airlines.* London: Regency House Publishing, 1997

Thomas, Lowell. *Famous First Flights that Changed History.* New York: Doubleday, 1968

Treadwell, Terry C. and Alan C. Wood. *The First Air War: A Pictorial History.* New York: Barnes & Noble, 1998

Trimble, William F., ed. *From Airships to Airbus (Vol 2).* Washington, D.C.: Smithsonian Institution Press, 1995

Wohl, Robert. *Aviation and the Western Imagination.* New Haven, Connecticut: Yale University Press, 1994

Wragg, David. *Wings Over the Sea.* New York: Arco Publishing, 1979

Wynn, Humphrey. *The Black Cat Squadron.* Washington, D.C.: Smithsonian Institute Press, 1990

ANNUAL PUBLICATIONS

Jane's All the World's Aircraft. London: Jane's Yearbooks

Jane's Fighting Ships. London: Jane's Yearbooks

Aviation Year Book. New York: Aeronautical Chamber of Commerce of America, Inc.

MAGAZINES

Aeroplane Monthly. London: IPC Media Ltd.

Flight Journal. Ridgefield, Connecticut: Air Age Inc.

Air & Space Smithsonian. Washington, D.C.: Smithsonian Business Ventures

GENERAL INDEX